T0327319

The Cruelest of All Mothers

CATHOLIC PRACTICE IN NORTH AMERICA

The Cruelest
of All Mothers

MARIE DE L'INCARNATION, MOTHERHOOD,
AND CHRISTIAN TRADITION

Mary Dunn

FORDHAM UNIVERSITY PRESS
New York   2016

Library of Congress Cataloging-in-Publication Data

Dunn, Mary, 1976–
    The cruelest of all mothers : Marie de l'Incarnation, motherhood, and Christian tradition / Mary Dunn. — First edition.
        pages cm. — (Catholic practice in North America)
    Includes bibliographical references and index.
    ISBN 978-0-8232-6721-7 (cloth : alk. paper)
    1. Mothers and sons—Religious aspects—Catholic Church.
2. Abandoned children—France—History. 3. Marie de l'Incarnation, mère, 1599–1672. 4. Martin, Claude, 1619–1696.
5. Catholic Church—France—History—17th century.
6. France—Church history—17th century. I. Title.
    BX2353.D86 2015
    271'.97402—dc23

                                        2015004708

for Aggie

Contents

Acknowledgments

I owe a debt of gratitude to the many people who have, along the way, helped bring this book into being. Thank you to John Seitz, who invited me to propose this project to Fordham in the first place, and to my editors, Fred Nachbaur and Will Cerbone, for their considerate (and considerable!) patience in waiting for the final product. Thank you, too, to my colleagues Grant Kaplan, Randy Rosenberg, and Bill O'Brien, whose thoughtful reading of and comments, advice, and suggestions on various chapters of this book were invaluable, and to Brenna Moore, with whom I have had countless inspiring and provocative conversations about motherhood, religious studies, and academic life. Thank you, finally, to Carla Zecher of the Newberry Library in Chicago, whose generous, careful, and thorough editing of and improvements on my translations of Marie de l'Incarnation's primary texts were critical to the final product.

I am grateful, too, to my wonderful and supportive family: first of all to my husband, Bobby Dunn; second, to my four children, Bobby, Frankie, Johnny, and Aggie, who, collectively, provided the initial and ongoing inspiration for my work on Marie de l'Incarnation; and finally to my mother, Judy Corley, whose assistance with my own children was critical to the completion of this project.

But because this is a book as much about my daughter, Aggie, as it is about Marie de l'Incarnation, these acknowledgments would not be complete without an expression of my gratitude toward the handful of professionals who have advocated for Aggie, cheered her on, and celebrated her triumphs over the course of the past year. Thank you to Jay Epstein, Aggie's optimistic and matter-of-fact pediatrician, and to Grace Hagan, Kelly Harris, Julie Grana, and Jo Russell-Brown, whose dedication and good cheer as therapists for children in St. Louis are deeply appreciated, probably more than they will ever know.

The Cruelest of All Mothers

Introduction

"I received your letter," wrote Marie de l'Incarnation to her son, Claude, "and everything that was in your packet when I was no longer expecting it." It was the summer of 1647 and nearly a decade since Marie had left her cloister in Tours, France, to found the first Ursuline convent in the New World. The Quebec in which Marie had settled in 1639 was still, eight years later, underdeveloped, poorly organized, and thinly populated—a struggling outpost pitifully vulnerable to Iroquois attacks. Marie's mind was not, however, on the state of colonial affairs at this particular moment in the summer of 1647. It was, instead, on the subject of her decision to abandon Claude in favor of religious life some sixteen years ago. "You reproach me," Marie continued in the letter from the summer of 1647,

> for a lack of affection, which I can't endure without an appropriate reply . . . You do, in fact, have some reason to complain because I left you . . . It is true that even though you were the only thing left in the world to which my heart was attached, [God] nevertheless wanted to separate us . . . Finally I had to yield to the force of divine love and suffer this blow of division which was more painful than I can tell you, but which didn't prevent me from considering myself an infinity of times the cruelest of all mothers. I ask you to forgive me, my very dear son, for I am the cause of your having suffered much affliction.[1]

Marie de l'Incarnation was born Marie Guyart just before the turn of the seventeenth century on October 28, 1599, in Tours, France.[2] The fourth of Florent Guyart and Jeanne Michelet's eight children, Marie was drawn to the liturgy and the sacraments from an early age and inclined to conversation with God the Father, Christ the Son, and the Blessed Virgin Mary. When she was just seven years old, Marie experienced the first of what would become a series of mystical encounters with Jesus Christ. One night, she recalls in the *Relation* of 1654, "in my sleep, it seemed to me that I was in the courtyard of a country school with one of my friends." "With my eyes toward heaven," she continues, "I saw . . . our Lord Jesus Christ in human form come forth and move through the air to me . . . As Jesus in his wondrous majesty was approaching me, I felt my heart enveloped by his love and I began to extend my arms to embrace him. Then he . . . put his arms about me, kissed me lovingly, and said, 'Do you wish to belong to me?' I answered, 'Yes!' And having received my consent, he ascended back into Heaven."[3] Deeply affected by this experience, Marie felt herself from that point on "inclined toward goodness," even if she still mixed her prayers with childish play.[4]

At the age of fourteen, eager to make good on her promise to belong to Christ, Marie proposed to her parents that she enter religious life among the Benedictines of Beaumont Abbey, which had been the only convent in Tours until 1608. Florent Guyart and Jeanne Michelet, however, had other plans for their daughter, and in 1617 Marie was married to Claude Martin, a master silk worker. My heart, Marie confesses to Claude in the supplement to the *Relation* of 1654, "was never in marriage."[5] She had married out of obedience alone, and with a "sincere desire to serve as an instrument of God in order to augment the number of predestined [souls]"—which is (Claude comments in his *Vie de la Vénérable Mère Marie de l'Incarnation*) "the true purpose of marriage" and its only justification.[6]

By her own account, Marie enjoyed a happy—though brief—union with Claude. Claude tolerated her "little devotions," even taking "pleasure in them because he was a good man who feared God."[7] Marie, for her part, continued to pray regularly, attend mass daily, and frequent the sacraments, but was never "so fixated on her devotions . . . that she neglected to care for her family."[8] Marie "made the fear of God reign in her house" and kept sin out of it.[9] She was careful to acquit herself of all her domestic duties, even caring for the bodies and (more important) the souls of the many craftsmen and servants who worked for her husband and lived with the couple in their home.

Within two years, the marriage had produced a son, Claude, born April 2, 1619. Neither Marie's *Relations* nor her letters reveal much, if anything, about Claude's early infancy. What we do know, however, is that a short six months after Claude's birth, Marie's husband died, leaving the nineteen-year-old widow with the daunting prospect of raising her new-born son alone. It takes but little imagination to appreciate how devastating her husband's death must have been for Marie (who was, no doubt, still not fully recovered from the physical and emotional upset wrought by Claude's birth). To make matters worse, when Marie's husband died his silk business was in shambles, burdened by accumulating debts and lawsuits that threatened to leave the family bankrupt.[10] In the midst of her affliction, Marie took comfort in these "holy words" from the Psalms: "I am with those who are in tribulation."[11] "I believed so firmly," she attests in the *Relation* of 1654, "that [God] was with me . . . that neither the loss of temporal goods, nor the legal proceedings, nor the prospect of scarcity, nor my son who was only six months old . . . [and] bereft of everything except me, worried me."[12]

Shortly after her husband's death, Marie committed her infant son to the care of a wet nurse—hardly an unusual practice in seventeenth-century France, where up to 25 percent of babies were breastfed by a hired hand—and took up residence in her father's attic.[13] For two years, she lived there in seclusion, reading, praying, and deepening her commitment to her spiritual growth. Finally, in the spring of 1621, Claude returned to his mother's side—having, by a stroke of good fortune, managed to escape the fate of the appalling proportion of early modern children who died while in the care of mercenary nursemaids.[14] Under these circumstances, one might expect Marie to have enjoyed a particularly joyful and affection reunion with the son from whom she had been separated for nearly two years. Marie, however, refused to caress Claude "as one does children, although I loved him dearly."[15] She intended, she explains in the *Relation* of 1654, to "detach him from me" so that he would feel less acutely her absence when the time came for her to leave him.[16] But the oppose happened, "for just as she never embraced him, so she never treated him badly." Where natural love is stronger and more deeply rooted, explains Claude in the *Vie*, "separation is harder and more difficult to do."[17]

Later that same year, Marie moved together with Claude to her sister's house. Marie's sister Claude and her husband, Paul Buisson, owned a thriving transportation business and had invited Marie to assist in managing their house and kitchen. Recalling those early years in the Buisson household in the *Relation* of 1633, Marie recounts how she "put up with a great number of humiliations . . . [acting as] a servant to my [brother-in-law]'s servants" and practicing an active apostolate of sorts as she cared for them in times of sickness and did her best to keep them from offending God.[18] Over time, Marie became increasingly involved in the administration of the Buisson's business. She describes in the *Relation* of 1633 spending "almost entire days in a stable that served as a store." Some days, she continues, "I was still at the port loading and unloading merchandise at midnight." She kept company with porters, carters, and "even fifty or sixty horses" with whose upkeep she was charged. There were times, Marie confesses, "that I felt so overburdened with responsibilities that I didn't know where to begin."[19]

Nothing, however, could distract Marie from her intensifying spiritual life. "I was constantly occupied by my intense concentration on God," she testifies in the *Relation* of 1633. "My soul was engulfed in this divine Majesty. Seeing me, people assumed I was listening with attention to everything they were saying, but . . . I would not have been able to repeat [what had been said] had someone asked." Nevertheless, she goes on, "when it was a question of business with which I was charged, our Lord gave me the grace to come out all right."[20] She would later reflect on her experiences in the Buisson household—"the hard work, the trials, all those disagreeable situations"—as "a preparation for Canada." "They were my novitiate," Marie wrote in the *Supplement* to the *Relation* of 1654, and "taught me to bear the difficulties and labors of New France."[21]

Over the course of the next ten years, Marie's inclination toward religious life would only sharpen. By 1624, she had undertaken vows of chastity, obedience, and poverty. She received communion daily, mortified her flesh with regularity, and consulted tirelessly with her spiritual director, Dom Raymond. But Marie was not satisfied. She longed to unite in mystical marriage with God "which stirred in her a more urgent wish for the religious life."[22] Claude, however, was still a young boy and Marie had no choice but to defer her desire. God, Marie writes in the *Relation* of 1633, "caressed me lovingly and assured me that he would grant me what I had been asking him for so insistently," but just not yet.[23]

Finally, in 1630, Mother Françoise de St. Bernard, who had just been elected prioress of the convent in Tours, invited Marie to join the Ursulines. Although Marie fretted about Claude, "who was not yet twelve years old and whom I saw stripped of all goods," God soon gave her to believe that "He would take care of what I wanted to leave out of love for him."[24]

And so, on January 25, 1631, Marie Guyart entered the Ursuline convent in Tours, abandoning the eleven-year-old Claude to the care of the Buissons against the wishes of her family, the admonitions of her neighbors, and her own persistent misgivings.

By all accounts, the young Claude did not adjust easily to his mother's absence. Shortly before Marie entered the convent, Claude ran away from home, provoked by a "profound melancholy . . . which was like a presentiment and a prediction of the misfortune that was about to befall him." In his own words, Claude "saw that his relatives who had knowledge of his mother's plan were looking at him fixedly with eyes of pity without saying anything to him, then turning back around they conferred together in low voices about this affair . . . Seeing nothing but sadness and gloom," he could stand it no longer and ran away to Paris to stay with the friend of his uncle.[25]

Three days later, Claude was discovered at the port of Blois and returned to his mother, at whose side he stayed until the moment of her departure. "Leaving our lodging to enter into the house of God, this child came with me totally resigned," recalls Marie in her *Relation* of 1633. "He did not dare to reveal his affliction to me, but I saw tears fall from his eyes which made me know that he was feeling in his soul. He made me feel such a great compassion that it seemed to me that my soul was being torn from me." "But," she concludes briskly, "God was dearer to me than all that. Leaving him therefore in his hands, I bid adieu to him joyfully. Then, receiving the benediction of my confessor, I threw myself at the feet of the reverend mother who received me freely for the love of Our Lord with much love and affection."[26]

Life behind the cloister walls was like a paradise for Marie. Everything—"the rules, the ceremonies, the enclosure, the vows"—seemed to Marie to be filled with the spirit of God.[27] Claude, however, found no such peace in the wake of his mother's departure. The boy was troubled, distraught, and doggedly persistent in his attempts to attract Marie's attention and persuade her to come home. Despite the rule of the cloister which, according to the terms agreed on by the Council of Trent, mandated the strict enclosure of all professed religious women, Claude found every opportunity to catch a glimpse of his estranged mother. "I saw," recalled Marie in a letter addressed to her son thirty-eight years after she joined the Ursulines, "how you came to cry at our parlor and the grill of our choir, how you passed a part of your body through the communion rail, how seeing by chance the big convent door left open by the workmen, you entered into our court and being warned that you ought not to do this, you went out backwards to see if you could see me."[28]

Not content to let his actions speak for themselves, Claude even sought out the assistance of his uncle who "had a particular talent for French poetry," and presented his mother with a poem on the subject of her withdrawal, written in the voice of the abandoned son.[29] Perhaps the most eloquent testimony of the affliction of the abandoned son, however, "was when a troop of young children your age came with you to the windows of our refectory, screaming and screeching that I be given back to you, and your voice distinct from the others, crying pitiably that your mother be given back to you and that you wanted to see her."[30] Never, Marie admits, "was I so embattled." I thought, she goes on, "that I would be thrown out of the house and that since I couldn't stand these things, all the more reason why our Reverend Mother and all the sisters wouldn't tolerate them, having no obligation to do so."[31]

Shortly after Marie made her profession among the Ursulines in 1633 she experienced a vision that would change her life and inspire her vocation in Canada. One night, Marie reports in the *Relation* of 1654,

> I dreamed that I was with a secular lady whom I had met . . . we came to a beautiful place . . . Advancing within, I saw at some distance to my left a little church of white marble, wrought with a lovely old architecture, on top of which the Blessed Virgin was seated. She was holding the Child Jesus on her lap. This place was very elevated, and below it lay a majestic and vast country, full of mountains, of valleys, of thick mists which permeated everything except the little building which was the church of this country and was exempt from the mists. The Blessed Virgin, Mother of God, looked down on this country, as pitiable as it was awesome . . . It seemed to me that she spoke about this country and about myself and that she had in mind some plan which involved me.[32]

The dream, Marie claims, remained incomprehensible until she confessed what had happened to her to the Jesuit Jacques Dinet, then serving as her spiritual director. Dinet identified for Marie the "pitiable" and "awesome" country of her dream as Canada. Around the same time, Marie received her first copy of the Jesuit *Relations* from Joseph Poncet, who had been teaching Claude in the humanities at the Jesuit school in Orléans. Poncet, unaware of Marie's dream and Dinet's interpretation, had enclosed along with the *Relation* a letter announcing his own eagerness to join the mission in New France and inviting Marie herself to join him.

From 1634 until her departure for the colony in 1639, Marie set herself to finding a way to get to New France. By 1638, she had made contact with Madeleine de la Peltrie, a wealthy widowed laywoman whose financial support would make possible the foundation of the Ursulines in Quebec, and on May 4, 1639, Marie finally set sail from Dieppe together with three additional Ursulines, de la Peltrie, and some others. After a nearly three-month journey across the Atlantic, they arrived in Canada toward the end of July. To Marie and her companions, Quebec—which counted only about two hundred and fifty settlers—"must have seemed less prepossessing than the meanest provincial village."[33] The Ursulines took up temporary residence in the lower town in a small house consisting of just two rooms, a cellar, and an attic.

Over the course of the next thirty-three years, Marie would found a school for the purpose of educating Native American girls, translate catechisms into indigenous languages, and serve some eighteen years as superior of the first Ursuline convent in the New World, negotiating with bishops, contracting with businessmen, and managing the affairs of her community of women. She would also maintain, over this same period of time, an extensive and intimate correspondence with the son she had abandoned so many years ago in favor of religious life. Giving shape and substance to the relationship between mother and son as it develops within this epistolary context is the memory of the abandonment. For Claude, who by 1641 had entered religious life himself among the Benedictines of St. Maur, the abandonment was a weapon of enormous persuasive power, deftly wielded in order to secure access to his mother's most intimate spiritual secrets. For years, Claude had been badgering his mother to make him "an account of the operations that it pleased the Divine Majesty to carry out on me."[34] And for years, Marie had deferred, resisted, and outright refused. Finally, in 1654, Marie acquiesced to her son's persistent requests and sent him the *Relation* of 1654, an autobiographical text that traces Marie's spiritual development from a young and preternaturally pious girl in seventeenth-century Tours to the celebrated mystic and founder of the Ursuline order in colonial New France. In a letter accompanying the *Relation*, Marie explained that "if I have made you wait, not giving you the satisfaction you desired nor heeding your pleas, although they proceeded from a true sentiment of piety, it was not for lack of affection." "This delay that you took for a tacit refusal didn't deter you at all," Marie continued:

> You beseeched me anew by means of the most insistent motives and the most touching reasons that your intellect could supply, accusing me of a lack of affection and testifying to me that I had abandoned you so young, such that you scarcely knew your mother; that not content with this first abandonment, I had departed from France and left you forever; that when you were a child you were not capable of the instructions I gave you, and that since you are of a more enlightened age today, I must not refuse you the lights God had communicated to me; that having embraced a condition similar to mine, we are both in God, and thus our spiritual goods must be shared; that in your present state I could not refuse you, without some sort of injustice and hardness, that which could console you and serve you in the practice of perfection that you had professed; and finally that if I gave you this consolation you would help me bless he who gave me such a substantial share of his graces and celestial favors.[35]

Marie shared all this with her spiritual director, who not only found "it fitting that I should give you this consolation, [but] even commanded me to do it."[36] In a letter written later that same year, Marie made clear to her son that the *Relation* of 1654 was for his eyes only. She commanded him to ensure that "these writings not be shared with or made known to anyone but you," begging him "to write on the cover, *Papers of conscience*, so that no one touches them and glances at them without scruple," and even to burn them "if you happened to fall ill and were in danger of death." "I trust," she concluded, "that you will keep the fidelity for which I am asking and that after I granted you what you asked of me, you will not refuse me what I desire of you."[37]

Claude published Marie's *Relation* in its entirety in 1677 under the title *Vie de la Vénérable Mère Marie de l'Incarnation*. Although he had originally intended to compose a biography of a more conventional sort, he was persuaded by "learned and pious people" to let his mother tell her own story, for to edit the text would have been to detract from the edifying simplicity of her prose and, indeed, "to correct the Holy Spirit who, after having made her do so many holy and heroic actions, guided her hand to put them down on paper."[38] Nevertheless, Claude could not resist tinkering with his mother's work, appending a number of "additions" to the text (culled from Marie's earlier *Relation* of 1633, her letters, and his own memory), dividing the *Relation* into books and chapters, and editing Marie's own prose—but only, he insists, in the interests of explaining, clarifying, and polishing— such that the resulting *Vie* amounts to the work of two authors.

Four years later, Claude published 221 of his mother's letters under the title *Écrits spirituels et historiques* (albeit, again, not without heavy editing).[39] For the next three hundred years—until the discovery of a handful of additional letters and a manuscript of the *Relation* of 1654 in the archives of the Ursulines of Trois-Rivières nearly a century ago—the Marie de l'Incarnation available to historians, theologians, and the interested public was the Marie de l'Incarnation packaged and produced exclusively by Claude Martin.[40] So total was Claude's editorial authority exercised over his mother's written legacy that it is hardly an exaggeration to suggest that Claude controlled the discursive production of Marie herself. In a very real sense, the poor abandoned son who had come "crying to the grill, asking that [his] mother be given back to" him, got her back, if only posthumously.[41]

When I began work on this book, my sons Bobby and Frankie were three and one years old, respectively. My world was—and is—one dominated by the ideology of "intensive mothering," a world in which mothers are selfless, children are priceless, and child rearing is "emotionally absorbing, labor-intensive, and financially expensive."[42] While I recognize the historically and culturally contingent nature of this model of intensive mothering, I couldn't—and can't—help but be mostly (if not completely) persuaded by its logic. And so, following Bobby's birth, I shifted my priorities from my professional development to my children's development. I took fewer trips to the library and more trips to the zoo. I measured my success not by whether I could make it all the way through de Certeau's *The Practice of Everyday Life*, but by the extent to which I could—over the course of a single demanding day—give my sons focused attention, loving patience, and enthusiastic companionship. I took to rising early (very early) in the morning, hours before Bobby and Frankie woke up, so that I could get some writing in and still have time to teach my children their letters, play in the leaves, read *The Runaway Bunny*, and take an unhurried walk around the block. I did (and do) this because I loved being with my children—most of the time, anyway. But I also did (and do) this because I thought (and think) it was important. I thought (and think) that it mattered whether I was around. You're lucky, our housekeeper Chrissy said recently, that you get to be with them all day like that. It makes a real difference, she said.[43]

Well, of course. In the world that both Chrissy and I inhabit, it is simply a matter of common sense that a mother's presence "makes a real difference." In our world, Marie de l'Incarnation's decision to abandon her son in favor of religious life is "'bizarre,' 'strange,' even 'deranged.'"[44] It is, in short, unthinkable. It cannot, however, be inexplicable. Although it would be easy to dismiss the abandonment as a symptom of mistaken belief, an instance of perverted practice—an example, in short, of religion gone wrong—mapping the abandonment onto the normative grid of the good and the bad would not do justice to the event in its complexities as the product of an embodied agent working within a particular historical and cultural context. Marie's decision to abandon her young son does, admittedly, offend the sensibilities of her twenty-first-century (American) interlocutors. Our world, after all, is one that privileges (exaggerates?) the relationship between mother and child as the most fundamental of all human relationships and, indeed, the most fundamental of all human experiences. It is, as Donald Winnicott, Heinz Kohut, and others remind us, in our interactions with our mothers that we learn how to love ourselves, how to love others, and how to love at all. Within the context of our world, the abandonment is jarringly out of place.

This, however, is precisely what makes the abandonment so ripe for explanation and a "most fruitful place to engage" the Christian tradition that (as I will argue in the pages that follow) gave rise to it.[45] This book is, simply put, an explanation of the abandonment. In adopting the terminology of "explanation," I intend to invoke Wayne Proudfoot's distinction between explication and explanation. For Proudfoot, *explication* demands that the scholar describe a particular religious experience in terms that "can be plausibly ascribed to the person to whom we attribute the experience."[46] *Explanation*, on the other hand, can—and should—go beyond the perspective of the religious insider. The explanation of the abandonment that I propose in Chapters 2–4 of this book is one with which Marie—and perhaps many of my readers—would no doubt disagree. The task of the scholar, however, is not to parrot the explication of the insider, but to offer an explanation of the religious experience that has the potential to "disturb, shock, or jolt us into an awareness that we did not have before."[47]

And yet, as Proudfoot reminds us, good scholarship is a two-step process. Good scholarship begins with explication and ends in explanation.[48] And so this book begins in Chapter 1 with an *explication* of the abandonment—with, in other words, a description of the abandonment in terms that can be plausibly ascribed to Marie herself. For Marie, the abandonment was a sacrifice performed in submission to the will of God and in imitation of Christ. It was not a decision motivated from within, but one imposed from without—a matter of divine will, not maternal will. In abandoning Claude, Marie had only submitted to God's orders, and this after much initial resistance.

The explication of the abandonment offered by Marie does not, of course, preclude an *explanation* of the abandonment as something else altogether. It is to the task of explanation, then, that Chapters 2–4 are dedicated. In Chapter 2, I propose that rather than reading the abandonment as an act of submission to God's orders, we might instead interpret it as an act of resistance against the norms of seventeenth-century French family life. In electing to abandon Claude "without any assured support," Marie behaved differently—and knowingly so—from her contemporaries who believed themselves categorically obliged to protect the patrimony of their children.[49] At least as much as it was an act of submission performed in deference to the uncompromising will of God, the abandonment was an act of resistance carried out by Marie in defiance of the expectations of her time and the standards of her place.

Rarely, however, does human agency resolve neatly into the binary categories of domination or resistance. An explanation of the abandonment that takes account of the complexity of Marie's agency as a mother and a mystic within the context of seventeenth-century Christian France must necessarily go beyond interpretations that read the event as an instance of *either* domination *or* resistance. In my attempt to make sense of the abandonment as the consequence of a more nuanced kind of agency—as, in other words, something more than simple domination, something other than mere resistance—I owe a debt to the work of French sociologist Pierre

Bourdieu. The way Bourdieu understands it, human agency is neither mechanistically determined (forced) nor spontaneously subjective (free). Instead, human agents act within the context of distinct social fields which generate within those agents certain dispositions, durable ways "of standing, speaking, walking, and thereby of feeling and thinking."[50] The "possibilities and impossibilities, freedoms and necessities, opportunities and prohibitions inscribed in the objective conditions" limit the range of human action.[51] Because, however, the objective social conditions which constrain human action "generate dispositions objectively compatible with these conditions," what agents *want* (subjectively) is equivalent to what is *possible* (objectively).[52] As Bourdieu puts it, "The most improbable practices are therefore excluded, as unthinkable, by a kind of immediate submission to order that inclines agents to make a virtue of necessity, that is, to refuse what is anyway denied and to will the inevitable."[53]

Following Bourdieu, I propose in Chapters 3–4 an explanation of the abandonment that situates Marie within the distinctive social field of seventeenth-century French Catholicism. In these two chapters, I argue that Marie's decision to abandon Claude in favor of religious life is best understood neither as an instance of simple domination nor as an instance of mere resistance, but rather as an instance of human agency informed by what had been possible within the Christian tradition and inflected by what was likely within the context of seventeenth-century French Catholicism. In Chapter 3, I draw the boundaries of a Christianity that left little room for actual maternal bodies and real maternal practice. Despite the proliferation of maternal metaphors in the language of affective piety and the ideal of spiritual motherhood in the lives of the saints, the material experience of mothering flesh and blood progeny merited little appreciation in the eyes of the Church Fathers. For the likes of Tertullian and Jerome, there was no more perfect index of humanity's enslavement to the things of this world, and no more perfect antithesis to humanity's potential for life resurrected in the next world, than the mother.

I go on in Chapter 4 to examine the ways in which the theological tendency toward the marginalization of motherhood gave rise to the conspicuous theme of the renunciation of children in hagiographic narrative. In the stories of holy mothers who relinquished their sons and daughters in favor of Christian discipleship, the renunciation of children testifies to the presence of heroic virtue in imitation of Christ. Whether illustrative of the holy woman's laudable virility, unconditional love for God, admirable faith, or commitment to the ideal of evangelical poverty, the renunciation of children within the context of hagiographic narrative operates in the last instance and in each instance as a proxy for the painful renunciation of self in the image of the crucified Christ. While Marie de l'Incarnation's decision to abandon Claude for religious life was no doubt informed by this distinctive hagiographic tradition, I argue in the second half of the chapter that it was at least as much inflected by a seventeenth-century French Catholicism saturated with spiritualities of abandonment that privileged self-surrender as the ultimate in spiritual practice. Within this context (informed by the hagiographic tradition and inflected by the spirituality of abandonment), the logic of leaving Claude for religious life must have seemed to Marie all but irrefutable. Confined within the boundaries of the possible and limited by the horizon of the probable, Marie had little choice but to abandon Claude in favor of religious life and make a virtue of this necessity.

In another time and place, however, it might have been possible for Marie to imagine motherhood itself—and not its renunciation—as sacrifice in imitation of Christ. In the fifth and final chapter, I draw on the work of Julia Kristeva to argue that maternal subjectivity is a sacrificial subjectivity that finds its closest analogue and ultimate model in Jesus Christ. For Kristeva, the maternal body is marked by an inexorable infolding of otherness that challenges binary notions of identity and difference. The "very embodiment of alterity-within," the mother—not unlike Christ himself, whose own subjectivity is a "strange fold" between humanity and divinity, vulnerability and omnipotence, mortality and eternity— confounds the Cartesian model of the autonomous, fixed, and tightly bounded self.[54] At the root of maternal subjectivity as Kristeva understands it (only "the most obvious example" of human subjectivity, generally) is a mother's "willingness to give herself up" in order to make room for the other within.[55] Much as the story of Christ's own sacrifice does not end with his death on the cross but looks forward to his resurrection and restoration to the right hand of the Father, however, so a mother's "willingness to give herself up" does not end in the annihilation of the mother in the service of the other, but in the enrichment of the mother through the inclusion of the other. Thus conceived, maternal sacrifice illuminates the ways in which the self-giving paradigmatically expressed by Christ's sacrifice on the cross is as much about love of the self as it is about love of the other, as much about giving as it is about receiving, as much about *eros* as it is about *agape*.

———

It is, and only can be, through the medium of comparison that that we might begin the project of explaining the abandonment. Indeed, to suggest that the abandonment *can* be explained presupposes the possibility— the necessity, even—of comparison. The conditions giving rise to Marie's decision to abandon Claude might be *different* from the conditions within which I find myself as a twenty-first-century American mother at work in the field of religious studies, but they cannot be altogether *other*. "'Otherness,'" Jonathan Z. Smith reminds us, "blocks language and conceptualization; 'difference' invites negotiation and intellection."[56] In order to understand the abandonment, then, again in the words of Smith, I had to "perform an act of reduction."[57] I had to reduce the abandonment "to the category of the known and the knowable." I had to declare the abandonment "an instance of . . . something [I had] seen before."[58]

And so, this book tracks back and forth between Marie's stories and my own. Whether I liked it or not, Marie has in a very real sense been my constant companion over the course of these last four years, during which I have given birth to two more children, wrestled with issues of work and family, and transformed my relationship with my Catholic tradition through the experience of this particular research project and the experiences of my everyday life as a mother of four—the last of whom, Aggie, was born unexpectedly with a rare genetic condition the summer I was to have turned in this book to my (very patient) publisher. In my attempt to understand the abandonment, I have encountered Marie in "the full and tragic necessity of [her] circumstances" and have studied them, written about them, and compared them "in the full and tragic necessity" of my own.[59] I have found—against my expectations—that Marie's story transected my own at countless points, that we had more in common than I had thought (or had wanted to admit), that I could, in fact, compare my notes with hers. And if I didn't share her beliefs (which I don't), I could at least understand what Marie did with her beliefs in "coping with the exigencies of life."[60]

Juxtaposition, Smith reminds us, is at the heart of religious belief and practice.[61] It is also at the heart of the *study* of religious belief and practice. The "initiating operation" of both religion and the study of religion, juxtaposition exploits the tension generated by the proximate placement of two things that don't go together, raising questions about the one and the other that are "not easily answered."[62] In what follows, I have self-consciously juxtaposed bits and pieces of my own narrative with Marie's, not (lest the reader misunderstand!) to claim any direct parallels between my experiences and Marie's, but rather as a means of generating fresh ways of thinking about Marie, the abandonment, and the Christian tradition.[63] I do not expect that all the questions raised by the juxtaposition of my story and Marie's will be easily answered by my readers. Indeed, I do not necessarily suppose that these questions *have* answers—or even that it's possible to identify just what these questions might be before they are asked. I am, however, wholly persuaded that the virtue of juxtaposition as a methodological tool inheres in its tendency to raise questions—unintended, unexpected, unfathomable questions—about both scholars and their subjects alike.

I have tried, in the process of making sense of the abandonment, to heed Robert Orsi's advice to stay "in-between . . . , at the intersection of self and other, at the boundary between [my] own moral universe and the moral world of the other."[64] An exercise in the dialectic of religious studies Orsi advocates, this book moves back and forth between the radical strangeness of Marie's stories and the mundane familiarity of my own. In what follows, I have brought the abandonment into conversation with my world, with the effect of making the abandonment more familiar and my world stranger.[65] Bringing Marie's world into conversation with my own has illuminated, in other words, both the ways in which my own world (in which the abandonment is unthinkable) is no more natural than Marie's world (in which the abandonment was almost inevitable), and at the same time how both worlds are possible.

I have tried to stay "in-between" in other ways, too. Following the lead of scholars like R. Marie Griffith, Saba Mahmood, and Julia Kristeva, I have labored to suspend my analysis of the abandonment between the crippling poles of domination and resistance, subordination and subversion, body and belief. Together with Manuel A. Vásquez, this book affirms the material reality of religious beliefs (of the sort that informed the abandonment) as "phenomena produced, performed, circulated, contested, sacralized, and consumed by embodied and emplaced individuals."[66] Thus, critical to my analysis of the abandonment is the contextualization of the event within the historical and religious milieus of seventeenth-century France and a Christian tradition that marginalized actual maternal practice as inimical to spiritual progress and incompatible with the work of salvation.

But there is more to it than that. Together with Orsi (and in the company of a host of others), this book approaches the study of religion in the conviction that there is something more to religious belief and practice than the material conditions that generate and sustain it. Religious events, as Orsi puts it, "are at once both thoroughly of culture and history" and at the same time "so saturated with need, memory, fear, desire, hope, denial, or terror . . . that these events slip the laws of culture and history and attain a reality that is more-than, excessive, abundant."[67] But how do we access (in the first instance) and account for (in the second) the "radical empiricism of the visible/invisible real" within the context of our secular scholarship on religion?[68] Building on the work of Constance Furey, who has called for a redirection of scholarly attention to intimate relationships as a possible "route around the impasse of debates about whether to investigate practices rather than beliefs, social norms in place of idiosyncratic voices, or action instead of meaning," Brenna Moore argues that we might apprehend something of the religious real by looking closely at the bonds between friends.[69] Religion, contends Moore, "is . . . rendered real between and among bodies, among family and friends in contexts of intimacy," contexts that include not just face-to-face contact between intimates, but dreams, memories, and "imagined conversations."[70]

Although not the explicit subject of this book, relationships are everywhere in the chapters that follow. In a very important sense, it was within the thick contexts of her relationships with others—Jesus Christ, the Virgin Mary, her Jesuit confessor, the Buissons, her Huron acolytes, and Claude himself—that religion was made real for Marie. In her interactions and exchanges with these multiple others, Marie experienced her religion, wrestled with it, and felt its weight. I have attempted in what follows to at once access and account for something of this "abundant empiricism," at least as it was adumbrated in the event and aftermath of the abandonment, by means of juxtaposing (that is, relating) what was most real to me in the course of writing this book with Marie's own narrative.[71] If it was (as I suspect, alongside Moore) in the contexts of her intimate relationships that religion became real for Marie, then it was within the contexts of my own relationships—with my children, my husband, my mother, my friends, my colleagues, and Marie herself—that Marie became real for me. And, so, as I said before, this book tracks back and forth between Marie's stories and my own—not (let me be clear) with the ambition to analogize or equate, but with the intention of gesturing more powerfully than the new materialism or new historicism alone could do to what was really real about the abandonment.

In what follows, I have self-consciously adopted a methodology that aims to illuminate not only the ways in which *religion* is a matter of both body and belief, but also the ways in which *scholarship about religion* is likewise a matter of body and belief. The majority of this book was researched, written, and edited in the wee hours of the morning before my children awoke and in the early afternoon when my children were napping. There were times, I confess, when I didn't feel like logging on to my computer and crafting some inspired paragraph about the vagaries of motherhood in seventeenth-century France (particularly after lunch and a full morning with Bobby, Frankie, Johnny, and Aggie, when all I really wanted to do was curl up in their beds alongside them). And there were times, too, when I was so engaged with whatever I was doing that I didn't feel like stopping when my children woke up or when it was time to get Bobby from school. But I did. And though I can imagine that, from the outside looking in, it might seem as if I was shortchanging both my children (fatiguing myself before they even arose) and my work (powering down in the middle of a thought), the opposite was true.

It might be easy, for the more academically minded, anyway, to see how my work satisfied an intellectual hunger that might otherwise have gnawed at me as I read *Chicka Chicka Boom Boom* to Johnny for the hundredth time or played "the bad guy" again and again (and again) in Frankie's game of pretend. Deep in the trenches of early childhood where anything can happen (and anything will) and some things happen over and over and over again, my work was—to paraphrase Virginia Wolff—like a room of my own to which I could retreat when time permitted and which sustained me, restored me, and energized me to great personal benefit and to the benefit of my family at large.

I suspect, however, that it might be harder to see how my children and all that time I spent mopping up messes, looking for turtles, pushing strollers, making forts, finger painting, swinging, disciplining, and crafting added anything of value to my work. It might, indeed, be easier to see how my children and all that time I spent with them detracted from my work. On account of my children, after all, I have presented papers at fewer conferences than I might otherwise have; I have attended fewer lectures than I might otherwise have; I have spent fewer hours in the library, served on fewer departmental committees, had fewer conversations with colleagues. And that isn't all. When our fourth child, Aggie, was born in June 2013, my eight-week maternity leave stretched into an extended and anguished multi-month hiatus that interrupted my labor on this book. During that time, I did little other than care for my family, sleep, and run. I didn't read much. I didn't write much. I just tried to keep it together. In no way, however, was this time wasted. In a very real sense, some of the most important work I did on this book, I did during that time. This book would not be what it is in the absence of the searing intensity of those material, corporeal experiences attending to Aggie and her brothers and wrestling with what it meant to be the mother of a child with special needs. This book, then, is more than just an explanation of the abandonment or an exercise in the dialectic of religious studies. In its appeal to lived personal experience as a valid source of knowing, it is also my acceptance of Adrienne Rich's invitation some decades ago to "think through the body" as a means of bridging the gap between the personal and the academic, private and public, body and soul, connecting, in other words, "'the prose and the passion' . . . and finally . . . annihilat[ing] those dichotomies" altogether.[72]

In proposing the explanation of the abandonment that I do in the pages that follow, I do not intend to suggest that Marie's explication of the event was mistaken, nor do I intend to foreclose the possibility of other, different, but equally persuasive explanations of the abandonment. Instead, I intend my own explanation as one among many historically situated, culturally contingent, and ineluctably subjective ways of reading the abandonment, albeit one (I hope) sufficiently grounded in "an intellectually defensible rationale . . . that can become part of the public debate" in my field.[73] In this sense, *The Cruelest of All Mothers* bears the mark of the postmodern, which is characterized by a self-conscious attention to the ways in which all knowledge is local, particular, and contextual.

But I confess: this is not at all where *The Cruelest of All Mothers* began— nor is it where it ends. I began work on this book four years ago, fired by the conviction that Marie's decision to abandon Claude in favor of religious life was bad—not bad conditionally, in this place, at this time, but bad absolutely, in all places and at all times. I was (and am) aware of the heavy historical baggage ported by normative distinctions between the good and the bad in the field of religious studies.[74] With the sound of the young Claude's cry outside the convent gate still ringing in my ears, however, I had wanted (and intended) to condemn Marie for the abandonment. And I had my theoretical weaponry ready. Armed with the logic that postmodernism's hyper-pluralism leaves open the possibility that "some . . . truth claims might actually be what they claim to be," I was ready to take a stance.[75]

Taking a stance, however, is not the task of the scholar of religious studies. The task of the scholar of religious studies is, instead, to suspend "the impulse to locate the other . . . securely in relation to one's own cosmos."[76] I don't fault myself for having an opinion about the abandonment. Nor do I fault myself for sharing it here. After all, as postmodern wisdom has it, both scholars and their subjects can't help but be "situated at . . . particular cultural location[s] that fundamentally shape" their perceptions of and perspectives on the world around them.[77] But the task of the scholar of religious studies requires more than just an affirmation of the postmodern. The task of the scholar of religious studies is to bring these multiple cultural locations into dialogic contact with one another, at once engaging the subject of study in conversation with contemporary culture and the tools of academic research and at the same time allowing herself to be engaged in conversation with the practices and epistemologies of places distant and times past. The challenge facing the discipline today, as Orsi puts it, "is . . . to get beyond 'otherizing' as its basic move."[78] Put differently, the challenge is how to maintain the delicate and critical balance (in) between authority and deference, between scholar and subject, between our world and theirs.

I think I might have been able to do this even if Aggie had never been born, or, indeed, if she had been born with all of her chromosomal bits and pieces. But I know that Aggie and her genetic difference has helped me to understand just what it means to experience "one's own world from the disorienting perspective of the other."[79] Over the course of the last eighteen months, I have found myself together with Aggie at St. Louis Children's Hospital more often than I would have liked (though, thankfully, less often these days). Together with Aggie, I have passed time in the waiting rooms of the neurologist, the geneticist, the audiologist, the ophthalmologist, the radiologist, the phlebotomist, and more. And in these waiting rooms, together with Aggie, I sat alongside the most unlikely of companions—tattooed grandmothers from rural Missouri, single moms from East St. Louis, Somali immigrants who spoke little English, people, in other words, whose worlds were utterly alien to me before Aggie was born but with whom I now share the common and profound experience of fighting against and coping with the reality of pediatric disability.

I can no longer condemn Marie for the abandonment. This is, in part, because in the process of writing this book I have done what any scholar worth her publisher's imprint would have done. I have labored to understand by means of thorough research and a vivid imagination what it must have been like for Marie to have been a mother, a widow, and a mystic in seventeenth-century Catholic France. But there is more to it than that. If, in what follows, I have succeeded in staying in between my world and Marie's, "I can only suppose" (to quote Marie) that it was at least as much on account of the corporeal accident of Aggie's birth and my viscerally lived and profoundly *real* maternal experience which brought me together with these others who, it turns out, are not in fact other at all.[80]

1

Explication: Representations of the Abandonment in the *Relations*, the Letters, and the *Vie*

It's hard to describe what it feels like to be told that there's something wrong with your baby. Bobby and I had been worried for a while about Aggie. She was only four months old, but she wasn't moving out of the newborn stage at the same pace that our three boys had. She rarely smiled. Her head was wobbly. And she still slept all the time. But I had been told that all babies develop at different rates, that girls are different, that—don't worry—by six months she'll blossom. So when Bobby and I brought Aggie in for a consultation with the best pediatric neurologist in St. Louis, I suspected we'd be told to go home and take our healthy baby with us. I suspected that Dr. Inder would gently rib us, scolding us for making a mountain out of a molehill.

But that's not what happened. We met Dr. Inder in the imaging center at St. Louis Children's Hospital, where Aggie was scheduled to get an MRI. I remember sitting between her and Bobby, holding Aggie (dressed in a delicate quilted pink crawler with tiny rosebuds and cream-colored lace trim) against my chest. I don't remember exactly what Dr. Inder said first. It might have been: You need to reset your expectations for this child. Or it might have been: Your job is to get Agnes to live independently one day. It doesn't matter. Whatever it was that Dr. Inder said first was shattering. Literally shattering. Everything I knew—about my family, my future, my world, and even myself—exploded in that instant. Nothing was left. The devastation was total, the annihilation complete.

It's hard to describe, as I said before, what it feels like to be told that there's something wrong with your baby. Imagine, though, to paraphrase Shakespeare, that life's a stage. Suddenly and without any forewarning the curtain falls on life as you know it, interrupting the action. There is darkness. And silence. Is that it? Is the play over?

But it's not, of course. After a while, the curtain rises again. The scenery has changed and the story is different. New actors enter stage left and stage right and you struggle to find your place among them. What part do you play? What are your lines? Gradually, you find your footing and you get comfortable—familiar even—with your new character. Gradually, too, you come to see that your character isn't really new at all, that this is who you've been all along. You are playing the same part, even if some of your lines are different. You come to see that mixed in among the new actors are, in fact, some old ones. You come to see that the scenery is not altogether alien and that the action really hasn't been interrupted. You come to see, in other words, that there is continuity between Scene 1 and Scene 2. You come to see that there was no rupture after all—just a twist (fantastically dramatic and wildly improbable, but still just a twist) in the story.

Paul Ricoeur proposes thinking about personal identity as two-dimensional, defined, on the one hand, by continuity and, on the other hand, by change.[1] For Ricoeur, personal identity consists of both *idem*-identity and *ipse*-identity. If my *idem*-identity accounts for the ways in which I stay the same as an embodied being in space and time (a response to the question: What am I?), my *ipse*-identity accounts for the ways in which I maintain a sense of myself as an agent capable of ethical and creative action (a response to the question: Who am I?). Personal identity, Ricoeur insists, emerges in the dialectic between *idem*-identity and *ipse*-identity, which is mediated by the medium of narrative. It is in the stories we tell about ourselves that personal identity takes shape. The stories we tell about ourselves are not only the media by which we express our selves, but also the media by which we shape our selves as we attempt to make coherent the disparate and sometimes discordant events of our past. As Ricoeur understands it, personal identity is narrative identity.

As narrative identity, personal identity is inherently labile. Emplotted as episodes in the linear trajectories of our personal narratives, the various events and experiences of our lives assume the appearance of inevitability (it had to happen this way) and necessity (if it hadn't happened this way, I wouldn't be who I am). But these events and experiences only appear inevitable and necessary because we have rendered them so within the structure of our own stories. In the stories we tell about ourselves, "the disruptive effects of the unforeseeable events" are denied and the discordant is made concordant, integrated into the "unity of a life considered a temporal totality which is itself singular and distinguished from all others."[2] Personal identity, Ricoeur argues, can only be understood in terms of this "dialectic of discordant concordance" which takes its place alongside the dialectic of sameness (*idem*-identity) and selfhood (*ipse*-identity).[3] Mediating between the poles of sameness and selfhood, narrative gives shape to a personal identity whose inherent instability is attested to by the countless "imaginative variations to which the narrative submits this identity."[4] The stories we tell about ourselves, in other words, can always be told differently, with the same events and experiences playing different roles, to different effects, of different magnitude. And indeed, until our stories have ended, our personal identities are subject to constant revision as we repeatedly adjust and adapt who we think we are in response to the unexpected contingencies of our lives.

Sounding a note in harmony with Ricoeur, Marya Schechtman pleads the case for autobiographical narrative as fundamental to the constructing of personal identity. Within the context of self-narratives, Schechtman argues, "individuals constitute themselves as persons by coming to think of themselves as persisting subjects."[5] A person's identity thus depends on the subjective decision to assume a particular position vis-à-vis the contingencies of life (a point well developed in Ricoeur's work). Personal identity, from this perspective, is something of an inside job (I am who I think I am). Where Schechtman's analysis of the politics of identity fruitfully supplements Ricoeur's, however, is at the intersection of the personal and the social. Personhood, Schechtman insists, "is an intrinsically social concept."[6] The project of identity formation must end in a product—a personal identity—that not only fits with the objective concept of personhood according to the terms of the individual's culture, but also "conform[s] in certain crucial respects to the narrative others tell of his life" (I am who they think I am).[7] For Schechtman, personal identity takes shape through the interplay of "a particular kind of subjectivity and orientation toward one's life" and the objective constraints imposed by the outside world.[8]

In crafting the stories we tell about ourselves, then, we navigate between the Scylla of continuity and the Charybdis of change by making our narratives intelligible not only to ourselves, but also to those around us. The stories we tell about ourselves are not, therefore, faithful representations of what really happened. They are, instead, filtered representations of what really happened, sifted through the sieve of our personal histories, our shared cultures, our languages, ideologies, and beliefs. Scholars of Christian hagiography have long since attended to the ways in which writings about the saints walk the line between fact and fiction, giving accounts of the lives of the saints who are, in most cases, real historical figures but whose life stories have, in all cases, been deliberately rendered to conform to the model provided by the life of Christ. What scholars of the humanities at large have only recently begun to realize is the extent to which all writing—even autobiographical narrative— occupies the territory claimed by traditional hagiography. All writing— like traditional hagiography—is representational, variously removed from the truth of what really happened by the conventions and codes that structure the way we think and write about ourselves.

To suggest, however, that autobiographical writing is representational is not to suggest that it is *mis*-representational. In his influential essay "Language, Epistemology, and Mysticism," Katz describes three theses on the interpretation of mysticism. According to the first, all mystical experiences are alike; according to the second, all mystical experiences are alike but are interpreted and expressed differently by the mystic in culturally inflected language; according to the third, there are types of mystical experiences (such that not all mystical experiences are alike), but these types are common across cultures even if they are interpreted and expressed differently by the mystic in culturally inflected language. Rejecting each of the three theses as unsatisfactory, Katz proposes instead that mystical experience itself "is shaped by concepts which the mystic brings to, and which shape, his experience."[9] The "forms of consciousness which the mystic brings to experience," Katz argues, "set structured and limiting parameters on what the experience will be . . . and rule out in advance what is 'inexperiencable' in the particular given, concrete context."[10]

What Steven Katz has argued about mystical experience in particular might be said about human experience more generally. Like mystical experience, human experience is determined by the "forms of consciousness" which an individual brings to the experience. Our personal histories, shared cultures, languages, ideologies, and beliefs do, indeed, shape our *representations* of what really happened. But just as—if not more— critically, they shape our *experiences* of what really happened by exerting a decisive influence on *how* we experience the events of our lives, a pro-

cess that begins prior to any attempt to formally represent the experience. Put differently, we are always representing what really happened,
even as it's really happening. Autobiographical narrative, then, can hardly
be accused of misrepresenting the truth, when the very hope in truth
(unadorned, disinterested, authentic) turns out to be a false one.

All this (I admit) is a very long (but necessary) prelude to the explication of the abandonment that follows. In what follows, I present an
account of the abandonment in terms that can plausibly be ascribed
to Marie herself, relying for the most part on the testimony provided by
Marie herself in her *Relations* of 1633 and 1654 and in her correspondence
with Claude. Marie's explication of the abandonment is not, as the above
discussion makes clear, a faithful representation of what really happened when she left Claude for religious life. It is, instead, a filtered
representation inflected by Marie's diverse historical, religious, and
cultural contexts—the absolutist regime of Louis XIV, the mystic inva-
sion of seventeenth-century France, European colonial expansion,
Counter-Reformation Catholicism, Bérullian spirituality, Christian dualism, and the hagiographic tradition (among others). It is, moreover, a
representation shaped profoundly by the idiosyncrasies of genre—in
Marie's case, the particular idiosyncrasies of spiritual autobiography—
and Claude's heavy editorial hand. Already experienced as an event whose
contours and proportions take shape through the influence of Marie's
particular "forms of consciousness," the abandonment re-presented by
Marie (and fine-tuned by Claude) in the *Relations* and letters bears the
double imprint of seventeenth-century conventions of female modesty
and literary humility and Claude's purposeful emendations.

An explication of the abandonment, then, that hopes to find in the *Relations* and the letters an unmediated and transparent account of what
really happened will invariably come up short. What the *Relations* and the
letters offer to the reader, instead, is a richly complex and multilayered
explication that positions the abandonment as a point along the plot line
of a temporally coherent, singular life, "distinguished from all others."[11]
At work in the stories Marie tells about herself is the dialectic of discordant concordance, as well as the dialectic of the personal and the social.
Not only does Marie integrate the disruptive event of the abandonment
into the narrative of her spiritual progress, but she also makes the abandonment sensible—as, indeed, she must—both to herself and to her reading

public. In what follows (after a brief discussion of genre and prove-
nance), I argue that over time Marie's doubts about whether the abandonment had been divinely inspired give way to a certitude that it had.
Over time, between the *Relation* of 1633 and her last letter to Claude in
1671, Marie comes to represent the abandonment unambiguously in the
familiar idiom of Christian sacrifice performed in submission to the will
of God. What is, if anything, only an implicit allusion to the sacrificial
dimensions of the abandonment in the *Relation* of 1633 becomes, in the
Relation of 1654 and in the letters, an explicit identification of the abandonment as an instance of sacrifice in imitation of Christ (an interpretation on which Claude enthusiastically expands in his *Vie de la Vénérable
Mère Marie de l'Incarnation*). Within the context of the *Relation* of 1654
and Marie's later letters to Claude, the abandonment takes its place as
an episode in a narrative of spiritual progress, in the absence of which
Marie's life story would not be what it is and Marie would not be who she
is. Rendered as an instance of Christian sacrifice performed in submission to God, in imitation of Christ, and against the wills of both mother
and son, the abandonment assumes in Marie's later writings the proportions of the inevitable and the dimensions of the necessary, healing the
rift in a personal narrative that threatens to fracture under the twin pres-
sures of mysticism and maternity.

———————

An inquiry into the substance of Marie de l'Incarnation's *Relations* of
1633 and 1654 must necessarily (and responsibly) begin with a discussion of
the genre of spiritual autobiography, of which the *Relations* are illustrative
seventeenth-century examples. Like the works of her peers—including
Madre María de San José and Jane Turner—Marie's *Relations* of 1633 and
1654 (as Kate Greenspan reminds us) are not "autobiographical in the
modern sense."[12] There might be, as Greenspan puts it, autobiographical
components to women's spiritual narratives, but the intention of these
texts was to "fit into a familiar pattern" and "to illustrate a point of general applicability." Originality, Greenspan avers, "was neither expected nor
valued."[13] Indeed, contends Greenspan, so unlike contemporary autobiographical writing are medieval and early modern instances of spiritual
autobiography that it is to the genre of "hagiography rather than autobiography" that we must look for comparison.[14] Tightly structured accord-

ing to a certain set of literary conventions, women's "autohagiography shares with traditional hagiography the desire to represent the subject's life as 'more exemplary than real.' "[15] Women like Madre Marí de San José, Jane Turner, and Marie de l'Incarnation did not aspire to draw the contours of themselves as unique and inimitable individuals, but rather to demonstrate the ways in which some broader universal (and usually theological) truth expressed itself within the context of their personal lives and experiences.

Among the literary conventions that structured women's autohagiography was the representation of the text as a response to a request made from the outside. In most cases, the seventeenth-century women who wrote spiritual autobiographies did so in obedience to the commands of their male superiors (often their spiritual directors), who ordered them to produce accounts of their interior lives—and frequently to specific ends. Marie was no exception. It was at the behest of her spiritual director, Father Georges de la Haye, who in an effort to lift Marie from the spiritual abyss into which she fallen commanded her to put into writing all the graces that she had received from God that Marie composed the *Relation* of 1633.[16] Similarly, Marie wrote the *Relation* of 1654 in response to pressure from Claude himself and "having been commanded by [her spiritual director, Father Jérome Lalemant] to put down in writing everything that I can about the graces and favors that his divine Majesty gave me regarding the gift of prayer."[17]

Characteristic of the spiritual autobiographies of seventeenth-century women, too, is a rhetorical style that has variously been called one of "femininity," "humility," and "modesty."[18] Seventeenth-century women writers repeatedly repudiate their own status as authors, lay claim to a "humble dread of publicity," and apologize for their own incompetence and ignorance and the insignificance of their written work.[19] Claiming to have written the *Relations* out of obedience alone, Marie goes on in a letter addressed to Claude accompanying the *Relation* of 1654 to assign responsibility for the text's authorship to none other than the Holy Spirit, who inspired her writing and guided her pen. In the same letter, she makes a plea for the worthlessness of the text, doubting that the *Relation* could add anything of value to Claude's spiritual development. "But if it is so," she concedes, "blessed be God forever for such a happy success, for if there is something good in these writings, it comes from him and not from me, who am but a miserable sinner."[20] Marie, moreover, had not been eager to share her spiritual secrets with Claude. She confesses to have written the *Relation* "with repugnance" and to have sent it to Claude "with difficulty."[21] Having "overcome" herself "to send you the writings that you have desired from me," however, Marie makes one thing clear: the *Relation* is for Claude's eyes alone.[22] "I trust," she concludes, "that you will keep the fidelity for which I am asking, and that after I granted you what you asked of me, you will not refuse me what I desire of you . . . If you happened to fall ill and were in danger of death, have [these papers] thrown into the fire, or . . . send them to my niece who will take care to keep them for me if I survive you. Such are my conditions."[23]

In her recent study on early modern women's writing and the rhetoric of modesty, Patricia Pender cautions against reading early modern women's professions of authorial humility literally. Early modern women's modesty rhetoric is best understood "not as an acknowledgement of exclusion and a literal assertion of ineptitude, but as the very mark of literariness as it circulates among early modern protocols of textual modesty and authority."[24] The protestations of incompetence and ignorance typical to the writings of seventeenth-century women function variously—to justify a woman writing in a man's world, to soften the assertions of authority in the text, to illuminate the "scope of the epideictic endeavor."[25] In the case of the genre of spiritual autobiography in particular, modesty rhetoric operates to gesture to the enormity of the spiritual experiences reported. When Marie laments—as she does repeatedly throughout the *Relations* and the letters—that she cannot find the words to describe her spiritual experiences ("I want to say what I can't express, and unable to express it, I don't know if I say it as I should"), the effect is not to draw the reader's attention to Marie's inadequacies but instead to draw the reader's attention to the magnitude—and authenticity—of those experiences themselves.[26] Although women letter writers delighted their seventeenth-century French reading public with the apparent sincerity of their unaffected prose, critical analysis of early modern women's correspondence reveals women's letters to be as consciously and strategically rhetorical as the letters of their male counterparts. Anything but unstudied and effortless, early modern women's writing was a carefully crafted means of self-fashioning—something of a "velvet glove that exhibits the contours of the handiness it conceals."[27]

If the literary conventions that structure Marie's *Relations* of 1633 and 1654 inflect Marie's explication of the abandonment, the imprint of Claude's heavy editorial hand threatens to altogether obscure it. Although it is to Claude that we owe the preservation of most of Marie's writings, Claude's interventions in his mother's texts—the extent of which is readily apparent where the existence of the original makes comparison possible—prove hardly insignificant. In the case of the *Relation* of 1654, which forms the basis of Claude's 1677 *Vie de la Vénérable Mère Marie de l'Incarnation*, Claude appended a number of "additions" to the text, divided the *Relation* into books and chapters, and modified Marie's own prose in ways that belie his claims to have merely explained, clarified, and polished his mother's autobiography.[28] We can only imagine that the *Relation* of 1633—which survives exclusively in bits and pieces as part of Claude's *Vie*—suffered a similar fate. Comparisons between Marie's few remaining original letters and those edited and published by Claude in 1681 under the title *Écrits spirituels et historiques* betray a similar editorial enthusiasm. Not only did Claude make more than mere aesthetic adjustments to his mother's writing, but in his attempt to separate his mother's letters into the categories of historical, on the one hand, and spiritual, on the other, Claude in some cases went so far as to separate portions of a single letter deemed historical from those considered spiritual, and to cobble together into a composite text sections from multiple letters.[29]

Just a few short months after her husband died, Marie experienced a dramatic vision that she would later identify as the moment of her conversion. Recounting the experience in her *Relation* of 1654, Marie writes:

> One morning when I was on my way to work . . . [engaged in] my usual prayer . . . I was suddenly stopped both interiorly and exteriorly . . . Then at that moment the eyes of my spirit were opened; all my faults, sins, and imperfections . . . were shown to me together and in detail . . . At the same moment, I saw myself completely drowned in blood and my spirit was convinced that this blood was that of the Son of God. [I was convinced, too,] that I was guilty for the shedding of this blood on account of my sins and that it had been poured out for my salvation . . . Sin, no matter how small it seemed, appeared horrible and terrifying to me.[30]

In the aftermath of this experience, Marie redoubled her religious devotions, frequenting the sacraments, praying constantly, and intensifying her practices of self-mortification. Over time, her yearning for religious life became increasingly acute until, at last, "life in the world [became] unbearable" for her.[31] Eventually, confident in God's assurances that he would provide for her young son (who had, for years, been the only thing holding her back), Marie resolved to enter religious life. She chose to enter among the Ursulines, who had come to Tours in 1622 "because they were instituted to help souls" and because "every time I passed in front of their monastery my spirit and heart jumped . . . [which suggested to me that] God wanted me there."[32]

Fifteen days before her entrance, however, Claude ran away from home. "For three days," Marie reports in the *Relation* of 1633, "I heard no news about him. I believed that he had surely drowned or that some depraved man had kidnapped him." Marie admits to being troubled by other "similar thoughts" and professes—in language characteristic of what Nicholas Paige calls an emerging "culture of interiority"—to have "suffered much more on the inside than I let show on the outside."[33] Like any good mother, Marie suffered on account of Claude's disappearance because she was concerned for his well-being. With a rare effusion of maternal sentiment, Marie confesses in the *Relation* of 1633 to bewildering feelings of grief upon learning of Claude's supposed demise. "I would never have believed," she writes in the *Relation* of 1633, "that the sorrow of the loss of a child could be so painful to a mother. I had seen him sick to the point that he almost died, and I gave him willingly to Our Lord, but to lose him in this way, it was something I was unable to understand."[34]

But what troubled Marie most of all about Claude's disappearance, was the possibility that it might further delay—or even frustrate altogether—her entry into religious life. Although Marie felt acutely the "painful pain" of the loss of her only son, it was the "privation of the thing of the world that I loved the most, namely, the good of religion," that touched her most deeply. Convinced that God had "allowed that to happen in order to hold me back in the world," Marie could only, in the end, "strip myself of all desire and stay naked at the foot of the cross, resigning myself with all my heart to what his goodness would ordain about it."[35]

Eventually, after three days—and extensive searches "from all sides"—Claude was discovered at the port of Blois and returned home to his mother.[36] In the interval between Claude's disappearance and his recovery, Marie testifies to having taken comfort in the company of "the very Holy Virgin" whose own son had gone missing that fateful Passover so many centuries before.[37] The whole time Claude was missing, Marie writes in the *Relation* of 1633, "I had engraved on my spirit the sorrow that the very holy Virgin felt, when she lost in the Temple the little Jesus, who was such a worthy son, whereas I, puny as I was, suffered for the loss of a little nothing." "This thought," Marie concludes, "consoled me."[38]

Upon Claude's return home, Marie "began hoping to soon enjoy the good that I thought I had lost."[39] Her sufferings, however, had not yet ended. In both *Relations*, Marie describes the criticisms levied against her by her family and friends who accused her of provoking Claude's flight in the first place. Everyone, Marie recalls in the *Relation* of 1654, warned me "that what had happened to him would happen again and that I would be guilty of his ruin." Claude's flight from home, insisted Marie's family and friends, "was an evident sign that God did not want me to become a religious," and, indeed, God's way of "chastising" Marie for even thinking about relinquishing her maternal responsibilities.[40]

For Marie, however, more persuasive than the censure of her family and friends were the words of Jesus preserved in the gospel of Matthew: "Whoever loves father or mother more than me is not worthy of me; and whoever loves son or daughter more than me is not worthy of me."[41] Fortified by her confessor (who "helped me a lot, assuring me that Our Lord would take care of my son and that I would enter freely in the sight of God"), Marie stepped over the convent threshold on the Day of the Conversion of St. Paul, 1631, leaving the eleven-year-old Claude behind.[42] Claude's distress upon his mother's departure seems to have made a lasting impression on Marie. In both *Relations*, she recounts how Claude accompanied her until the last moment, crying "bitterly." If, in the *Relation* of 1633, it was Claude who labored (in vain) to hide his grief from the eyes of his mother ("He did not dare to testify to me his affliction, but I saw the tears fall from his eyes, which let me know what he was feeling in his soul"), it is Marie who managed (successfully) in the *Relation* of 1654 to conceal her anguish from the watchful public: seeing Claude, she admits, "it seemed to me that I was being split in half: nevertheless I did not let it show."[43] Marie's memory of the circumstances of her departure seems not to have dulled even as late as 1669. In a letter addressed to Claude that year, Marie recalls how "you came with me and in leaving you, I felt that my soul was being sundered from my body with extreme pains."[44]

Marie's abandonment of Claude was, by her own account, made all the more dramatic by her decision to leave her son with no material support. I thought, Marie explains in the *Relation* of 1633, that "I was leaving more, in leaving my son whom I loved very much, than if I had left all imaginable possessions, and above all, leaving him without support."[45] Claude elaborates on his mother's decision in his *Vie de la Vénérable Mère Marie de l'Incarnation*. Deferring, like Marie, to evangelical command, Claude reminds his readers that Jesus Christ had instructed his followers to leave their fathers, their mothers, and their children. This, Claude continues, "must therefore be done." Claude's mother was not, of course, the first to abandon her family for religious life. But all those good Christians had, Claude explained, left their children with "their goods and their possessions," supporting and providing for their children as if they had still been with them, and so left them "in such a way that they did not really leave them." If ever Jesus's counsel was "practiced in its perfection," concludes Claude, it was assuredly by his mother who left Claude "without goods, without support, without industry, abandoning him to the sole providence of the one who called her."[46]

In both *Relations*, Marie reports an immediate feeling of "complete peace" upon entering the convent, which seemed to her a true "paradise of delights."[47] "Words cannot describe," she writes in the *Relation* of 1654, "how sweet religious life was to me after a commotion like the one I had left, and [how sweet it was] to find myself a novice whose only task was to observe the rule."[48] Marie's long-awaited peace, however, was soon disturbed by the young Claude's calculated and tenacious efforts to win his mother back. On one occasion, Claude "came to the church when we were saying mass and passed part of his body through the window of the communion grille," demanding again that his mother be returned to him.[49] He then "went to the parlor and pestered the nun in the attending box to give me back or to let him enter with me. I was sent to see him. I calmed him down and consoled him. I was given some little presents to give him. When he left, he thought I was going to the dormitory. The nuns in the attending boxes outside noted that he walked out backwards, his eyes fixed on the windows to see if I would be there . . . until he lost sight of the monastery."[50] Claude even managed to find a way breach the walls of his mother's cloister. "Seeing by chance, the big convent door left open by workmen," Claude wandered into the convent's most interior courts, once making "so many turns without knowing where he was going that he finally found himself in a room where the whole community was gathered, about to sit down to eat."[51] "I leave you to imagine," Claude comments in the *Vie*, "what kind of impression the unexpected presence of a son can make on a mother under such extraordinary circumstances."[52]

Supplementing Marie's account of the assaults she endured upon entering religious life with additions to his *Vie de la Vénérable Mère Marie de l'Incarnation* furnished by his own memory, Claude recounts how he sometimes "threw his coat or his hat" into the convent choir and on one occasion presented his mother with "some lugubrious verses on the subject of her retreat" penned by her brother-in-law in the voice of the abandoned son, and "all this in such tender terms and with such animated affections that one would have had to be made of something other than flesh not to be moved by it."[53] To all appearances, Marie read these verses with "an unshakable confidence" that elicited the admiration of her fellow Ursulines. On the inside, though, her heart ached, visible only to "the eyes of God and the angels."[54]

"But the strongest blow" of all, Marie admits in a letter written in 1669, was when Claude, in the company of his sympathetic peers, besieged the monastery demanding Marie's return. I heard your voice, Marie recalls, "distinct from the others wailing pitiably that your mother be given back to you and that you wanted to see her."[55] This particular episode was not one Marie could easily forget. She describes it not only in her correspondence with Claude, but also in both *Relations*, where she is careful to craft the episode as an instance of peer pressure. It was not Claude's idea to besiege the convent, Marie insists in both the *Relation* of 1633 and the *Relation* of 1654, but that of his friends who succeeded in "affecting [Claude] very strongly" and in "throw[ing] him into such an affliction that he almost never moved from our grill where he made complaints and asked for me."[56] Elaborating on the incident in the *Vie*, Claude likewise casts it as an "innocent conspiracy" engineered by his friends who, "seeing him deprived of lots of little comforts that mothers give their children . . . [and seeing] him one day strongly stricken with sadness" were moved by compassion. "They set themselves to consoling him," Claude continues, "and in order to do it effectively they said to him: you have neither this nor that, because you have no mother; but come, let's go ask for yours. We will make noise, we will break down the doors, we will make them give her back to you."[57]

In thus representing the siege of the monastery, mother and son collude to absolve Marie from the guilt of having abandoned Claude. Cast as a schoolboys' prank, a childish scheme—at any rate, someone else's idea— the *Relations* and the *Vie* alike foreclose the possibility that the episode could have been, in fact, an indication of Claude's genuine affliction. The witnessing public, however, was not so sure. The spectacle of "an army of children" laying siege to a cloistered convent attracted the attention of passersby. Some "laughed about it as a game of children." Others, however, "had compassion about it" and sided with the children in accusing Marie of an unnatural insensitivity "for leaving a son at such a tender and weak age."[58] Indeed, the criticisms that Marie had endured from the outside before entering religious life continued unabated after she joined the Ursulines. Everyone, she writes in the *Relation* of 1633, "blamed me for leaving thus a child who was not yet twelve years old, without any assured support . . . Others said that I was a cruel mother or a mother with little heart, who, to content myself, had carelessly abandoned my son."[59] Even Marie's fellow Ursulines were "keenly touched by grief and compassion" for Claude.[60]

In implicit contrast to her family, friends, and fellow Ursulines who had proven themselves all-too-readily susceptible to Claude's emotional appeals, Marie stood firm in her commitment to religious life. What bothered Marie most about Claude's assaults on the convent was not the indication they gave of how much Claude was suffering in her absence, but the threat that they posed to her religious vocation—a point she makes three times over, first in the *Relation* of 1633, then in the *Relation* of 1654, and finally in a letter dated July 30, 1669. I thought, Marie admits in the *Relation* of 1633, that the community "would soon cast me out of the house and that since I could not stand all these things, all the more reason why our Reverend Mother and all the sisters couldn't stand them, having no obligation to do so."[61] Marie's fears, however, were soon put to rest by the assurances of none other than God himself, who promised her ("climbing one day the steps to our novitiate") that "I would be a religious in this house."[62]

Marie's claims of "peace and certitude" to the contrary, a close reading of the *Relations* and letters reveals the very real ways in which Marie continued to have misgivings about her religious vocation long after en-

tering the convent. Marie's doubts about whether God was, in fact, calling her to religious life began—at least according to the testimony provided
by the *Relations*—in the weeks before she entered the convent. Although
she did, indeed, take comfort in the gospel story of Jesus in the Temple,
Marie confesses in the *Relation* of 1633 to have had "many other [thoughts
about Claude's disappearance] . . . that troubled me, and tended to make
me believe that all the inspirations that I had received to give myself to
God and to leave the world had been temptations rather than true inspirations."[63] So uncertain was Marie about the authenticity of her vocation
that she found herself "powerfully united with Our Lord for several days"
following Claude's return home. Over the course of these few days, Marie
discussed with God the details of his plans for her. She was ready "to
obey [God] in everything," but asked for his guidance on the questions of
her religious vocation and her decision to abandon Claude. Pleading with
God to relieve her doubts, Marie could only importune ceaselessly, "Hey!
Do you want this, O my Love? Hey! Tell me, do you want this?"[64]

Marie's misgivings about the abandonment continued up to—and
beyond—the moment of her entry into religious life. On the eve of her departure, Marie testifies in the *Relation* of 1654 to her concern for "my
son, who was not yet twelve years old" and whom she had opted to leave
bereft of all material possessions.[65] The devil, she reports, "pressed me
about that, making me see that I had been foolish to have thus left my
own interests, having done nothing for myself or for my son, and that, to
have wanted to leave him in this state would be to ruin him, and finally
to engage my conscience powerfully."[66] Later, after Marie had been with
the Ursulines for some time, the devil "attacked" her again,

> persuading me that I was the cause of [Claude's academic troubles] . . . ;
> that I was obliged to return to the world to give order there; that other-
> wise, I would be the cause of my son's misfortune; that it seemed
> indeed that it was to content myself that I had entered into religious
> life; that it was not the spirit of God that made me leave the world, but
> only the inclination of my self-love; that finally this child would be
> ruined, that I would forever have only disappointment about it, and that
> I would be the cause of his ruin.

"My understanding was so obscured by all these thoughts," Marie concludes, "that I believed that all this would surely happen, and that

however certain I believed myself to be in religious life, these were only imaginings."[67]

It was only when Claude himself entered religious life in 1641 that Marie claims to have put to rest any lingering doubts about the abandonment and her own religious vocation. In a letter written to Claude just three years before her death, Marie describes how she suffered on his account, "fearing that my estrangement from you would lead to your ruin and that my relatives and friends would abandon you." One time, she continues, "the devil gave me a strong temptation that this had happened by means of certain incidents with which he filled my imagination . . . I thought then that I would die of sadness." Marie's misgivings, however, were fleeting, for "shortly after, I learned about your retreat from the world into holy religion, which revived me like a dead person coming back to life."[68]

Aggie took her first steps—her first wobbly, tottering, lurching steps—on August 5, 2013. She was thirteen months old. Any baby's first steps are exciting. But Aggie's? They were astounding. They were breathtaking. They were, in truth, nothing short of incredible. Aggie would walk, Dr. Inder had confirmed that day in the imaging center, but it probably wouldn't be until she was three years old. So when Aggie did walk on August 5, 2013, at the age of thirteen months, I was revived like a dead person coming back to life. All my doubts, my fears, my dark imaginings about what Aggie could do and who she would become evaporated in the heat of her triumph.

My euphoria lasted for some weeks afterward. But then, slowly, slowly, the old familiar apprehension returned. What if this milestone wasn't really all it was cracked up to be? Just because Aggie had walked on time (well within the range, in fact, of what was typical) didn't mean that her struggles were over. There might, indeed, be light at the end of the tunnel, but I couldn't see it yet. I found this disappointing.

Up and down. Up and down. I had been told it would be like this.

Read against the grain, the letters suggest that Marie's misgivings about the abandonment never really did abate. Over the course of her thirty-one-year correspondence with Claude, Marie returns repeatedly to the subject in an attempt to justify her decision and to obtain absolution from the abandoned son himself. In a letter dated September 6, 1641, Marie pleads with her son to acknowledge the abandonment as the primary (and necessary) cause of his spiritual success: "You were abandoned by your mother and your relatives. Hasn't this abandonment been useful to you?"[69] Some thirteen years later, Marie answered for Claude: "For if I abandoned you in your childhood, moved by his grace, without leaving you with any support other than his totally pure providence, he took you into his paternal protection and richly provided for you, giving you the honor of calling you to his service at a time preordained by his eternal counsel . . . You have therefore won much in losing me, and my abandonment has been useful to you."[70]

Even as she sought to secure Claude's absolution for the abandonment, Marie rendered the decision one of little consequence to her young son. To begin with, Marie insisted, the separation was only temporary. Reflecting on the abandonment, Marie admits to Claude in a letter written in the summer of 1647 that she "consider[ed] myself an infinity of times the cruelest of all mothers" and that she had been "the cause of your having suffered much affliction." She goes on to ask Claude's forgiveness, displacing responsibility for the abandonment to God and reasoning that "life is short and that, by the mercy of the One who thus separated us in this world, we will have an entire eternity to see each other and celebrate each other in him."[71] Moreover, in withdrawing from the world, Marie was not—all appearances to the contrary—leaving Claude without a mother. The child would suffer none of the disabilities of the orphaned, for Marie had placed him "in the hands of the Mother of Goodness, trusting that since I was going to give my life for the service of her Beloved Son, she would take care of you."[72]

In constructing such an elaborate defense of the abandonment, Marie doth protest too much (methinks). The decision to abandon Claude in favor of religious life had been anything but easy for Marie—and anything but obvious. Over time, however, the abandonment assumes the position of the necessary and the coordinates of the inevitable, taking its place in Marie's own narrative as a sacrifice performed in submission to the unambiguous will of God and in conscious imitation of Christ. Over time, between the *Relation* of 1633 and her last letter to Claude in 1671, Marie's doubts about whether the abandonment had been divinely inspired give way to a (professed) certitude that it had. By the end of her life, Marie had succeeded in taming the unruly event of the abandonment—one that had threatened to undermine both her identity as mystic and her identity as mother. Rendered a sacrifice in submission to the will of God and in imitation of Christ carried out (critically!) against the wills of both mother and son alike, the discordant event of the abandonment is made concordant within the temporal totality of Marie's singular life story.

To be fair, allusions to an interpretation of the abandonment as a sacrifice performed in submission to the will of God and in imitation of Christ are not altogether absent from the *Relation* of 1633. There, Marie represents the abandonment as an act carried out in obedience to Christ's evangelical command and in deference to "the will of Our Lord."[73] Repeatedly, too, throughout the *Relation* of 1633, Marie invokes the language of the cross to describe her maternal sufferings on Claude's behalf. For Marie, Claude's flight from home on the eve of her entry into religious life was a "most painful" cross. His assaults against the convent were, likewise, "crosses," and Marie's fear that she would be expelled from the convent a "cross quite heavy." Although the news of Claude's debauchery at school only made "my cross heavier," Marie did not shrink from her agonies but instead appealed to God to let her "suffer still more for my son." Offering herself to God as a martyr willing to give up her own life for the salvation of her son, Marie asked God to "make me suffer all the crosses that it pleases you if this child ever offends you." For, she explained, "I would prefer to see him die a thousand times than to see him offending you in the world, and not being one of your children. Oh! I very much want to be on the cross, martyred in all ways, provided that you take care of him."[74]

But there is ambiguity here. Recall that repeatedly in the account of the abandonment given in the *Relation* of 1633, Marie admits to profound misgivings about her religious vocation—wondering whether God really *was* calling her to religious life and whether God really *was* asking her to leave Claude—with the effect of undermining and destabilizing her representation of the abandonment as God's will. By way of contrast, in her letters to Claude (the earliest of which postdates the *Relation* of 1633 by eight years), Marie gives voice to none of the uncertainties that threaten to disrupt the narrative of the abandonment in the *Relation* of 1633. As early as 1641, Marie explains to Claude that despite her aversion to leaving him, she "had to obey his divine will, which wanted things to happen thus."[75] Thirteen years later, she refuses even to inquire into God's motives for the abandonment, reasoning to Claude that "it's not for us to enter into the domain of his providence or to penetrate the profound secrets of his operations on us, but only to conclude that he wanted it thus, without having regard for his creature."[76] Gone entirely are any traces of doubt about the abandonment. In marked contrast to her own testimony in the *Relation* of 1633, Marie claims in a letter to Claude dated August 16, 1664, that "I never did anything with such generosity and with so much confidence in God as when I left you out of love for him."[77]

What was only implicit in the *Relation* of 1633, moreover, is made explicit in the *Relation* of 1654. There, in the context of a passage in which she describes her second thoughts about leaving Claude for religious life, Marie boldly declares the abandonment itself nothing short of a sacrifice. "I loved my son with a very great love," she insists, "and leaving him constituted my sacrifice."[78] Carried out against her own inclinations and against the powerful pull of her natural affections for Claude, the abandonment was an act performed in submission to God's will. "I blinded myself voluntarily," Marie confesses in the *Relation* of 1654, "and committed everything to his Providence."[79] Marie extends her representation of the abandonment as a sacrifice in imitation of Christ in her correspondence with Claude. Like the sacrifice of Christ, the theological significance of which lies not so much in the fact of the crucifixion as in the fact of the resurrection, the significance of Marie's own sacrifice was apparent not in the moment of the abandonment but in what happened after. In her letters home to Claude, Marie spares no ink in detailing the fruits of the abandonment. It was, she insists, the primary cause of Claude's spiritual success among the Benedictines of St. Maur, an inexpressible "boon" that guaranteed Claude "the great and inestimable happiness of the religious profession."[80] It was also the only conceivable reason for her own spiritual gifts, for which Marie could give no other justification than "you, whom I abandoned for his love at a time when, according to all human reason, you needed me most."[81] And, indeed, it was on account of the abandonment alone that mother and son—separated from one another in the flesh—were now united together "in the bosom of this totally lovable God" by virtue of a shared vocation in religious life.[82]

Against all expectations, the abandonment—like the painful and igno-minious death of Christ on the cross—had turned out to be good news.

Taking his mother's cue, Claude develops the sacrificial interpretation of the abandonment in the *Vie de la Vénérable Mère Marie de l'Incarnation*, finding precedent for what Marie had done in the models of Abraham, Jacob, and Christ himself. "The most difficult part of her sacrifice," Claude confirms, "was to abandon her son whom she was going to leave young, without means, without industry, without support."[83] Identifying himself as "an Isaac, an only child, whom God gave to [Marie] in order to test her faith and her love," Claude compares his mother to Abraham, insisting that in both cases, God provided the strength and courage to sacrifice the be-loved child against reason, natural law, and ecclesiastical norms. He goes on to justify Marie's action as one of obedience to a supernatural light, affirming that "the light that caused Patriarch Abraham to see that he could himself immolate his own son . . . was the same that made this generous soul see that she could abandon her own, after God had declared to her so many times that this was his will."[84] Marie, Claude insists, abandoned her son, her only son, whom she loved, not on account of per-sonal desire or even indifference, but against the inclinations of natural affections no less powerful than those of Abraham himself.

For Claude, the story of Jacob—the Hebrew patriarch whose favorite son Joseph was sold to Midianite slave traders by his jealous brothers—likewise provided an illuminating parallel to the circumstances of his own abandonment. Recalling how, after his mother joined the Ursulines, he occasionally entered into the choir and "threw his coat there or his hat" in view of his mother, Claude comments that "the sisters had been able to say to [Marie] what Joseph's brothers said to their father Jacob, 'See if these are the clothes of your son.'"[85] To a Christian audience attentive to the parallels between Joseph's story and Christ's own story, Claude's allu-sion to Genesis 37 would have been heavy with sacrificial implications.

Claude, however, did not stop there. In his account of the schoolboys' siege of the Ursuline monastery Claude makes explicit his interpretation of the abandonment as a sacrifice offered not only in the company of Israel's greatest patriarchs, but also in imitation of Christ. When his friends and classmates surrounded the monastery clamoring for Marie to return to Claude, "the heart of this strong but nonetheless tender mother found itself much more powerfully afflicted, for among this confusion of cries, she heard distinctly the voice of her son, like an innocent ewe who distinguishes among a thousand [the cry] of her own sheep."[86] Claude's thinly veiled allusion here to the paschal lamb of John's gospel puts the finishing touches on his representation of the abandonment as an instance of Christian sacrifice.[87] His mother's decision to abandon him had not been a careless one motivated by selfish interests, but like the sacrifice of the Lamb of God himself a loving parent's generous gift of her only beloved son.

As the contours of abandonment as the unequivocal will of God sharpen over the course of Marie's correspondence with Claude, Marie slips into place alongside Claude as its reluctant and resistant victim. Admitting the legitimacy of Claude's grievances against her in a letter from the summer of 1647, Marie insists that she, too, would complain "if I could about he who came to bring a sword to earth, making such strange divisions."[88] In defense of the profundity of her maternal sentiments, Marie explains that "even though you were the only thing left in the world to which my heart was attached, he nevertheless wanted to separate us when you were still at the breast." Like Claude, who did not give his mother up easily to religious life, Marie "struggled to keep [Claude] for nearly twelve years." Finally, however, overcome by the will of God (who was "unmoved by the tender feelings I had for you"), Marie "had to yield to the force of divine love and suffer this blow of division which was more painful than I can tell you."[89] Like Claude, Marie resisted the abandonment; like Claude, Marie grieved over the separation; like Claude, Marie was the victim of God's uncompromising demands.[90] In the place of the opinion of outsiders (who had accused Marie of maternal negligence and malignant self-interest for having abandoned Claude), Marie offers to Claude in the *Relation* of 1654 and in her letters an alternative interpretation of the event. The abandonment was not, as the witnessing public may have suspected, an injury inflicted by an indifferent mother on her *unloved* son, but the result of the imposition of divine will on a resistant mother and her *beloved* son—the double victims of a sacrifice of biblical proportions.

Rendered a sacrifice performed in submission to the will of God, in imitation of Christ, and against the inclinations of both mother and son, the abandonment operates within the context of Marie's life story to heal the fracture in a personal identity split between the facts of motherhood and mysticism. By styling the abandonment thus, Marie exculpates herself from the guilt of having wronged Claude. The way Marie tells it, the abandonment was not her fault, but God's. It was, after all, only out of obedience to God's "absolute will" that Marie finally resolved to leave Claude. Against those who accused her of having abandoned Claude out of self-interest, Marie insists that the abandonment had actually been *contrary* to her own interests (which "concern[ed] the obligation of a mother toward a son").[91] Eager to defend the intensity of her maternal sentiments and the authenticity of her maternal identity, Marie renders herself, like Claude, the victim of a sacrifice ordered from above. "Know then, once more," she commands Claude in a letter dated July 30, 1669, "that when I separated myself from you, I died while still alive."[92] In crafting the story of the abandonment as one of sacrifice performed in submission to God's will, Marie can have it both ways. Within the context of the *Relation* of 1654 and Marie's later correspondence with Claude, motherhood and mysticism are no longer discordant facts that bedevil the logic of Marie's narrative identity, but two aspects of one life brought together in harmony through the idiom of Christian sacrifice.

———

Marie's representation of the abandonment as a sacrifice performed in submission to the will of God followed a social script that would have been readily familiar to a Christian audience well versed in the gospel narrative and the legends of the saints. The story of a family rent by the force of divine love, of obedient submission to the will of God, of the painful (but productive) suffering wrought by the experience of sacrifice was an old one. In rendering the abandonment in the idiom of Christian sacrifice, Marie made sense of the event within the broader context of her personal narrative. For Marie, the abandonment was not just inevitable (God's will) and necessary (the exclusive cause of the spiritual successes of both mother and son), but meaningful, too. Freighted with theological significance, the abandonment takes shape in the *Relations* and in the letters as an instance of ethical and creative action—an index (in Ricoeur's terms) of *ipseity*. It was, in the context of the story Marie tells about herself, constitutive of her very identity as, at once, a mother bound irrevocably to her only beloved son and a mystic chosen specially by God for a "lofty vocation."[93]

To suggest that Marie's representation of the abandonment as a sacrifice performed in submission to the will of God and in imitation of Christ is scripted is not to suggest that it is somehow inauthentic. The stories we tell about ourselves, after all, do not just express our experiences but actively operate to shape those very experiences themselves. In a chapter from his acclaimed meditation on the enterprise of religious studies, *Between Heaven and Earth*, Robert Orsi writes about his grandmother's devotion to St. Gemma Galgani, a turn-of-the-century stigmatic from Lucca, Italy. Born, like Gemma, in Tuscany around the end of the nineteenth century, Orsi's grandmother found in Gemma Galgani someone with whom she shared the common experiences of suffering and pain, abuse at the hands of family members, and a frustrating longing for an absent lover. Taking his grandmother's relationship with Gemma as an index of the broader dynamic between Catholic saints and their devotees, Orsi argues that "making lives in relation to sacred stories proceeded on both conscious and unconscious levels." Not only was "the saint . . . a straightforward model of the good life," but "in deeper and unnoticed ways, the movements of the most extraordinary desire, pain, and joy in a saint's life opened and oriented those who lived their lives in relation to these narratives to similar and unexpected levels of experience and emotion."[94] Catholic devotees like Orsi's grandmother, in other words, did not just find in the stories of the saints echoes of their own life experiences. They actively *experienced life itself* in conversation with the stories of the saints.

If Orsi is right (and I think he is), the idiom of Christian sacrifice functions not only as the means by which Marie discursively represents the abandonment in the *Relation* of 1654 and her correspondence with Claude, but furnishes the medium through which she actually experiences the abandonment. Just as Orsi's grandmother recognized "something of herself . . . in Gemma's story and something of Gemma's in hers," so Marie saw parallels between her own story of suffering, sacrifice, and salvation and those of Christ and the saints. In apprehending the abandonment as a sacrifice performed in submission to the will of God and in imitation of Christ, Marie made sense of the event to herself and to the witnessing public—and not just *post hoc* but *per hoc*, too.

Or, at least she tried to. Reflecting on his own family's history, Orsi doubts whether "the religious idioms that shaped the stories . . . [my grandmother told] made [her life] any more comprehensible or bearable."[95] Meaning-making, Orsi insists, "is the wrong register in which to think about" the relationships between religious people and their sacred narratives. What sacred narratives offer is not a reservoir of ready meanings that explain away life's inconsistencies and agonies, but "companionship on a bitter and confusing journey."[96] If we shift our focus from the meanings made by religious narratives to the processes of meaning-making, Orsi argues, we will "see . . . the wounding."[97]

Attending to the process by which Marie makes meaning of the abandonment in the *Relations* and the letters helps us to see just how unstable Marie's rendering of the abandonment as Christian sacrifice really is. Marie's repeated articulation of the abandonment in the idiom of sacrifice— obliquely at first in the *Relation* of 1633, then directly in the *Relation* of 1654 and in the letters—does not reveal her conviction that the abandonment really was a sacrifice performed in submission to the will of God, but rather her fear that it wasn't.[98] At work in the *Relations* and the letters— and, indeed, Claude's *Vie de la Vénérable Mère Marie de l'Incarnation*—is a process of meaning-making that is never quite finished. For both Marie and Claude, the abandonment remained incomprehensible, its ambiguities never quite resolved by the *Relations*, the letters, and the *Vie*. It was, in Orsi's language, an open wound that no amount of sacrificial narrative could ever quite heal.

On a warm, sunny Saturday in May, Bobby and I sat on our driveway watching the joggers and the bikers and the parents pushing baby strollers on the path in the park across the street. Our four children played nearby—Johnny with an oversized Bruder transport truck and Frankie with an assortment of Legos. Little Bobby was decked out in St. Louis Cardinals gear from head to toe, waiting to go to his first baseball game of the season. And Aggie was on a blanket between us, practicing crawling on all fours, a skill she had mastered just the day before. It had been only six months since that encounter with Dr. Inder in the imaging center, and the wound of Aggie's unexpected diagnosis was still raw.

Do you think Orsi's right, I asked Bobby. Is it enough that we have companionship on life's bitter and confusing journey? Is it enough to know that we're not alone? Is meaning-making really the "wrong register" within which to think about people (religious or not) and their stories (sacred or not)? I can't think, I confessed, of another way of dealing with tragedy and suffering other than trying to make it meaningful. What else can we do when the going gets rough than give the rough-going a meaning, a purpose, a raison d'être so that we can *keep* going?

There are, as one might imagine, a whole host of online communities—blogs, chat rooms, Facebook groups—populated by the families of children who share Aggie's particular genetic condition. Within these communities, stories of struggle and success, sorrow and joy, fear, dread, and optimism circulate readily and rapidly, offering easy companionship to anyone who wants it. But I don't want it. For me, these stories only multiply the bitterness and confusion of my own journey. The companionship offered by stories like these does not make my going any easier, but to the contrary, makes it harder. When I read these stories, it is as if I bear the weight of not just my own tragedy but the weight of the tragedies of countless others. And it's enough to make me feel like I *can't* go on.

In the aftermath of Aggie's diagnosis, I tried out various ways of making sense of what had happened. Aggie had been born with a deletion in her seventeenth chromosome in order to bind our family more tightly together, in order to teach our boys compassion, in order to show us how to love more deeply, feel more sharply, think more creatively. This had happened to render our lives even richer and more vivid than they would otherwise have been. This had happened for a reason. And a good reason, at that. All these interpretative possibilities were, of course, ways of making Aggie's diagnosis mean something. I didn't need to believe that there really *was* a meaning (I am, I admit, too much of a postmodernist for that), but I needed to believe that I could *make* a meaning out of it. I needed to find a way of making the discordant event of Aggie's diagnosis concordant with the temporal totality of my own singular life story. What meanings I make of Aggie's diagnosis might change (and have changed) over time and, at any one time, I might make it mean more than one thing. The meanings I make of Aggie's diagnosis are, in other words, neither fixed nor singular. But meaning-making is at the heart of what I do when I think about what happened.

And I suspect it was so for Marie, too. I suspect (strongly and without much doubt) that when Marie turned to the idiom of Christian sacrifice as a means of explicating the abandonment she was engaged in a process of meaning-making. Although Marie might, indeed, never have succeeded in settling the meaning of the abandonment once and for all, meaning-making is precisely the right register in which to think about what's going on in the *Relations* of 1633 and 1654 and in Marie's correspondence with Claude. In the story of Christ's own sacrifice performed in submission to the will of God, Marie found not just companionship—plain and simple— on a bitter and confusing journey, but meaningful companionship. Sacred narratives, after all, are powerful narratives because they are purposeful narratives. The stories of Christ and the saints and other holy men and women are stories with happy endings. They are stories that promise redemption and resurrection, salvation and deliverance—and all this not in spite of but *because of* tragedy and suffering. They are stories that, in the end, make it all mean something.

2

Explanation: Contextualizing
the Abandonment within
Seventeenth-Century French
Family Life

The way Marie tells the story in the *Relations* of 1633 and 1654 and in her letters home to Claude, the abandonment was a sacrifice performed in imitation of Christ and in submission to the unambiguous will of God. Much as Christ himself had pleaded with God to "take this cup from me" (Luke 22:42), so Marie had resisted delivering "the blow of division" that God had commanded her to carry out. Marie's sacrifice of Claude, much like Christ's own sacrifice, had been contrary to both natural instinct and human reason. But in the end Marie, much like Christ himself, had overcome herself in obedience to God's uncompromising will. According to Marie, the abandonment was not her idea, but God's idea.[1] God had acted; Marie had only reacted; God had commanded, Marie had obeyed; God had dominated, Marie had submitted. Thus understood, the abandonment fits readily into a binary framework which parses human action as either domination or resistance.

In her masterful analysis of the evangelical Women's Aglow Fellowship, R. Marie Griffith calls for "fresh ways to think about power and resistance."[2] The testimonies of healing wrought by prayer offered by the evangelical women of the Aglow Fellowship conform—much like Marie's explication of the abandonment—to an established set of narrative conventions. According to these conventions, healing (from illness, from abuse, from grief) is found in a "total surrender of the will and an unending struggle to 'know' God and please him"—a posture that ought to be replicated by women in the home.[3] Although the narrative accounts that circulate among members of Aglow hew closely to the script of female submission, Griffith finds "a high degree of innovation" in Aglow's interpretation of just what female submission means.[4] Even within the tightly circumscribed spaces of healing narratives, evangelical women find ways to "continuously redraw and renegotiate the boundaries of power and authority."[5] Encoded in the accounts of female surrender, Griffith notices women's "assertions of power over bad situations" as they "center their narratives on their own capacity to initiate personal healing and cultivate domestic harmony."[6]

There is a story Griffith tells about a woman named Mary who found herself in an unhappy marriage with a husband she describes as unappreciative and demanding. On the verge of seeking a divorce, Mary "asked Jesus to come into her heart, forgive her sins, and be the master of her life." Shortly thereafter, Mary "was baptized in the Holy Spirit" and, from that point on, was better able to control the anger she felt toward her husband. The next time her husband chided her for not having his lunch ready, Mary was able to simply apologize: "Cal," she said, "I've irritated you by not having your lunch ready. I'm sorry." Mary's decision to submit to her husband was conceived and executed by Mary herself. Mary had taken control of her personal happiness and failing marriage by choosing— willingly and deliberately—to submit to her husband. Thus, Mary testifies, "we were able to grow in love for each other and for Jesus, until now, five years later, we are able to minister to others."[7]

Like the evangelical women of Aglow Fellowship who at once adopt and adapt a narrative of female surrender, Marie de l'Incarnation conceals the exercise of her own agency under the cover of a Christian script of sacrifice performed in submission to the will of God. I would not go so far as to argue that Marie does this deliberately or with any trace of subversive intention (she does not). But I would argue—and I do in the pages that follow—that Marie's agency as the author of the abandonment is best understood, like the agency exercised by Aglow women through the medium of prayer, not as simple submission (or, alternatively, resistance), but as a maneuvering in the interstices between submission and resistance.

On its face, the story of the abandonment in the *Relations* of 1633 and 1654 and in Marie's letters is one of unequivocal submission. It is a drama, as we have seen, in which God plays the leading role as the all-powerful sovereign to whose will Marie ultimately can't help but surrender. Belying her claims to passivity, however, the *Relations* and the letters fairly bustle with Marie's activity in executing God's orders. In the months preceding the abandonment, Marie busied herself with discerning just which religious community she would enter, arranging for Claude's education among the Jesuits of Rennes, and securing special permission to join the Ursulines without a dowry. The *Relations* and letters also betray the critical evidence of Marie's creative initiative in interpreting just what the abandonment entailed. Nowhere, after all, in the *Relations* or in the letters does Marie claim that God had ordered her to leave Claude without any goods or possessions. This last bit was Marie's own inspiration, for "according to my interior sentiments, I thought I was leaving more in leaving my son whom I loved a lot, than if I had left all imaginable possessions and above all if I left him without support."[8]

Her own rhetoric of submission notwithstanding, Marie's response to God's command that she forsake "her very dear and beloved son" was hardly one of passive acquiescence.[9] It was, instead, one of active collusion and creative elaboration. It was also one of calculated resistance. In what follows, I argue that in abandoning Claude "without any assured support," Marie defied—and knowingly so—the conventions of seventeenth-century French family life.[10] Scholars have squabbled about just what the seventeenth-century French family looked like, and especially about whether parents loved their children, whether children loved their parents, and how love was expressed between parents and children. If the available evidence makes one thing clear, however, it is that early modern French parents were charged with the absolute and essential obligation to protect the patrimony of their children. More than anything else, parents in seventeenth-century France were expected to meet the material needs of their children—feeding them, clothing them, making arrangements for their futures, and ensuring the stable transmission of goods from one generation to the next. Within this historical context, the abandonment was at once an act of submission to the uncompromising will of God and, at the same time, an act of resistance against the norms of seventeenth-century French family life. If, in leaving Claude for religious life Marie submitted to God's will, in leaving Claude *with nothing* Marie resisted the social practices of her contemporaries. Put differently, encoded in Marie's own account of surrender is an assertion of a certain kind of power over and against the expectations of her time and the standards of her place.[11]

In the beginning, when Aggie was first diagnosed, I had allowed my imagination to run wild. Or maybe I just couldn't keep it from running wild. It ran, really, in all directions—to the abyss of what this disability might mean for the future of our family (A child in a wheelchair? A child who can't talk? A child who never grows out of diapers?), to the apex of what was possible for Aggie, missing genetic material and all. I had even allowed myself to wonder whether, absent from my own genetic material—or indeed Johnny's, because he, too, had a conspicuous mole on his left lower leg and an unusually large right cerebral ventricle—was that same bit of the long arm of the seventeenth chromosome. Maybe, I had allowed myself to wonder, we are a family just particularly well adapted to make do without this handful of genes. Maybe, I had reasoned, encoded in our family's unique genetic constitution were tools (especially sturdy and versatile tools) that Aggie could use to compensate for what she lacked. Truth be told, I still believe this. And don't fault me—it's to Aggie's advantage that I do. But when I shared these thoughts with my best friend, she could only reply, I think you're having a hard time accepting this.

———

A few years ago when I was giving a paper on the subject of the abandonment at St. Louis University, someone among the roomful of faculty and students asked me, "But was it really abandonment?" That, of course, was a very good question. After all, Claude was eleven years old at the time of the event in question, hardly an infant and, by early modern standards, almost a young man. Within the context of our own time and place, eleven-year-old children are still very much children, in need of the constant, solicitous attention of their parents (and particularly, according to the logic of intensive mothering, the constant, solicitous attention of their mothers), whose natural love would not tolerate premature separation from their offspring anyway. The abandonment might, indeed, have been unthinkable for most of us. But would it have been unthinkable for Marie's contemporaries? Measured against the standards of maternal care in seventeenth-century France, did Marie fail to fulfill her responsibilities toward Claude in leaving him—without material support but in the care of his aunt and uncle—to answer the call of her religious vocation? Situated within the historically and culturally specific context of Marie's time and place, was it really abandonment?[12]

To tender an answer to this question invites engagement with two lines of scholarly inquiry on the subject of families in medieval and early modern Europe—the first having to do, specifically, with the phenomenon of child abandonment and the second having to do with the nature of the family and childhood. As John Boswell and others have shown, the incidence of child abandonment was anything but rare in former times.[13] Medieval and early modern European parents relinquished control over their children for a host of different reasons and under a host of different circumstances. Pressured by poverty, shame, greed, and other factors, parents donated their children to religious houses, sold their children as servants to the rich, and placed them with "relatives, feudal subordinates, other rulers, or other householders, to be reared from early childhood through adolescence."[14] In the most egregious (but far from uncommon) of instances, parents simply "exposed" their children, leaving them somewhere outside the home to be discovered (or not) and rescued (or not) by the "kindness of strangers."[15] Although Church and state alike made sporadic attempts over the course of Western European history to curb and control the phenomenon, child abandonment remained a fact of life in medieval and early modern Europe, a necessary evil ("in the absence of any other acceptable means of family limitation") "to be regulated and coped with rather than opposed absolutely."[16]

Juxtaposed with the practices of her more negligent parental peers, what Marie did in giving Claude over to the care of her sister and brother-in-law, arranging for his education, and maintaining regular and even intimate contact with him over the course of her decades-long religious career was anything but an obvious case of abandonment. It was, instead, something more like fostering—a fairly ordinary arrangement for a fairly independent young adult. Given the social practices of her contemporaries, Marie can hardly be accused of having abandoned Claude outright. But what of other, more subtle forms of abandonment? Within the context of seventeenth-century France, after all, abandonment implied not simply desertion, but neglect. Antoine Furetière's 1690 *Dictionaire Universel* defines abandonment as "disregard, the desertion of something," giving as an example someone who "abandoned his house to be pillaged."[17] If Marie did not neglect Claude so absolutely as to expose him to the mercy of strangers, can she nonetheless be accused of having neglected her maternal responsibilities vis-à-vis Claude in other ways? What were mothers in seventeenth-century France expected to do for their children anyway? How were they supposed to treat them? Were they supposed to love them? Teach them? Discipline them? Provide for them? And how did Marie compare?

The terms of the conversation about the nature of the family and childhood in the history of Western Europe were set by Philippe Ariès's *L'Enfant et la Vie Familiale sous l'Ancien Régime* (translated into English as *Centuries of Childhood*) in 1960.[18] Famously (and, by now, infamously), Ariès argued that until the seventeenth century Western European society knew nothing of childhood as a separate stage of life. Largely indifferent to the fate of their offspring, medieval parents harbored no special sentiment toward their children.[19] Instead, children were treated as adults-in-the-making, members of an undifferentiated society which made no effective distinction between the young and the old.

Against the grim backdrop of the medieval European family (which, David Herlihy argues, "has become the negative stereotype against which later families are compared"), Ariès drew the contours of the modern family.[20] If the medieval family was conspicuous for its lack of sentiment about children and childhood, the chief attribute of the modern family was an evident appreciation for what was special about children and childhood. No longer considered latent adults, children were treated to an educational program that became, over the course of the modern period, increasingly specialized. The manuals and handbooks of the modern period testify to the development of what David Hunt calls a "detailed program for the raising of children" and to the growing tendency of parents to invest heavily—both materially and emotionally—in their children's futures.[21]

If for Ariès the advent of the modern family was a matter of decided ambivalence (he found much to appreciate about the newfound sentimentality toward childhood, but mourned the loss of the family's ties to the broader community and the freedom and tranquility enjoyed by children in times past), historians who came after were decidedly less ambiguous. For the likes of Lloyd DeMause, Edward Shorter, and Lawrence Stone the rise of the modern family was an occasion for celebration—largely on account of a perceived improvement in the relations between parents and their children.[22] Curiously (since Ariès never made the claim that medieval parents lacked affection for their children), in the decades following the publication of *L'Enfant et la Vie Familiale sous l'Ancien Régime* the debate about the nature of the family and childhood in Western European history became one about whether parents loved their children and how much.[23]

And so it remained, until the 1983 publication of Linda Pollock's *Forgotten Children: Parent–Child Relations from 1500 to 1900*. Convinced that "it stretches the evidence entirely too far to maintain that children were undifferentiated from adult society or that harshness, at best indifference, was their lot," Pollock rejected Ariès's contention that medieval Europe knew nothing of childhood and challenged the scholarly consensus that medieval parents had no affection for their children.[24] There has always been a notion of childhood as a separate stage of life, Pollock insisted, and Western European history abounds with evidence of the strength of affective ties between parents and their children—even if parents in modern times showed their affection differently than in times past. Against the weight of scholarly opinion that represented the history of the Western European family as one of change, Pollock proposed the hermeneutic of continuity.

In the aftermath of Pollock's seismic intervention in the debate about the family and childhood, most historians now agree that there was, indeed, a notion of childhood in medieval Europe—even if that notion bears scant resemblance to the notion of childhood in the modern West. Shulamith Shahar, for example, takes as a given "that a concept of childhood existed in the . . . Middle Ages," but contends it was a profoundly ambivalent one for medieval Europeans.[25] On the one hand, the medieval literature on children and childhood emphasizes the natural goodness and innocence of children and represented childhood as a period of blessed naïveté and unequivocal faith. On display in the devotion to the child Jesus (whom contemporary artists tenderly represented laughing, playing, weeping, and nursing at his mother's breast), the medieval appreciation for what was special about children accentuated the ways in which children possessed admirable purity and innocence largely lacking in their adult counterparts.

On the other hand, however—and perhaps overwhelmingly so—medieval commentators drew attention to what was wrong with children and to the dark side of childhood.[26] Medieval theologians reminded parents that it was through the act of sexual intercourse (which was, of course, necessary in all cases but one for the production of children) that the original sin of Adam and Eve was transmitted from one generation to the next. Not only were children tainted from the moment of conception by the stain of original sin, medieval commentators insisted, but they also tended to exhibit the worst in human behavior—jealousy, avarice, rage, and aggression. Helpless and irrational in ways that bore comparison to other, more beastly members of the animal kingdom, children were creatures distinguished (following Aristotle) by what they *lacked*. The evidence, as Hugh Cunningham puts it, is indisputable "that in [the Middle Ages] . . . childhood was recognized as a separate stage of human existence"—if an unfortunate stage that ought to be passed through as quickly as possible on the way to adulthood.[27]

Just as most historians now agree that medieval Europeans recognized childhood as a separate stage of existence, so most historians now also agree that medieval parents had—and showed—affection for their children. For Steven Ozment, the emotional tenor of letters exchanged between parents and their children provides eloquent testimony of the affective ties that bound medieval families together.[28] For Pollock, it is the sustained contact between parents and their children long after the children left home.[29] For Yvonne Knibiehler and Catherine Fouquet, it is the proliferation of ex-votos left at shrines and other holy places.[30] Other scholars have found in Christian practice and the hagiographic tradition evidence of a passionate attachment to children and to the notion of family. Gesturing to the cult of the infant Jesus (which flourished in the twelfth century) as the locus within which medieval Europeans could express "sentiments concerning childhood, sacred and profane," David Herlihy contends that Christian devotional practice "exploited real attitudes towards babies."[31] For Herlihy, the lives of the saints "show beyond question that the medieval family was not an emotional desert."[32] Although it is indeed true that Christian hagiography tended to exploit the theme of antagonism between the saint and his family (repeating, ad nauseam, the stories of the families who stood between the saint and his unconditional love for God), the writings about the saints also made ready use of motherhood, fatherhood, childhood, and spousal relations as metaphors for the expression of spiritual ecstasies and mystical experiences.[33] As Herlihy puts it, "In their struggle to achieve sanctity, the saints break free from family entanglements, but not at all from familial sentiments."[34]

These days, the conversation about the history of the family in Western Europe is less about *whether* families today are similar to or different from families in times past, and more—and more productively—about *how* families today are similar to or different from families in times past. The conversation has shifted, in other words, from a discussion of whether medieval Europeans had a sense of childhood and whether medieval parents loved their children, to a discussion of how the medieval and modern concepts of childhood compare and how medieval parents expressed their affection for their children in comparison to their modern counterparts.[35] By most accounts, the medieval take on childhood (which was ambivalent at best, unfavorable at worst) gave way by the modern period to a sense of childhood as the best time of life. Unlike their medieval predecessors who had viewed "the small child as a predatory and frightening creature," modern parents began to appreciate their children as a source of enjoyment.[36] The proliferation of books, toys, games, and clothing specially created and intended for children testified to a cultural sense of just how different from adults children were—and happily so. For modern parents, childhood deserved to be savored and children deserved to be nurtured. By the modern period, the business of raising children had become a serious one, a task requiring constant parental vigilance and one with critical consequences to the child's future.

Had it ever. The number (and diversity) of after-school classes offered by Bobby's elementary school is staggering. Learn basic principles of engineering with Bricks 4 Kidz! Hone your multiplication skills at Math Lab! Master the fundamentals of Okinawan Karate-do! And learn Japanese at the same time! Bobby is involved in a handful of activities, but for the most part I try to keep these seductive offers at arm's length. It is tempting— and convenient—to believe that the more you sign your child up for, the more he'll know and the better he'll do. Every eight weeks when Forsyth School rolls out a new listing of after-school options, I am (I admit) briefly seized by a moment of maternal anxiety. Should Bobby do Rock Climbing 101? What about Junior Mad Science? Or Mandarin Chinese? Is he missing out on some critical developmental opportunity by wrestling in the backyard with his brothers instead of learning how to paint like Georges Seurat? I realize—I really do—that my concerns are the luxuries of the affluent. My friend Emma, who sends her children to a public school in St. Louis, reminds me that her daughters' peers are worried about much bigger things—like where they're going to live, what they're going to eat, how they're going to get to school. Fair enough. But isn't it still true that to whom much is given, much is expected? Isn't it my maternal obligation to see to it (as best I can) that my children do more than "just fine"? That they exhaust their potential? That they, in fact, max out?

———————

If the concept of childhood transformed over the course of the modern period, so did notions of familial affection and its modes of expression. Jean-Louis Flandrin notes that conduct books on domestic morality written between the fourteenth and the sixteenth century rarely make mention of love within the context of the family at all.[37] And while the subject does begin to appear in manuals dating to the end of the sixteenth century, explications of love within the home are mostly confined to an absence of hatred and a fulfillment of obligations until the close of the eighteenth century. In a manual for confessors written in 1713, for example, the moralist Antoine Blanchard discusses the subject of domestic affection only in its negative dimensions, condemning wives' indifference toward their husbands and children's hardheartedness toward their parents.[38] Where conduct books composed prior to the eighteenth century do dwell on more positive expressions of love, it is only to condemn their excesses. Blanchard, for example, urges confessors to determine whether parents harbored "too much attachment for one of your children at the expense of the others," and condemns husbands for "form[ing] an attachment for some woman other than your wife."[39] As Jean-Louis Flandrin puts it, "Far from uniting the family, affection and sentimental attachments were suspected of provoking all kinds of disorders."[40] In the eyes of premodern theologians, domestic affections were among the most pernicious of worldly entanglements.

By the latter half of the eighteenth century, however, notions of domestic love had transformed from an absence of ill-feeling to the presence of "an inwardly felt tenderness or . . . an impulse of the heart which impels one to do all that one can—and not just what one ought—for the person one loves."[41] As a consequence of the churches' loosening grip over domestic morality more generally, families were, in Flandrin's words, "left . . . free" to love one another.[42] Catechisms penned between 1765 and 1815 begin to make mention of love within the context of the family in terms that still ring true today: love meant respecting the vocation of one's children, keeping society with one's spouse, and doing everything one could for someone.[43] Certainly by the end of the eighteenth century, the Western European family had become a "companionship family," founded on the strength of the conjugal tie and the natural resource of maternal love.[44]

Some historians date the emergence of the modern family not to the eighteenth century but to the seventeenth century or even earlier. As early as the twelfth century, Phyllis Gaffney argues, Western European attitudes toward childhood had begun to subtly shift. Looking closely at the representation of children in old French narrative, Gaffney contends that the emergence of romance as a genre reflects a "slow conversion of sensibility towards the young."[45] In place of the strong, fearless, and precocious child–hero of the epic poem, children in old French romances are vulnerable and immature, and childhood (which "has moved to centre stage") is a time of development, self-discovery, and nurture.[46] For Ariès, too, the first signs of changing views on children and childhood were apparent well before the definitive advent of the modern family. As early as the thirteenth century, Ariès points out, realistic portraits of children and clothing and games designed specifically for children give evidence that the slow process that would eventually end in the modern family had begun.

For most historians, however, it would take the demographic and economic transformations of the early modern period as well as the influences of cultural and religious forces to effect the metamorphosis of the family from a loose collection of extended kin to a tight grouping of parents and children bound together by tender affection. Inspired by the humanists' emphasis on the importance of mutual love between parents and children, early modern Protestants and Catholics alike drew attention to the responsibility of parents to ensure—by means of discipline and education—the salvation of their children's souls.[47] Martin Luther, for example, argued that there was no more valuable school for the development of a child's character than the family. In an early modern Europe fractured by religious difference it was, more than ever, on the shoulders of mothers and fathers that the weighty task of educating children in the ways of both God and the world rested. By the end of the early modern period, European parents had begun to regard childhood as a precious stage of life. And they were doing it for longer. With money to burn and time to spend, Europe's emerging middle class seized the opportunity to indulge their children—materially, emotionally, and otherwise—well beyond the period of "hurried infancy" tolerated by their medieval ancestors.[48]

I noticed it first at Thanksgiving. Little Bobby wanted nothing to do with me. Albeit a full head shorter than his ten- and eleven-year-old cousins, he had declared himself one of the big guys. He brushed past me, his cheeks flushed from playing football outside in the late November chill. I tried to grab him for a kiss. He pushed me away, indignant. Little Bobby's growing up, I said to (big) Bobby on the ride back home. He doesn't just not *need* me anymore, he doesn't *want* me anymore. But this, of course, was the way it was supposed to be. About a year ago, when we were in the hospital with Aggie (where she had been admitted, officially, for "feeding difficulties" and, unofficially, for the express purpose of getting our insurance company to pay for this complex genetic test known as the chromosomal microarray), my sister-in-law had dropped in for a visit. Liza's presence was a comfort, as it always is. An emergency room physician and the mother of two young boys, Liza is good at knowing when to worry and when not to worry. She's just being a girl, Liza had joked, as Aggie slept soundly (IV catheter dangling from her head) in the round metal crib next to us. Just wait until she's a teenager! Even then, back before we'd received the results of the microarray, back when it was still possible that there might be nothing wrong, back when we might still reasonably accuse ourselves of hypervigilance or overreaction, I knew enough to yearn for Aggie's rebellious adolescence. I knew enough to want Aggie to talk back to me, to lie to me, to sneak out of the house to hang out with her boyfriend. I knew enough to dismiss the sentimental fantasy of endless childhood (so unfamiliar to our medieval ancestors!) as seriously misguided and foolishly shortsighted. The only problem with children, an elderly man had said to me once in passing, is that they grow up. These are the words of a father who has never faced the possibility that one of his own children might *not* grow up.

How, then, ought we to situate Marie and Claude and the event of the abandonment in relation to the historiography of childhood and the family in Western Europe? Did Marie's decision to leave the eleven-year-old

Claude stand out as anomalous within the context of seventeenth-century France? Measured against the standards of her time, did Marie neglect the obligations of a mother to her son? Was it, in short, really abandonment?

We are, admittedly, in a difficult spot with Marie and Claude and the relationship between them. Marie entered religious life in 1631, well after Catherine of Siena had cautioned the Countess Benedette Salimbeni against the "disordered love" for their families to which women, in particular, were susceptible.[49] To be sure, the Europe within which Marie bore, raised, and later left Claude was no longer one convinced of the inadequacies and animalistic attributes of children as in times past. And yet, it was not yet the Europe within which the floridly affectionate letters of Madame de Sévigné to her daughter were published, promoted, and celebrated as the exemplary expression of maternal love.[50] It was not yet the Europe within which Rousseau's *Julie ou La Nouvelle Héloïse* glorified the domestic affections and the passionate excesses of heartfelt love. The Europe of the early seventeenth century was, instead—as handbooks like Richelieu's 1640 *Instruction du Chrétien* make clear—one within which Christian moralists were just beginning to draw attention to the duties parents owed their children (and not just, as before, those children owed their parents).[51] Chief among the parental duties identified by seventeenth-century manuals and handbooks were the duties to educate, love, and materially support one's children. Seventeenth-century parents like Marie were expected, at the very least, to provide their children with instruction both sacred and secular, to have and show affection for their children, and to feed and clothe and guarantee the futures of their children.[52]

Since at least the Middle Ages, the Church had drawn attention to the responsibilities of parents—particularly mothers—as the first and most important teachers of their children, a point reinforced by the popularity of representations of St. Anne teaching the Virgin Mary to read, walk, pray, and write. Despite the fact that written sources have Mary leaving home at the age of three to live out her childhood in the temple, European artists persisted in portraying the education of the Virgin as the occupation of her mother Anne well into the seventeenth century.[53] Like Anne had done for Mary, mothers in the Christian West were expected to teach their children about things both sacred and secular. A mother's direct educational obligations toward her son, however, ceased when the boy reached the age of seven and entered into the society of men. From that point on, the education of boys became the responsibility of the boy's father or a male tutor, the presumption being that continuing maternal education would only "soften" boys who needed the influence of adult males to learn how to become men.[54]

It is reasonable to suspect (as Claude's biographer Dom Guy Oury does) that Claude's early instruction at his mother's side might have suffered when Marie moved together with Claude to the Buisson household. It is hard to imagine, after all, that Marie would have had either the time or the energy to devote herself to Claude's instruction in the midst of her administrative responsibilities with the Buisson's business and her increasing occupation with prayer. The quality of Claude's early education notwithstanding, however, Marie can hardly be accused of neglecting her pedagogical obligations toward her son as a consequence of the abandonment. By the time Marie left Claude for religious life, the boy was already eleven years old and well beyond the age at which most boys of his time and place would have left home for a more formal education anyway. Under these circumstances, Marie's decision to arrange for Claude's education by the Jesuits of Rennes was anything but a dereliction of maternal duty. To the contrary, in giving Claude over to the care of professional (male) tutors, Marie was only doing what was expected—and, indeed, required—of her by the standards of seventeenth-century French family life.

If seventeenth-century French parents were expected to educate their children, they were also expected to love their children—even if theological treatises and domestic handbooks rarely elaborate on the subject.[55] Just what parental—and, specifically, maternal—love meant to Marie and Claude and others in seventeenth-century France, however, bears consideration. Given the demographic, social, and economic realities of life in seventeenth-century France, neither Marie nor Claude could reasonably have believed that maternal love meant the abiding presence of a mother at her child's side. The facts of famine, plague, and armed conflict, after all, rendered the early modern family a shifting network of relations between kinsmen who occupied the spaces left vacant by deceased husbands and wives, mothers and fathers. The reality of premature death in early modern Europe meant that, not uncommonly, it was on the shoulders of uncles, stepfathers, grandmothers, and others that the burden of parental responsibilities fell. Indeed, that Claude lived with his maternal aunt and uncle after his mother entered religious life would have been far from unusual in seventeenth-century France, where the guardianship of orphans was typically assumed by the brother of the departed.[56] Even if mothers and fathers did survive to usher their children into adulthood, the social customs of child rearing in seventeenth-century France suggest that maternal love was not—and could not have been—expressed by a mother's commitment to assume the role of exclusive caregiver vis-à-vis her children. Not only were early modern French mothers like Marie in the striking habit of putting their infants out to nurse (only to welcome them back home when they were weaned two years later), but some also arranged for schooling and apprenticeships away from home for children as young as seven.[57] Parents and children in early modern Europe found themselves separated from one another for a variety of other reasons, too. In times of natural disaster or civil unrest, parents sent their children to live, at least temporarily, with relatives far from home—and they did this not because they didn't love their children, but because they did. Within the context of early modern Europe, the domestic affections did not just make room for the separation of children from their parents, but occasionally demanded it as the best way to protect and provide for children. Measured against the standards of her own time and place, then, Marie can hardly be accused of indifference toward Claude simply because she absented herself from him physically.

And yet, read as testimony of the contours of seventeenth-century expectations of familial affection, the *Relations*, the *Vie*, and the letters betray something of a generational conflict between mother and son on the subject of maternal love. If, for Marie, it was enough that she satisfied her obligations to educate Claude and provide for his future, Claude expected something more from his mother—something more heartfelt, something more inwardly felt, something more tender. To be fair, allusions to a heartfelt affection and tenderness for Claude are not altogether absent from Marie's writings. Marie, for example, was only too aware that a mother's love expressed itself in physical caresses, embraces, and a unique maternal tenderness (although she seems not to have appreciated such displays of maternal affection as of any material consequence to Claude's future).[58] Moreover, at several points in the *Relations* and in the letters, Marie admits to feelings of compassion for Claude as well as to sensations of physical pain upon leaving Claude—first for the Ursuline convent in Tours and then later for the wilderness of the New World. Abandoning Claude—"the only thing left in the world to which my heart was attached"—had caused Marie "strange agonies known to God alone" and made her feel such pain that "it seemed to me I was being split in half . . . [although] I did not let it show."[59]

Whatever affection Marie had for Claude, however, was not enough to keep her from religious life. Nor was it enough to overshadow the "sense of calm" instilled in her upon receiving God's promise that "he would take care of you" after she had entered religious life.[60] What seemed to bother Marie most about leaving Claude for the convent was not that her absence would deprive him of the tender affections owed a mother to her son, but that she might fail in her obligations to educate him and to secure for him something of a comfortable future. Shortly after Marie entered religious life, Claude began to misbehave at school. He "did not want to study any longer, or do anything else, [such that] it seemed like he would never be good for anything."[61] So disruptive had Claude become that the headmaster of the Jesuit seminary at Rennes threatened to send him home. Marie confesses in the *Relation* of 1633 to have suspected that "I was the cause of all this trouble" and to have worried that "I would be the cause of my son's misfortune . . . that . . . this child would be ruined . . . and that I would be the cause of his ruin."[62] Concerned that she would be sent back into the world to set Claude straight, Marie attributed Claude's debauchery to divine chastisement "or, indeed . . . a trap that the demon set for me to impede my profession."[63] If Marie worried that in leaving Claude for religious life she might put at risk his education, she also feared that he would amount to nothing absent her maternal solicitude. "It seemed to me," Marie admits to Claude in a letter written toward the end of her life, "that in leaving you so young, [I risked that] you would not be brought up to fear God and that you could fall into bad hands or under some influence where you would be in danger of ruin . . . [and that] I would be deprived of a son whom I wanted to raise only for the service of God, staying with him in the world until he was capable of entering into some holy religious order."[64] On both counts, however, God "who always pitied my weakness assured me interiorly that he would take care of this child."[65] With God's guarantee that he would provide both for Claude's education and his future, Marie was at "peace and . . . troubled myself no longer," confident that her maternal responsibilities toward Claude would be satisfied from above.[66] And, indeed, just two years after she migrated to New France, Marie got word of Claude's "retreat from the world into holy religious life," which "revived me like a dead person back to life."[67]

If, for Marie, it was enough that she made good on her obligations to see that Claude was educated and settled in life, Claude expected more. Despite the knowledge that he would be supported by his aunt and uncle and educated by the Jesuits of Rennes, Claude resisted his mother's departure, protesting that he would no longer be able to see her. In his *Vie de la Vénérable Mère Marie de l'Incarnation* Claude reports a conversation he had with his mother on the eve of her entry into religious life. Taking her son aside, Marie explained to him that her inclination for religious life had only intensified with the passage of time and that she had, until now, resisted it "because being as young as you are, I have not wanted to leave you, believing that my presence was necessary for you to learn to love God and to serve him well." Asking for the young Claude's consent to her departure, Marie reminded her son that "God wants this . . . and if we love him, we must also want it. It is for him to command and for us to obey." That being the case, Marie concluded, "don't you earnestly want me to obey God, who is ordering me to separate myself from you?" Claude, he reports, "was dumbfounded, and in his astonishment, all that he could say was this response of a child: But I won't see you anymore!"[68] Many years later, Claude would again make the connection between maternal love and maternal presence, accusing his mother of lacking affection for him by having abandoned him twice over. For Claude—as for his peers who pitied him for going without the "little comforts mothers give their children"—a mother's love had an affective dimension that could not be replicated by others.[69]

Repeatedly throughout his *Vie* Claude labors to ascribe to Marie the inward, heartfelt tenderness he thought fitting for a mother. Eager to affirm at once Marie's stability in religious life and at the same time the strength of her natural maternal affections, Claude reads between the lines of Marie's *Relations* to find evidence of his mother's passionate love for her only son. Claude's unexpected presence in the cloistered convent "pierced" Marie's heart with "sentiments of love and pity"; the sight of his coat and hat in the choir "gave . . . mortal ravages to her soul"; the poems Claude delivered to his mother in the voice of the abandoned son inflicted on her heart "very painful blows." "But what touched this generous and invincible soul most vividly," Claude avers, "was an army of children . . . who went to besiege the monastery. At the same time that this group of children besieged the monastery, the heart of this strong but nevertheless tender mother found itself much more strongly besieged, for among this confusion of cries she heard distinctly the voice of her son. With this blow, strength had to give way for a moment to the tenderness by which this invincible heart was totally penetrated, and by which all other courage than her own would have let itself be defeated."[70] The way Claude tells it, the abandonment (and what followed after) gave proof not of Marie's tepid affections for her only son, but of the profundity of her ardor for God and the solidity of her commitment to religious life. His mother, Claude insisted, had loved him with the emotional intensity expected of mothers in modern times—an intensity which, indeed, only magnified the dimensions of her maternal sacrifice in abandoning Claude. A model mother and a model Christian, Marie had loved—truly, madly, deeply— both God the Father and Claude her son.

In addition to educating and loving their children, seventeenth-century French parents were also expected to materially support their children— an obligation that extended well into the child's adult future. Beginning with the strategic selection of godparents at their children's birth, seventeenth-century mothers and fathers labored to ensure that their children would enjoy comfort and security as independent adults, negotiating skillfully within their social networks to coordinate advantageous marriages, arrange apprenticeships, and secure respectable positions for their offspring. More than anything else, however, parents' obligation to materially support their children meant securing the stable transmission of goods from one generation to the next. Regional, class, and religious differences notwithstanding, if there was one thing seventeenth-century French families had in common, it was a concern to protect the patrimony of their progeny.

French legal records—from petitions for spousal separation, to arrangements for the guardianship of children, to edicts on the remarriage of widows—are univocal in their prioritization of the economic welfare of the family and, especially, the material well-being of children. Even in an early modern France in which divorce was prohibited, courts readily granted petitions for spousal separation given evidence that a husband had mismanaged family property and jeopardized the financial security of his children.[71] At the center of debates over the appointment of guardians for children who had lost one or both parents, likewise, were questions of just how the children's inheritance ought to be managed and who ought to manage it.[72] Edicts barring the remarriage of widows give additional proof of a cultural imperative to protect the economic interests of children in early modern France. According to an edict issued in 1483, a widow was prohibited from remarrying during the year following the death of her husband upon pain of losing the rights to her dowry, all goods acquired during her prior marriage, and guardianship over her children. Nearly a century later, the Edict of Second Marriages (1560) imposed similar restrictions on the remarriage of widows. Animating both edicts was the cultural suspicion that remarried widows might recklessly fritter away their children's inheritance and foolishly give their children's patrimony over to their new husbands.[73] Tellingly, by the terms of the 1560 edict, widows were not prohibited from marrying again if they had no children from their previous marriages. Nor did the edict mandate the removal of the widow's children in the event of remarriage, but only the widow's right to manage the material goods of her children. Even Francis de Sales, whose disciple Jeanne de Chantal famously stepped over the prostrate body of her youngest son to enter religious life, did not go so far as to advise widows to relinquish their material responsibilities toward their children: "The widow with children in need of her skill and guidance, especially as regards their soul *and the establishment of their life*, cannot and should not abandon them in any way."[74]

Like her contemporaries, Marie took steps—even after entering religious life—to find gainful employment for the twenty-one-year-old Claude. In a letter written to Claude dated September 10, 1640, Marie chastises her son for his "negligence" and informs him that she has written "to several of our friends on your behalf to try to find you a suitable situation in case your plans do not work out."[75] By the following year, however, Marie had second thoughts. "When I passed through Paris," Marie admits to Claude, "it would have been easy for me to place you. The Queen, Madame the Duchess d'Aiguillon and Madame the Countess Brienne, who did me the honor of looking upon me with favor . . . wouldn't have refused me anything I desired for you." Deeply suspicious of the spiritual risks of worldly rewards, Marie ultimately rejected the Duchess's offer of help. She "thanked Madame the Duchess d'Aiguillon for the good that she wanted to do for you" and resolved instead to leave Claude in the hands of the Virgin Mary alone.[76]

While Marie's eleventh-hour decision to reject the Duchess d'Aiguillon's offer to help place Claude in a position of respectable employment was, indeed, an unusual one within the context of early modern France, her determination to bequeath to Claude "neither gold nor riches . . . but only the poverty" of Jesus Christ was downright extraordinary and outrageously transgressive.[77] And Marie knew it. Not only does she admit to having suffered criticisms from the outside for leaving the eleven-year-old Claude "without any assured support," she also confesses to having been troubled on the inside by the thought of "my son, who was not yet twelve years old, denuded of all goods."[78] "The devil pressed me about that," Marie continues in the *Relation* of 1654, "making me see that I had been foolish to have thus left my own interests, having done nothing for myself or for my son, and that, to have wanted to leave him in this state would be to ruin him, and finally to engage my conscience powerfully."[79]

To be fair, the way Marie saw it—or, at least, would come to see it with the luxury of hindsight—her decision to leave Claude without goods and possessions was a strategy intended to encourage his entry into religious life. Writing to Claude in 1654, Marie insists that "if I abandoned you in your childhood . . . without leaving you with any support other than [God's] totally pure providence, he took you into his paternal protection and richly provided for you, giving you the honor of calling you to his service at a time preordained by his eternal counsel."[80] In the eyes of her contemporaries, Marie's decision to leave Claude without material goods and possessions must have seemed a blatant breach of maternal duty. In "ask[ing] . . . only the poverty of his Son for us both," however, Marie had opted (and wisely so) to trade Claude's material well-being in this life for the enduring spiritual comfort of eternal life. All appearances to the contrary, she had not neglected but actually *exceeded* her obligation to provide for Claude's future, extending her maternal solicitude from this life to the next.

So, then, was it really abandonment? In leaving Claude for religious life, did Marie neglect the responsibilities of a mother toward her son within the context of her time and place? Measured against the standard of her seventeenth-century French peers, how did Marie compare? Did she meet expectations? Or did she come up short?

By anyone's calculation, Marie had seen to it that Claude was educated. And she loved him, too—even if she didn't show it in the way Claude wanted her to. But she neglected to provide for Claude's future, and deliberately so, at that. In sharp contrast to her seventeenth-century French peers who sought to protect the property of their progeny at all costs, Marie took active steps to withdraw from Claude all goods and possessions, depriving him of his rightful patrimony. Measured against the standards of her time and place, Marie's was not just a sin of omission, but, worse, a sin of commission. In truth, it was not because she had denied Claude her loving presence in leaving him for religious life that Marie considered herself "an infinity of times the cruelest of all mothers," but because she had left him bereft of all material support.[81] Put differently, it was not so much Marie's decision to *leave* Claude for religious life, but rather her decision to leave Claude *with nothing* that stands out as anomalous within the context of seventeenth-century France. This, at the very least, was neglect. This, at the very least, was abandonment.

This, at the very least, was also resistance. To suggest that in withdrawing material support from Claude Marie resisted the conventions of her time and place is not to suggest that she purposively repudiated the practices of her contemporaries as a means of lodging a protest against the values they held dear. It is, rather, to draw attention to the ways in which the abandonment—Marie's own explication of the event notwithstanding—was about more than simple submission.

In *Politics of Piety*, her well-received study of women's support of the mosque movement in Egypt, Saba Mahmood calls for a rethinking of human agency. Against the weight of feminist tradition which locates women's action as either submission to or resistance of the conditions of their oppression, Mahmood urges her readers to recognize the ways in which agency plays out in the spaces between the binary poles of "subordination and subversion."[82] What women's submission to the virtues of modesty and humility within the context of the mosque movement makes clear to Mahmood is that agency is not just "the capacity to realize one's own interests against the weight of custom, tradition, transcendental will, or other obstacles."[83] Instead, agency assumes more complex configurations, shaping not only "those acts that resist norms but also the multiple ways in which one *inhabits* norms."[84] Within the context of the mosque movement, "norms are not only consolidated and/or subverted . . . but performed, inhabited, and experienced in a variety of ways," operating for Egyptian women as "socially authorized forms of performance . . . through which the self is realized."[85] Two examples from Mahmood's text might help to elucidate her broader theoretical point: In their arguments for a woman's right to lead prayer, the women of the mosque movement do not raise the banner of gender equality but invoke instead the opinions of the juridical schools of Islam (three out of four of which, Mahmood notes, support women's right to lead women in prayer). In their discussions of the rule of modesty, similarly, women do not contest the justice of the rule but instead how it ought to be executed and whether it requires women to wear the veil. Women in the mosque movement are not engaged in the business of subverting the norms that would seem to cripple their agentival capacities, but instead find ways in the lived practice of submission to those norms to exercise more subtle forms of agency.

Where Mahmood's work has been helpful in my appreciation of the sort of agency implicated in the abandonment is in its insistence on the "uncoupling [of] the notion of self-realization from that of the autonomous will."[86] Marie's decision to abandon Claude in favor of religious life was, indeed, one made in resistance to the norms of seventeenth-century French family life. But it was, at the same time, one made in submission to the will of God. Even if, as we have seen, Marie did act in abandoning Claude, she did not act alone. The abandonment had not been an exercise of autonomous will, dreamed up, planned out, and carried through by a self-interested Marie who wanted nothing more than to chart her own course in life. If anything, Marie wanted the opposite. Shortly after entering the convent, the devil attacked Marie, "persuading me . . . that it was to content myself that I had entered into religious life, that it was not the spirit of God that made me leave the world, but only the inclination of my self-love." All that time, Marie "feared only having offended God" and would have "preferred a thousand times not to be a religious than to displease God in the least thing."[87] For Marie, however—as for her latter-day counterparts in Egypt's mosque movement—submission did not mean incapacitation but operated instead as "a socially authorized form of performance" that enabled a particular kind of activity. Whether we describe Marie as "inhabiting" a Christian norm of submission (to borrow from

Mahmood's vocabulary) or the Christian norm of submission as "making room" (to use R. Marie Griffith's language), the point is the same: in submitting to God's will that she abandon Claude in favor of religious life, Marie found a limited sort of freedom. At last unburdened by the "only thing in the world to which my heart was attached," Marie felt her soul "melt . . . in thanksgiving for the fact that my heart and affections could open out toward God alone."[88]

He didn't open his eyes today, my mom said. It was June 9, my parents' anniversary. They had been married forty-one years. My dad had been in a nursing home for just over two. It hadn't been easy for my mom to put dad in the nursing home. She had struggled to keep him at home and manage his worsening dementia on her own. But then he had become unpredictable, violent even, and too big for her to handle. After much investigation of the various possibilities, my mom had settled on the Missouri Veterans Home—a place populated exclusively by veterans of the United States Armed Forces, and staffed by employees and volunteers alike eager to give back to those men (and women) who had served them and their country. Even though the Veterans Home is a full thirty minutes away from where my mom lives, she goes to visit my father every day. Every day. She leaves her house at 10:30, arrives at the home at 11:00, and wheels my father (who hasn't, incidentally, spoken a word in at least a year and has, as far as we can tell, no sense of where he is or who he is or what's going on around him) to the lunchroom. There she feeds him by her own hand, wipes his face, and wheels him back to his wing where she writes in a journal about their visit and leaves, to return home by 12:45.

This is not, of course, how my mother imagined that her retirement would play out. And this is not, of course, what she wanted. In fact, my mother had resisted almost everything about my father's decline into dementia—she had wondered in the beginning whether he just wasn't trying hard enough to remember, whether, if he just ate more salmon or took a brisk walk each day, he'd feel better and think sharper. Or, maybe the prescription drug Aricept would help? Maybe he could get into some experimental research program? Maybe there would be a miracle? In the end, though, my mom submitted to my father's disease. And she has found a way of inhabiting this norm of submission that, in my estimation (and,

I would contend, in anyone's estimation), is exemplary. My mom couldn't fix my dad (as hard as she tried). She couldn't cure him, she couldn't restore him, she couldn't put him back together again. But she could find a way of moving around in the small spaces left open by the norm of submission. She could find a way—and has found a way—of acting and doing in the midst of the inexorable.

I remind myself of this when I think about Aggie.

3

Explanation: The Marginalization of Motherhood in the Christian Tradition

When I was in graduate school, I was assigned to read the bestseller *Expecting Adam*, Martha Beck's memoir about bearing and raising a son with Down syndrome. Beck's story, as she tells it, is one of "two driven Harvard academics" who find meaning and miracles in the experience of parenting their special-needs child. Fundamentally a narrative of resistance to a coldly rational and achievement-oriented Harvard culture, *Expecting Adam* is the story of parents who, in "allow[ing] their baby to be born . . . [were] themselves . . . born, infants in a new world where magic is commonplace, Harvard professors are the slow learners, and retarded babies are the master teachers."[1] Part of the book's allure is Beck's representation of herself as a "thoroughly Harvardized" skeptic who is unwittingly converted from her world of logic, reason, and hard facts by the force of supernatural experiences in connection with her special-needs son.[2] It turns out, however, that miracles and magic did not exactly break in uninvited to Beck's world. The daughter of a prominent Mormon scholar and product of a devout LDS upbringing, it turns out that Beck was unusually well situated to perceive the divine operations and the angelic machinations she reports.

One of my friends, also a mother of a son with Down syndrome, relies not on God and angels (as far as I know) to make meaning of her maternal experience, but on metaphors culled from the athletic and military contexts—which, I assume, is no accident even if it is not entirely conscious. An accomplished sportswoman in her own right, Rebecca grew up in a family dominated by the athletic activities of her two older brothers, both of whom (not incidentally) later served in the United States Armed Forces. Rebecca's husband is also a former marine. Rebecca's approach to her son's condition is highly strategic and tactical. Together with other parents, Rebecca attends conferences on Down syndrome, runs races in support of the cause, and participates in clinics. She has, in her own words, gotten "in the game." She has become a member of the team, an officer in the corps.

So what about me? How have I made sense of Aggie's own diagnosis? Not unlike Martha Beck, I have found, if not meaning, then at least companionship in my religious tradition. I have taken comfort in the gospel story of Jairus's daughter (*Talitha koum!*), whom Jesus healed in the most impossible of circumstances. I have found consolation in the compassion of the Virgin Mary and in her capacity for intercession. I have taken solace—and found much food for thought—in Christian ideas about sin, suffering, redemption, and salvation. I have, on a more profane level, relied on my experience as a competitive distance runner to fuel my endurance (in the absence of any degree of raw athletic talent, I had managed to grit my way through fourteen marathons—so why not this, too?). And when the going has gotten tough, I have remembered my adolescent thirst for exotic adventure (hadn't I always wanted to trek through Bhutan, camp overnight in the Andes, rough it in Gabon?) and reminded myself that navigating the uncharted wilderness of Aggie's infancy is every bit as intense and dangerous and scary and exciting and—I expect—ultimately rewarding as these more land-bound expeditions. Sometimes I wonder how, in the end, I will tell the story of Aggie's infancy. Will it be a sacred one? Or a secular one? Will it be about grief? Or gratitude? Victory? Or defeat? Discovery? Or devastation? What, in the end, will I make it all mean?

Much as I continue to play around with various interpretative schemes in making sense of Aggie's diagnosis, so Marie must have flirted with explaining the abandonment in a diversity of ways, only to settle on the Christian idioms of sacrifice and submission. In the end, Marie tells the story of her decision to abandon Claude in favor of religious life as one of sacrifice in imitation of Christ and in submission to the uncompromising will of God. Belying Marie's claims to have only acquiesced—against her own inclinations—to divine demands imposed from without, however, is the evidence of her own active agency in shaping the story as one of sacrifice and submission. Just as I could tell Aggie's story in many variations, so Marie could have told the story of the abandonment differently. But she didn't. She had chosen the narrative of sacrifice and submission over and above all other possible narratives. If we take narrative seriously as a medium for the exercise of human agency (which I think we should), then what remains of Marie's own interpretation of the abandonment as an instance of divine domination?[3] If, in other words, it was Marie who elected to craft the story of the abandonment as one of submission in the first place, then what practical room is left for reading the abandonment as Marie's domination from without?

A fair amount, I argue in this chapter and the next. It is true that Marie chose to shape the story of the abandonment as a Christian sacrifice performed in submission to God's will, but this was a choice tightly circumscribed within the boundaries of a Christian tradition that offered but few alternatives. Marie did not so much make the abandonment meaningful through recourse to the Christian idioms of sacrifice and submission as much as the abandonment was "made by the meanings embodied, expressed, and available" in the Christian tradition.[4] As there was for Gemma and Guilia (recall, Orsi's grandmother and the Tuscan saint to whom she was devoted), "there was a narrative waiting for [Marie] that had little to do with [her] agency or intentionality." Like Gemma and Guilia—and, indeed, like Martha Beck, my friend Rebecca, and me, too—Marie was caught up in the "narrative flow," "held in the grip of available meanings."[5] Born into a religious and cultural matrix that rendered motherhood incompatible with Christian discipleship, what choice did Marie have but to abandon Claude in favor of religious life and to have made a virtue of this necessity? It is true that Marie chose to tell the story of the abandonment as one of sacrifice in imitation of Christ and performed in submission to the will of God, but how could it have been otherwise? Marie's was a Christianity, after all, in which the practice of conceiving, bearing, and mothering actual biological children had no place in the economy of salvation.

If, in Chapter 2, I proposed an explanation of the abandonment that—contra Marie's own explanation—located the event somewhere between submission (to God's will) and resistance (to seventeenth-century French standards of parental care), I advance in this chapter and the next an alternative interpretation of the abandonment as an instance of human agency that is at once autonomous (but not absolutely) and at the same time scripted (but not completely). Drawing on the work of French sociologist Pierre Bourdieu, I propose in these next two chapters an explanation of the abandonment that situates Marie within the distinctive social field of seventeenth-century French Catholicism. Circumscribed within the boundaries of a Christian tradition that left no room for actual maternal practice (Chapter 3) and that, in its seventeenth-century French incarnation, made a theological virtue of abandonment (Chapter 4), Marie's decision to abandon Claude in favor of religious life was hardly autonomous. Whatever agency Marie exercised in abandoning Claude was an agency informed by what had been possible within the Christian tradition and inflected by what was likely within the context of seventeenth-century French Catholicism.

In this chapter, I examine the etiology of Christianity's marginalization of motherhood, arguing that it is the Jesus of the gospels (whose startling command to "hate father and mother, wife and children, brothers and sisters" has inspired generations of Christian exegetes) with whom the exclusion of motherhood and maternal bodies from the Christian tradition originates.[6] For Jesus, and for Paul after him, the ties that bound mothers to sons, fathers to daughters, sisters to brothers, and children to parents proved dangerous distractions on the eve of the end-times, the successful navigation of which required nothing less than an undivided heart. Whatever forms Christian sexual ethics assumed in the ensuing millennia—and, as Peter Brown has persuasively demonstrated, these were many and varied—rules and regulations about the body, sexuality, and reproduction betrayed a persistent and deeply rooted distrust of the family. It is my contention in the pages that follow that the ideal of sexual renunciation, which by the fourth century had become a marked feature of Christianity, developed as a response to a more fundamental suspicion toward the family as an impediment to personal salvation. In other words, it is my contention that the problematization of the family came first, and a mistrust of sexuality and sexed bodies (the primary vectors for the reproduction of the family) followed.

Within this theological milieu maternal bodies and maternal practice fit uncomfortably, if at all. While, as I will elaborate below, Christianity did make room for maternal metaphors in the language of affective piety and the ideal of spiritual motherhood in the lives of the saints, the actual experience of mothering real flesh and blood progeny merited little appreciation. Beholden to the demands of her offspring (whether in utero—where they pushed and kicked and made their mothers' bodies bleed, sweat, and contract—or ex utero—where they required energy and attention, money and marriages), there was no more perfect index of humanity's enslavement to the things of this world, and no more perfect antithesis to humanity's potential for life resurrected in the next world, than the mother.

———————

Pierre Bourdieu's career as an ethnographer and social anthropologist began in Algeria in the late 1950s. By his own account, Bourdieu was, in the beginning, a "blissful structuralist."[7] Influenced by the likes of Claude Lévi-Strauss, Bourdieu found in structuralist analysis an irresistible means of making sense of social practice. For the young Bourdieu, structuralism's allure lay in its guarantee that social phenomena were readily intelligible to those who could grasp the (binary) systems of signification that gave logic to human practice. Bourdieu's 1963 essay on the Kabyle house is an excellent example not only of Bourdieu's early commitment to structuralism but also of structuralist analysis more generally.[8] In this essay, Bourdieu described the houses inhabited by the Kabyle, a Berber people living in northern Algeria, as very orderly and highly structured, "a microcosm of an entire cultural world, [and] a condensed universe full of meaning."[9] The way Bourdieu saw it, the organization of the Kabyle house reflected and sustained the "generative framework of Kabyle culture and cosmology," the key to which could be found "in the binary oppositions which it embodies"—inside/outside, east/west, back/front, light/dark, dry/damp, upper/lower, male/female, human/animal, cooked/raw.[10]

Very quickly, however, Bourdieu became disenchanted with the usefulness of structuralism as an explanatory mechanism for understanding the logic of social practice. Structuralism, Bourdieu had discovered, did little to account for what human actors did or to predict what they would do in any given situation. The rules according to which structuralism supposed human actors operated revealed more about the perceptions and expectations of the sociologist observers than about the logic of native practices. What was really going on, Bourdieu began to suspect, had more to do with strategies (which make room for improvisation and adjustment) than rules (which presuppose mechanistic application). Social practice, Bourdieu began to see, was not as simple as applying compulsory rules automatically and unthinkingly to the circumstances of life. The objective analysis perfected by structuralism was not sufficient to account for the logic of practice.

At the same time, however, Bourdieu knew that social practice was not entirely conscious, deliberate, and intentional. Human actors were not exactly autonomous, free to choose this or that course of action. The possibilities for social practice, Bourdieu realized, were not limitless. Instead—and this is what scholars widely consider Bourdieu's most valuable contribution to sociology—social practice unfolds somewhere between objectivism and subjectivism, somewhere between the extremes of social determinism and individual autonomy. The logic of social practice, Bourdieu insists, is resembles the logic of a game. Like the game of football, the social game has rules that determine what players can and cannot do. But like action on the football field, social action is not deliberately orchestrated or organized in conscious application of these rules. It is, rather, "a mastery acquired by the experience of the game . . . which works outside conscious control and discourse . . . in the way that . . . techniques of the body do."[11] In the game of social practice, players engage in strategic action, knowing "without knowing—the right thing to do."[12]

Critical to Bourdieu's conceptualization of social practice is the notion of habitus. Habitus, a term that appears prior to Bourdieu's appropriation of it in the work of Hegel and Durkheim among others, is an "acquired system of generative schemes objectively adjusted to the particular conditions in which it is constituted," a system, in other words, "of durable, transposable dispositions, structured structures predisposed to function as structuring structures, that is, as principles which generate and organize practices and representations that can be objectively adapted to their outcomes without presupposing a conscious aiming at ends or an express mastery of the operations necessary in order to attain them."[13] The schemes and dispositions which constitute the habitus are embodied, inflecting the way social actors walk, talk, and carry themselves more generally. They are not conscious or intentional stances taken up vis-à-vis the social world; instead, their "power . . . derives from the thoughtlessness of habit and habituation."[14]

The notion of habitus allows Bourdieu to bridge the gap between a concept of human agency that emphasizes the autonomy of the subjective actor on the one hand, and one that emphasizes the authority of the objective environment on the other. Although the habitus is unique to each individual—shaped by the idiosyncrasies of personal experience, class, gender, and economic resources, inter alia—there is a dialectical relationship between the habitus and the objective environment, such that the objective conditions of social life inform and force the adjustment of the habitus to what is probable or possible within that environment. As Bourdieu puts it, "the dispositions durably inculcated by the possibilities and impossibilities, freedoms and necessities, opportunities and prohibitions inscribed in the objective conditions [of social life] . . . generate dispositions objectively compatible with these conditions and in a sense preadapted to their demands."[15] Habitus, then, gives rise to social practice by predisposing actors toward a limited set of options: "The most improbable practices are . . . excluded as unthinkable, by a kind of immediate submission to order that inclines agents to make a virtue of necessity, to refuse what is anyway denied and to will the inevitable."[16]

The importance of the objective environment to Bourdieu's understanding of social practice is captured by the notion of the social field. A social field, Bourdieu explains, is "a network, or a configuration, of objective relations between positions objectively defined . . . in the structure of the distribution of power (or capital) whose possession commands access to the specific profits that are at stake in the field, as well as by their objective relation to other positions."[17] A social field, in other words, is an arena within which actors compete over access to resources, jockeying to maintain or improve their position vis-à-vis the resources that define the field. Social practices are never generated in isolation but instead always "in and by the encounter between the habitus and its dispositions, on the one hand, and the constraints, demands and opportunities of the social field or market to which the habitus is appropriate or within which the actor is moving, on the other."[18]

Taking my cue from Bourdieu himself, who cautions against a rigid application of "this or that technology of . . . analysis as the penultimate badge of scientificity," I have been careful in what follows not to structure my reading of Marie de l'Incarnation and the abandonment according to the rubric suggested by Bourdieu's understanding of human agency.[19] I am less concerned in what follows to identify the various component parts of Marie's habitus (informed, no doubt, by her childhood visions and premature widowhood, among other things) and to delineate the boundaries of the social field of Christianity (marked, to be sure, by competition for theological authority, ecclesiastical power, and ultimate salvation). I am, instead, interested in making use of Bourdieu's work as a helpful medium for thinking about the dynamics of freedom and constraint at play in Marie's decision to abandon Claude in favor of religious life and to explicate the event in the idioms of Christian sacrifice and submission to God's will. In what follows, I have allowed Bourdieu's notions of habitus and social field to loosely guide my interpretation of the abandonment as neither an instance of domination (the Scylla of social determinism!) nor of resistance (the Charybdis of existential autonomy!), but as an instance of a human agency confined within the boundaries of what was possible and, indeed, necessary within the context of the Christian tradition.

I am not, of course, the first to notice the tendency of the Christian tradition toward the marginalization of motherhood and the exclusion of the maternal body.[20] Much of Clarissa Atkinson's career, for example, has been devoted to identifying and accounting for Christianity's fraught relationship with mothers. Jane Schulenburg, too, has noted the incompatibility between motherhood and constructions of Christian sanctity in the Middle Ages. Training her lens on early medieval hagiography, Schulenburg argues that representations of motherhood in the lives of female saints betray a discomfort with maternal experience—rendering it at once a sacred calling and at the same time inferior to a life of virginity and an obstacle to spiritual growth. Similarly, Anneke Mulder-Bakker's edited volume on sanctity and motherhood in the Middle Ages addresses the problem of the representation of motherhood in the lives of the saints. Few saints' lives, notes Mulder-Bakker in the introduction to *Sanctity and Motherhood*, tell the stories of women whose maternal practices provided the context for the exercise of saintly virtues. Indeed, in most cases, medieval women became saints despite having been mothers. With few exceptions, artists in the Middle Ages did not represent female saints together with their children, but in their roles as abbesses, nuns, or sovereigns instead.

The explanations offered to account for the marginalization of motherhood within the Christian tradition have varied. Atkinson, for one, points an accusing finger at Neoplatonism and its presumptions about the antagonism between body and soul (which left mothers, beholden to the demands of their own bodies as well as to those of their children, at a decided disadvantage).[21] Schulenburg, for her part, places the blame on the prioritization of virginity as the female virtue par excellence (to which motherhood was, of course, irredeemably opposed).[22] Others have faulted Paul (whose ordering of the spirit over the flesh lent itself to subsequent misinterpretation as an antipathy toward the body), still others, Augustine (whose yoking together of original sin and sexual reproduction reinforced the associations between motherhood and the Fall), and yet others, Aquinas (whose revival of Aristotle made the convictions about women's natural defectiveness and inherent subordination part of mainstream Christianity). While there is, no doubt, some truth to each of the preceding arguments, I lay the burden of Christianity's unease about mothers at the feet of none other than Jesus (the Jesus, at least, of scripture) himself. More than Paul's dichotomization of the spirit and the flesh, more than the influence of Platonic dualism, more than the revival of Aristotelian anthropology, Jesus's own articulate subordination of the biological family to the exigencies of Christian discipleship provided the foundation for the enduring exclusion of motherhood from the center of the Christian tradition.

To a Jewish audience, Jesus's subordination of the family would have been unusual (though not entirely alien). Family, after all, is fundamental to both the biblical narrative and to the biblical theology that takes shape through that narrative. It is, in particular, the story of one specific family—its marital intrigues, its fraternal conflicts, its filial dramas—that dominates the Hebrew Bible. The stories of fathers and mothers, wives and children, brothers and sisters are not peripheral to the theology of the Hebrew Bible, but absolutely central to the character of the biblical God as it unfolds in human history. Indeed, one of the most salient recurring motifs of the Hebrew Bible is that of the barren woman who conceives miraculously (though not virginally), giving proof of a biblical God who intervenes to propagate the family and sustain it.

By the first century, however, the notion that family obligations might hinder spiritual progress had begun to take root among certain radical Jewish groups. For those like the Dead Sea Scroll sect, the imminent end of the world required a strict celibacy, the practice of which was presumed conducive to an undivided heart. There was, as Peter Brown has pointed out, nothing novel about the ideal of the undivided heart in the first century, which stood metonymically for the whole human person (body and soul) in harmony with God. Nor was there anything novel about the notion that sexual relations (even sexual temptations) impeded the culti-vation of the undivided heart. But in a first-century Palestine abuzz with expectations of the imminent apocalypse, these themes assumed a par-ticular urgency.

It was within this historical context that Jesus's exhortations to "hate father and mother, wife and children, brothers and sisters . . . [and] be my disciple" were received by his Palestinian–Jewish listening public.[23] For Jesus, as for his radical Jewish counterparts, there was no better way to prepare for the end of the world than to align one's heart with the will of God. If, to the Dead Sea Scroll sect, sexual relations were the chief impediment to an undivided heart, to Jesus—and to Paul after him—it was the biological family created and sustained through sexual rela-tions.[24] There was no time, when the end of the world was nigh, to marry and to bury. There was time only to "hear the word of God and do it."[25] The heavenly kingdom promised by Jesus was not, moreover, one marked by family harmony and the reunion of loved relations. "I have come," Je-sus proclaims in the gospel of Matthew, not "to bring peace to the earth . . . but a sword . . . I have come to set a man against his father, and a daughter against her mother, and a daughter-in-law against her mo-ther-in-law; and one's foes will be members of one's own household."[26] At the end of time, Jesus predicted, the flesh and blood ties that bound members of the biological family together would give way to spiritual connections forged between believers united in a shared religious faith.

Under the influence of the patristic fathers of the first few centuries after Christ, the evangelical suspicion toward the family gave way to a more general suspicion toward sexual activity and sexed bodies.[27] By the fourth century, among Christian theologians, "sexuality [had] edged itself into the center of attention, as a privileged symptom of humanity's fall into bondage."[28] For the Encratites (who were, admittedly, on the extreme end of the theological spectrum), sexual activity "made plain humanity's present separation from the Spirit of God."[29] For Gregory of Nyssa, it was the sexually differentiated bodies of men and women. For Augustine, it was sexual desire. If early Christian theologians found in sexual activity the causes and effects of humanity's fall, they located in sexual renunciation the possibility of humanity's salvation. By the fourth century, among Church fathers in both East and West, sexual renunciation "came to be linked on a deep symbolic level with the reestablishment of a lost human freedom, with a regaining of the Spirit of God, and, so with man's ability to undo the power of death."[30] Patristic theologians from Tertullian to Origen to Augustine saw in the practice of sexual continence a means of making way for the gift of the spirit, recovering the original integrity of the human person, and anticipating the promise of the resurrection.

As a number of scholars—most notably Michel Foucault—have argued, the Christian sexual ethic that emerged out of the early Church was in many ways continuous with the Greco-Roman cultural milieu within which it was elaborated in the centuries following Christ.[31] Contrary to popular opinion, ancient Greece was not a "sunny 'Eden of the unrepressed'" and early Christian morality not a reaction to pagan promiscuity.[32] Rather, Greek sexual morality around the time of Christ intersected with (and arguably influenced) its early Christian counterpart in a number of important respects.

To begin with, by the second century before Christ the Greeks had come to suspect that sexual activity was dangerous—not just in excess (a point Plato had made long ago), but (as Origen and Ambrose and Augustine would argue some centuries later) in any amount. Philosophers like Galen and physicians like Soranus insisted that sexual intercourse depleted the body's heat, a sufficient quantity of which was necessary to maintain virility. An excessive loss of the body's heat might not turn a man into a woman, but it did risk making him *like* a woman—cooler, softer, and lacking in self-restraint.

Second, from this generalized suspicion of human sexuality grew an impulse (with parallels in Christianity) to subject sexual activity to a rigorous control. Part of a broader program geared toward the cultivation of the self, the regulation of the sexual urge in the Greek context demanded a consideration of the age and temperaments of the consenting partners as well as the timing and duration of the sexual act in an effort to coordinate the sexual urge as perfectly as possible with the needs of the body.[33]

Third, from this generalized suspicion of human sexuality, too, grew the twin impulses to chastity and abstinence which would, of course, be richly elaborated in the Christian context in the centuries to come. Against the grain of an earlier sexual ethic that had celebrated "the political and virile domination of desires" and had regarded virginity as physically unhealthy, later Greek sexual ethics made room for the practice of sexual renunciation.[34] For the likes of the Pythagoreans and Orphists, there was no more eloquent testimony to the virtues of moderation and self-control than the untouched virginal body.

Finally, for all their hesitations toward human sexuality, second-century Greeks (like early Christians) nonetheless recognized the value of sexual relations within the boundaries of marriage. In contrast to their philosophical predecessors (like Plato) who had advocated the abolition of marriage and the communal pooling of women, Stoics like Musonious, Antipater, and Hierocles recognized in marriage and in marital intercourse a "means for mutual friendship . . . between husbands and wives."[35] Sexual fidelity encouraged attachment, affection, and respect between spouses; sexual infidelity threatened the opposite. In further anticipation of early Christian sexual ethics, the Pythagoreans even went so far as to limit sexual relations not only within the confines of marriage but also for the sole purpose of procreation.

Early Christian attitudes toward sexuality, then, were in many ways continuous with Greek sexual ethics in the Hellenistic period. But they were not identical. Christian sexual ethics and Greek sexual ethics were, Foucault argues, based on profoundly different conceptions of the self. According to Foucault, while the Greeks understood the self as a cooperative unity of body and soul, early Christians imagined the self as the site of conflict between body and soul. Greek sexual ethics—and Greek codes of conduct more generally—aimed to encourage body and soul to work together in the task of regulating and administering the self. Christian sexual ethics, Foucault argues, were oriented instead toward facilitating the soul's mastery over the body as part of the grander project of transforming the self. Christian sexual ethics, therefore, had more to do with "rules" (about which sexual activities were permitted and which forbidden); Greek sexual ethics had more to do with questions of "use" (concerning when, where, and how often one ought to indulge in sexual activities). Animating Hellenistic sexual ethics was not, Foucault insists, a fear of the sins of the flesh, but rather a desire to develop "a technique of existence" which sought to distribute sexual acts "in the closest conformity with what nature demanded."[36]

Although I do not agree with Foucault's assessment of early Christian conceptions of the self (by and large, Christians were not such dualists as Foucault supposes, a point to which I will return below), I find the distinction Foucault draws between the Greek emphasis on the *regulation* of the body and the Christian emphasis on the *transformation* of the body insightful and revealing of the main fault line between Greek and Christian sexual ethics. What separated Greek sexual ethics from Christian sexual ethics was not the line between eroticism and asceticism, nor even the line between license and restraint, but the line between the saecula and the eschaton. In contrast to their Christian counterparts, Greek sexual ethics were profoundly secular in orientation. Plato's ideas about sex, for example, took shape within the broader context of his focus on the welfare of the city. For Plato, sexual activity—properly regulated and limited by eugenic concerns—was the means by which the city reproduced itself, generating the healthiest and the fittest future citizens. Within the context of Plato's republic, the young and the vigorous were not just *permitted* to engage in sexual relations but were, indeed, *obliged* to procreate for the benefit of the city. For the Stoics, too, controlled sexual activity had a salutary social function. Sexual intercourse was a useful means of cultivating friendship between consenting partners—even if, as the later Stoics would have it, the consenting partners were limited to a husband and wife bound in monogamous matrimony.[37] Even virginity was possessed of social and secular import for the Greeks of the second century. More than anything else, for the Greeks of the second century virginity had value as badge of social honor and as an indicator of future fidelity between spouses united in companionate marriage.

In marked contrast to the secular orientation of Greek sexual ethics, early Christian sexual ethics had everything to do with the imminent apocalypse and a nascent eschatology. If, for the Greeks, the regulation of the sexual appetite was intended as a means of determining how best to live in this world, early Christian efforts to control and constrain sexual activity were intended as preparations for life in the next world and, indeed, as a means for opting out of this world. Among early Christians, the practice of sexual renunciation—which, by the fourth century, had become the defining feature of Christian sexual ethics—was, as Peter Brown has cogently argued, multivalent. To some in the early Church, it was a strategy for cultivating an undivided heart; to others it was the key to liberating the faithful from social entanglements; to still others it was a means of recovering humanity's original integrity; and to yet others it was an anticipation of the promise of resurrection.[38] But fundamental to the notion of sexual renunciation, however conceived, was an enduring conviction in the incompatibility between human sexuality and human salvation. For early Christians eager for life in the next world, there was no better way to bring an end to life in this world than to refuse—through the practice of sexual renunciation—to reproduce it.

Within a scheme of salvation thus understood, there was little room for the biological family. For all their attention to sexual activity as the "privileged ideogram" of humanity's alienation from God and sexual continence as the singular key to humanity's reunion with God, underlying early Christians' suspicion toward sex was a more primary (and evangelically rooted) wariness about the family.[39] In the eyes of the Church Fathers, it was the family—not sexual activity and not sexed bodies—that enmeshed human beings in the present world. Mothers and fathers, children and servants, aunts and uncles and distant relatives were enslaved by the demands of family life. The family required endless amounts of time, attention, and material resources, leaving little—if anything—to God. When there were mouths to feed, educations to manage, and marriages to arrange, what remained to nourish the spirit and make way for the kingdom of God? This, I would contend (and not any generalized antipathy toward the female body), is what Tertullian had in mind when he insisted that Heaven had no place for mothers. Why else, Tertullian reasoned, would Christ have prophesied "'Woe to those that are with child and that give suck,' if he did not mean that on the day of our great exodus children will be a handicap to those who bear them?" The privilege of serving Christ at the time of the Second Coming, Tertullian concluded, was reserved only to those with "none of the heavy baggage of marriage in their wombs or at their breasts."[40] These, after all, were those who had the time to think about and prepare for the eschaton. Several centuries later, Jerome made the point even more starkly. In a letter written to the widow Furia in 394, Jerome cautioned that the pull of the natural affections—to which mothers were particularly susceptible—were dangerous in a world preparing for the imminent day of judgment. "Too great affection towards one's children," Jerome warned, "is disaffection towards God."[41] To Jerome, love was a zero-sum game; the family's gain was God's loss.

———

A few weeks ago—the twenty-third Sunday in ordinary time, to be exact—I was sitting in the pew with Bobby, our three boys, and Aggie, alternately

retrieving dropped Matchbox cars, warding off incipient squabbles between the boys, and doing my best to (silently) encourage Aggie to reach
up and maintain her grip on some plastic rings I'd found in the basket
behind us. The priest was delivering a homily on the gospel which, as co-
incidence would have it, was the passage from Luke that has Jesus ex-
horting his disciples to "hate father and mother, wife and children,
brothers and sisters." "Did you hear that," Bobby asked me. "What do you
think?" Did I hear that? What did I think? I think I *didn't* hear that. I had
been too busy with—and too distracted by—my children to listen.

In the eyes of early (and later) Christian theologians, it was mothers—
more than others—who were loaded down by the weight of the world.
Mothers, more than others, were distracted by the "wailing of [their]
infant[s]" and the "brats . . . crawling upon [their] breast[s] and soiling
[their] neck[s] with nastiness."[42] If the task of preparing for the end of the
world demanded an undivided heart, there was no more vulnerable group
than mothers—whose affections for their children were regularly and
roundly condemned as excessive and incompatible with Christian devotion.[43] Indeed, in the lives of some saints, motherhood is singled out as a
source of worldly temptation that threatens to seduce holy women away
from the things of God. Ivetta of Huy's hagiographer, for example, presents the saint's moral transgressions as the (natural) consequences of a
misguided concern for her children.[44] It is the saint's maternal interest in
providing for her two sons in the aftermath of their father's death that
leads to Ivetta's unwitting commission of usury and her near seduction
by a lustful man who had only pretended to care for the welfare of her
children. The passions of Perpetua and Agathonike, likewise, represent the
maternity of these early Christian martyrs as not just possible but maxi-
mally powerful sources of temptation. In both accounts, it is the would-
be martyr's maternal status that is invoked by the witnessing public as a
means of persuading the woman to desist from her determination to die
for Christ and to "sacrifice for the Emperor's prosperity."[45]

Moreover, it was on the bodies of mothers that the most damning evidence of humanity's alienation from God was inscribed. From the pun-
ishment imposed on Eve for having eaten the forbidden fruit, which
included the curses of sexual desire and painful childbirth, it was but a

short step to the association of motherhood itself with female incapacity, original sin, and the Fall of humankind. Indeed, Augustine affirmed, it was through the act of sexual reproduction (the necessary corollary to motherhood in all cases but one) that the stain of original sin was transferred from a mother to her children.[46] Corrupted, concupiscent, and changeable, the maternal body stood as a shrill reminder of the original sin and just how far humanity had fallen from what God had intended at the outset of creation. According to the eleventh-century mystic Hildegard of Bingen, God had intended both men and women to reproduce as virgins in paradise. According to Augustine, God had at least intended men and women to reproduce without concupiscence. In either case, on the continuum of human sexuality thus conceived, mothers were the antitheses of virgins—sexual (as opposed to chaste), sinful (as opposed to stainless), controlled by (as opposed to in control of) their bodies.[47] In contradistinction to virgins whose bodies most closely resembled the bodies of the resurrected dead who "neither marry nor are given in marriage," the bodies of mothers, insisted the sixth-century poet and hymnodist Fortunatus, were "sluggish . . . with an imprisoned embryo . . . depressed and worn out by its awkward weight . . . When the belly swells from its wound and sensual dropsy grows, the woman's exhausted health hangs by a hair. The raised skin is so distent and misshapen that even though the mother may be happy with her burden, she becomes ashamed."[48] It was on the bodies of mothers, more than others, that the ugly realities of the fallen flesh played out most dramatically.[49]

For Church Fathers like Jerome, Augustine, and others, sexual activity, the biological family, and the corruption of the present age were linked together in a chain of causation that forestalled the advent of the eschaton. Despite the patristic tendency to draw a sharp distinction between this world and the next, however, most Christians were not dualists.[50] Within the context of the early Church, the issue was neither the material body (as Schulenburg supposes) nor the material world (as Atkinson and Foucault suppose), but the biological family and its potential to seduce the attentions of the faithful away from their obligations to transform the world. The historical matrix within which Christianity emerged, after all, was hardly a fertile environment for the development of a dualist anthropology. To begin with, the biblical Judaism out of which the Christian tradition emerged was marked by a profoundly unitary anthropology.

According to biblical anthropology, the human person was a singular unity of body and soul. Body and soul operated together in the human person either in alliance with God or in rebellion against God—a monism captured by the biblical metaphor of the heart. Indeed, as Peter Brown points out, whatever dualism there was in biblical Judaism was not a dualism that fractured the human person but a dualism that gestured to the yawning chasm between a finite and fallible humanity and an infinite omnipotent God. Even supposing (as we no doubt should) the influence of Hellenistic anthropology on developing Christian conceptions of the human person, one would be hard-pressed to argue that there was anything more than the imprint of what Brown has called a "benevolent dualism."[51] In contrast to their forefather Plato (who had conceived of the body as the prison of the soul), Greeks around the time of Christ proposed a cooperative relationship between body and soul. For the Greeks of the Hellenistic period, body and soul were not antagonists locked in a battle for the absolute sovereignty of the one over the other. Instead, the soul was engaged in a struggle to master itself so that it could serve as a responsible guide for the body "according to a law which [was] that of the body itself."[52]

Although various heretical groups throughout Christian history tried (and failed) to articulate accounts of the human person as the embattled site of a conflict between body and soul, orthodox Christian theology maintained an enthusiastically inclusive perspective on the human person.[53] Consistent with a faith in the incarnated Christ and a confidence in the promise of bodily resurrection, Christian soteriology made room for both body *and* soul. For all its apparent hostility toward the body, Christian asceticism was not premised on an implicit antagonism between body and soul but was, instead, geared toward the ultimate salvation of the body in cooperation with the soul. It is, I admit, tempting to read the self-mortifications of Anthony and Dorotheos of Gaza (among others) as expressions of an antipathy toward the body as a hindrance to the soul. But as Peter Brown points out, their bodies were "grippingly present to the monks" in the Egyptian desert, the "cumulative experience of ascetic transformation [having] . . . revealed, if anything, the inextricable interdependence of body and soul."[54] It is, perhaps, even more tempting to read the extreme food asceticism of medieval women like Catherine of Genoa as proof that a dualist anthropology (or, indeed, at least a dualist gynecology) had gained traction by the Christian Middle Ages. Carolyn Walker Bynum, however, has persuasively argued that when women like Lidwina and Hadjewich refused to eat, they were not fleeing from physicality but instead attempting to "plumb and to realize all the possibilities of the flesh." It was, Bynum concludes, "a profound expression of the Incarnation."[55] All appearances aside, Christian asceticism had little to do with dualism and much more to do with making use of the body as an instrument of salvation and seeing in the body the potential for conversion in the model of the resurrected Christ. Indeed, even Origen (whose theology owes a particularly heavy debt to the notoriously dualistic Plato) was a vigorous proponent of the transformation of the body. Despite his suspicion of human sexuality and the pleasures of the flesh, Origen remained confident that human bodies—albeit radically transformed human bodies—had a place in the world to come.

Much as Christian theology anticipated the transformation of the body in the model of the resurrected Christ, it also anticipated the transformation of the world—and along with this, the transformation of the family. To suggest, therefore, that the defining feature of Christian sexual ethics (in contrast to its Hellenistic counterpart) was its eschatological orientation risks misleading readers insensitive to the profound fluidity of Christian conceptions of this world and the next. Christian ideas about the eschaton were not premised on the abandonment of this world in favor of the next, but on the conversion of this world into the next. Fundamental to Christian notions of redemption was a confidence that humans could (and one day would) become divine, and that earth could (and one day would) become heaven. And when earth did become heaven, there would still be a place for the family. The way a number of early Christians understood it, the biological family would give way in the world to come to a spiritual family united freely by a shared faith in Christ. The second-century bishop Marcion, for example, envisioned an eschatological community undetermined by blood ties and marital obligations. But for Marcion, as for others, this eschatological community could not come into being unless and until human beings unfettered themselves from the chains of conventional society—including their marriages, their children, and their extended relations.[56] Basil of Caesarea and Gregory of Nyssa, too, anticipated a reformed society consisting of believers whose common renunciation of the biological family and ministrations toward the poor would "stand as a pointed rebuke to the habits of conspicuous expenditure that had made the ancient city what it was."[57] Around the turn of the fifth century, Jerome appealed to Jesus's own words in support of an eschatological vision of the family transformed. Pleading with Heliodorus to return to the ascetic way of life he had left behind to assume ecclesiastical office, Jerome insisted that "the battering-ram of natural affection which so often shatters faith must recoil powerless from the wall of the Gospel. My mother and my brethren are these whosoever do the will of my Father which is in heaven. If they believe in Christ let them bid me God-speed, for I go to fight in His name. And if they do not believe, let the dead bury their dead."[58]

Inspired, no doubt, by Jesus's own unambiguous subordination of the biological family to the demands of the faith, by the Middle Ages one of the most enduring themes of Christian hagiography had become that of the saint whose natural affections for her mother and father, sons and daughters, had been transformed and extended to a broad community—a new family—chartered by a common Christian devotion. The tone having been set by the Acts of Paul and Thecla (which told the story of the first-century virgin who rejected her fiancé and defied her mother to follow Paul through Asia Minor), the lives of Christian holy men and women time and again recounted the bitter struggles of saints against their parents, their spouses, and even their children who wanted to keep them in the world. In the lives of these holy men and women, loyalties that had once been commanded by the saint's biological family were transferred to an inclusive network of relations united in spirit rather than by the ties of the flesh or marriage. Francis of Assisi, for example, famously renounced his inheritance and his own father in the public square of Assisi, going on to gather around himself a community of *fratres minores*. Paula, the fourth-century wealthy widow and mother of five, left her two youngest children for a new life in the Holy Land, where she founded a monastic order of women who lived together as sisters in Christ. Even Maxellendis, the seventh-century French virgin who was murdered by her betrothed for refusing to marry him as a mark of her fidelity to Christ alone, was received in heaven as a part of the spiritual family of martyrs who had offered up their own lives out of love for Christ.

A corollary to the motif of the family, the theme of motherhood had become a popular one in the lives of holy women in particular by the

Middle Ages. For all its historic hostility toward motherhood as antitheti-
cal to Christian discipleship, by the Middle Ages the Christian tradition
had made some room for mothers and the maternal experience.[59] As suggested by the growth of the cults of the Virgin Mary and her mother, Anne,
the rise of affective piety, and the increase in the number of saints who
were married with children, motherhood—if not a means—was, at the
very least, not an absolute bar to sanctity within the context of the medieval Church. The Carolingian period, for example, finds Haimo of Auxerre
insisting that married women please God as much as virgins do. In educating their children in matters of faith and religion, mothers performed
the work of God. Several centuries later, Jacques de Vitry would again draw
attention to the teaching role of mothers, praising "holy women serving
the lord devoutly in marriage . . . women teaching their sons in the fear
of the Lord [and] keeping . . . an undefiled wedding bed."[60]

Late medieval devotional texts and iconography relating to St. Anne
make much the same point. As the mother of the Virgin Mary, Anne was
primarily responsible for instructing her daughter in prayer, charity, and
moral virtue—and merited veneration for having so perfectly executed her
maternal responsibility. The Virgin Mary, too, by the end of the Middle
Ages had become the subject of a lively devotional cult that centered
around her maternity. Venerated not only for her purity (which had occupied the attentions of previous generations of Christians), but also (and
increasingly) for her intimacy with Christ, Mary played the role of the
loving mother who willingly interceded between her devotees and God. By
the thirteenth century, Christian artists had begun to explore the more
affective dimensions of Mary's relationship with Christ, experimenting
with new postures and gestures that expressed the emotional—and
material—closeness between mother and son. One particularly prominent
theme in late medieval Marian iconography was that of the Virgin mother's
breasts, symbols of maternal love and nurture.

Inflecting the tenor of late medieval Marian devotion was the elaboration of what religious studies scholars have called affective piety. Characterized by dramatic emotional display and imaginative engagement with
the events of the Christian narrative, the language of affective piety made
use of maternal experience as a means of knowing God and participating
in the life of Christ.[61] Lay and monastic, male and female, medieval Christians played the role of mother to the infant Jesus—in sometimes very

tangible ways. The Beguines of northern Europe, for example, focused their maternal attentions on an actual Christ doll, bathing him, dressing him, and caressing him before "cover[ing] him with precious blankets, and [laying] him to rest in cradles ornamented with the most expensive and precious handmade . . . details."[62] Likewise, Christian devotional texts and religious art of the later Middle Ages not infrequently depicted Christ himself as mother. Like a mother, Christ (as Bynum puts it) "bled, . . . bled food, and . . . gave birth."[63] When medieval Christians like Aelred of Rievaulx and Julian of Norwich connected the maternal body and Christ's body, they meant to compare Christ's life-giving death on the cross with a mother giving birth, the nourishing qualities of Christ's body and blood with a mother's milk, and Christ's expansive love for humankind with a mother's unconditional love for her child.[64]

Finally, inspired, perhaps, by the growing popularity of devotion to the Holy Family and the language of affective piety, the Middle Ages gave rise to a number of female saints whose maternity seems to have presented no hindrance to their sanctity. The tenth-century life of Rictrude, for example, represents the saint as an exemplary mother. Rictrude had married for the purpose of bearing children, fulfilling the divine command in Genesis to increase and multiply. When her husband died, Rictrude refused to marry again, renounced her worldly possessions, and withdrew to a convent. She remained, however, actively involved in the lives of her children, dedicating her three daughters as virgins betrothed to Christ. As Ineke van't Spikjer puts it, Rictrude's *Vita* "does not create the impression that she is a saint *in spite of* her motherhood . . . on the contrary, . . . motherhood takes its place as a natural relationship alongside of spiritual *familiaritas* or is integrated into it."[65] Holy women like Elizabeth of Thuringia, Ivetta of Huy, and Birgitta of Sweden—all of whom had been married with children—likewise attracted the devotional attention of late medieval Christians. Although few mother–saints of this period (or any period, for that matter) are represented iconographically together with their children, "'something happened,'" as Anneke Mulder-Bakker puts it, "with respect to sanctity and motherhood" in the later Middle Ages.[66] And whatever it was that happened, Mulder-Bakker insists, happened owing to "the 'cultural force' of the laity."[67] It is no accident that Jacobus de Voragine's widely popular late-thirteenth-century *Legenda Aurea* departs from hagiographic tradition to include among twenty-one female saints a near majority who are not virgins. Indeed, it must have been to appeal to a lay audience, Mulder-Bakker reasons, that Voragine chose to recount in the lives of his saints episodes culled from their experiences of family life.

By the end of the Middle Ages, then, the Christian tradition had witnessed the recovery of a certain kind of "compatibility [between] . . . holiness and physical maternity."[68] And yet! And yet, the fact of motherhood continued to weigh uncomfortably on the bodies of Christian women. It is true that the Virgin Mary and her mother, Anne, merited the veneration of the faithful precisely because of their maternal status. But these were exceptional—and inimitable—cases. For both Mary and Anne, maternity had not come at the cost of bodily integrity. Not only had Mary been a virgin when she conceived Christ, but late medieval artists frequently represented the conception of Mary herself as the result of a mere kiss exchanged between Anne and her husband, Joachim. And even if Anne had conceived Mary through regular sexual intercourse (a position the Church officially maintained), by the late fifteenth century it was widely accepted that the conception had still been immaculate.

It is true, too, that Christian hagiography had made some room for mothers and maternal practice over the course of the Middle Ages. But the life of Rictrude stands out as an exception to the rule according to which the experience of biological motherhood gave way to the practice of spiritual motherhood—much as the natural family gave way to the spiritual family—in the *vitae* of medieval mother–saints like Elizabeth of Thuringia, Ivetta of Huy, and Birgitta of Sweden. In each of these saintly lives—and in a host of others not considered here—motherhood operates primarily in a spiritual dimension, structuring and giving meaning to the saint's charitable activities. Elizabeth of Thuringia, for example, "gathered [the poor] to her as if they were her own children." So kindly and sweetly did she act toward those she sheltered in her house that they "ran to her as children to a mother" and "all called her mother."[69] She fed and nurtured the sick, the lame, and the needy and upon her death, they "cried as if she had been a mother to them all."[70] Similarly, Ivetta of Huy elicits the admiration of her own hagiographer as the "sapientissima materfamilias," having successfully "transposed her tasks as a housewife and mother into the spiritual sphere" as the head of her Beguine community and manager of a leprosarium-turned-hospital.[71] Finally, Birgitta of Sweden was said to have educated, converted, and counseled others as well as served the poor "with a tender compassion and the greatest of maternal charity."[72]

The "warm, liberating, and generative spiritual motherhood of all" practiced by these maternal saints, however, does not take its place alongside flesh and blood motherhood but rather demands its renunciation.[73] In the lives of these saints and others, the performance of maternal acts of charity vis-à-vis the sick and the needy precludes the holy woman's maternal ministrations toward her own biological children. In the case of Elizabeth of Thuringia, for example, it was only after she sent her two children away to be cared for by relatives (and, "in the presence of certain Franciscan brothers, renounced her parentage, her children, her own free will, and all of the pomp of this world") that Elizabeth could apply herself to the nurturing and nourishing of others.[74] In the life of Margaret of Cortona, similarly, the holy woman's "maternal piety" for the needy came at the expense of the attentions and affections she owed her own son. Accustomed to depriving herself and her son of food and other "things given to her for her use," Margaret spared no effort in tending to the needs of the poor. Indeed, declares Fra Giunta Bevegnati, Margaret "thoroughly fulfilled the Gospel message, when on account of love for her beloved spouse Jesus she expelled her only son, preferring, out of love for Christ, pilgrims, the poor, the notorious."[75] The *Revelations* of Birgitta of Sweden make explicit the mutual exclusivity of spiritual motherhood and its biological counterpart. It was in exchange for relinquishing her maternal responsibilities over her own eight children that Christ honored Birgitta by making her his bride and the spiritual mother of his own sons and daughters.[76] In the lives of these saints and others, it was not the actual messy experience of birthing, nourishing, and nurturing biological children that deserved approbation, but rather its virtual and considerably tidier spiritual counterpart.

————————————

Considerably tidier, indeed. A friend of mine, then the mother of a one-year-old child, received the following advice from an older male colleague who wanted to encourage her in the beginning of her academic career. Just make it clear to your children, her colleague had told her, that you are simply not available at certain times. This is hardly workable advice for a breast-feeding mother whose nursling knows no boundaries between his needs and her wants, and only marginally better advice for a mother of slightly older children whose own needs and wants are nearly constant and immediate. There is a story I have read to my boys—I can't quite recall the title—about a mother who, wanting a little space from her children, climbs a tree and rests there. Her children, however, refuse—innocently enough—to leave their mother to herself and persist in demanding her attention. So the mother manufactures a game of pretend which involves her children in various tasks, each of which takes some time to complete and each of which buys her a few precious moments of peace. Even from her aerie in the branches this mother is occupied by the care of her children. Motherhood—real, flesh and blood motherhood—respects no neat boundaries between work and play, self and other, activity and rest.

———————

There is an interesting conversation going on among religious studies scholars at work in the areas of Christian spirituality and sexuality having to do with just how to understand the relationship between the two. There are some, like Rosemary Radford Ruether, who argue that "the degradation of . . . sexuality . . . shaped a mystical spirituality for men and women built on sexual sublimation."[77] The spirituality of Christian mystics like Rupert of Deutz (who envisioned himself embracing Christ "whom my soul loved" and who, "in the midst of the kiss opened his mouth so I could kiss more deeply") and Mechthild of Magdeburg (who imagined herself naked in the "hidden chamber of the immaculate Godhead" engaged with Christ in "mutual intercourse") was built on a "powerful urge for a sexuality united with affective love for spouse and children [that was] rigorously repressed on the physical level" and reconstituted in ways that "despised rather than rehabilitated those visions' negated physical counterpart."[78] Grace Jantzen, too, makes the case that the erotic imagery at play in the writings of male mystics like Bernard of Clairvaux stands in as a substitute for a material eroticism, betraying disgust (rather than appreciation) for the body.[79] The use of erotic imagery, Jantzen insists, "was at the expense of the valuation of real sexual relations. It used the language of passion, but forbade any actual physical passion in an effort to channel all desire away from the body and towards God. Human sexuality was therefore seen not as a way of knowing something of divine Eros, but as a distraction and corruption, distasteful and gross."[80]

Then there are others, like Merry Weisner-Hanks and Carolyn Walker Bynum, who see in the tradition of erotic mysticism "a kind of counter-discourse within Christianity to the much more common disparagement of the body and the senses."[81] For Bynum, human sexuality is at home in Christian spirituality, sometimes so much so that in the writings of late medieval mystics "asceticism and eroticism . . . fused . . . completely."[82] It seems inappropriate, Bynum suggests, "to speak of 'sublimation' " when it comes to the sexuality of medieval holy women.[83] When medieval holy women kissed the wounds of Christ or swooned before the cross, "sexual feelings were . . . not so much translated into another medium as simply set free."[84] Virginia Burrus, too, has made much the same point with regard to the tradition of Christian hagiography. The lives of the saints, Burrus argues, are "the site of an exuberant eroticism."[85] For Burrus, what's going on in Christian hagiography is not the sublimation of human sexuality, but its amplification. Hagiography, argues Burrus, "conveys a sublime art of eroticism" that, far from repressing sexual desire, actually stokes it by refusing "the telos of [its] satisfaction."[86]

So what about motherhood? Ought we to read allusions to maternal experience and the maternal body in the language of affective piety and the lives of the saints as an index of the inclusion of mothers within the Christian tradition (much as Bynum and Burrus do with regard to sexuality) or as an index of their exclusion from it (à la Ruether and Jantzen)? Did representations of Christ as mother (and, indeed, as a child) depreciate the value of the labor performed by the flesh and blood mothers of biological children? Did the admiration of the nourishing and nurturing carried out by saints toward the poor and the needy supplant an appreciation of the material practices of ordinary Christian women vis-à-vis their own children? Or did, instead, the language of affective piety and the motif of spiritual motherhood redound to the benefit—or perhaps even reflect the status—of real Christian mothers in late medieval Europe?

On the one hand, the usefulness of motherhood and maternal practices for thinking about Christ and the saints must surely have come from somewhere. Surely, the adoration of Christ as a mother who births, feeds, and loves the faithful and the veneration of saints who ministered maternally to the sick and the poor betrays a cultural appreciation for the sort of work performed by the countless anonymous Christian mothers in relation to their own offspring. What other grounds could there be, indeed, for attributing to none less than the God who became man himself and those who lived their lives in imitation of him the characteristics and functions of a mother? Arguably, when we read into Christianity a bifurcation between the reality of biological motherhood and the ideal of spiritual motherhood we are not exposing the dualism that supposedly lies at the heart of the tradition, but instead revealing our own tendencies toward dualistic thinking (much as Bourdieu suspected of structuralism and academic sociologists). After all, as Bynum has shown, the dualisms—between body and soul, male and female, materiality and spirituality—that "modern commentators have emphasized so much were far from absolute" in the Christian tradition.[87]

On the other hand, the persistent privileging of virginity over and above maternity would seem to suggest that flesh and blood motherhood was, at best, an inferior female vocation—though a vocation nonetheless (Augustine, after all, had included among the three goods of marriage the production of children). Unlike virgins whose bodies retained their original integrity, who had managed to resist the temptation of concupiscence, and whose attentions were directed toward God alone, mothers had been corrupted by lust and were in constant danger of losing sight of the things of the next world on account of their enmeshment in this world. Within this context, then, it is possible to read the ideal of spiritual motherhood not as a complement to or a reflection of biological motherhood, but as a replacement of biological motherhood and an improvement on it. Bolstered by the theology of Church Fathers like Origen who wrote of the spiritual fecundity of the soul that conceives and gives birth to the Word of God, spiritual motherhood arguably superseded biological motherhood as the highest calling of the Christian woman. In a poem written for the Frankish nun Radegund in honor of the consecration of her spiritual daughter Agnes as abbess, Fortunatus developed the theme of virginal conception and suggested the inherent superiority of spiritual motherhood to its biological counterpart. Referring to Agnes, Fortunatus addressed Radegund, "Your womb did not make this child for you, but grace did; not the flesh, but Christ gave her in love. The Author brought her to you to be with you forever . . . Happy posterity that will never cease and which will remain undying with its mother!"[88] Thus stripped of its dangerous associations with the corrupted, concupiscent, and mortal flesh, the idea of motherhood was rescued by the Christian tradition—but, it would seem, only at the expense of actual motherhood experienced by decidedly non-virginal women engaged in intimate physical relationships with real biological progeny.

So which is it, then? Sublimation or celebration? There is room, I think, for seeing both at work in Christianity's relationship with motherhood. And in the end, I'm not sure there is much practical difference between the one and the other anyway. Whatever room the Christian tradition made for motherhood was so cramped and uncomfortable that it might as well not have made room at all. It is hard to argue against the logic that real maternal practices and actual maternal bodies must have informed the language of affective piety and the ideal of spiritual motherhood. But the relationship between the real and the actual, on the one hand, and the rhetorical and the spiritual, on the other, was mostly a unidirectional one. What flesh and blood mothers did gave meaning and merit to the deeds of Christ and the saints, but the actions of Christ and the saints did not give meaning and merit to the deeds of flesh and blood mothers. In the end, then, whatever room Christianity made for motherhood was one that excluded the maternal practices of real mothers soiled by the "nastiness" of their "brats" and exhausted by the wailing of their infants. In the end, whatever room Christianity made for motherhood could not accommodate both Marie de l'Incarnation and her young son Claude together.

4

Explanation: Maternal
Hagiographies and Spiritualities
of Abandonment in
Seventeenth-Century France

Let me return, by way of beginning this chapter, to Anneke Mulder-
Bakker's observation that "'something happened' with respect to sanctity and motherhood" in the later Middle Ages.[1] Beginning in the
twelfth century, we find the first representations of a quartet of martyred
mothers with their children—Felicitas and Symphorosa together with
their seven sons, Julita holding her son Quiricius on her lap, and Sophia
surrounded by her three children.[2] It is around the same period that
St. Anne, second only to her virgin daughter Mary in maternal fame,
began to garner the attention of the Christian faithful. And between the
thirteenth and fifteenth centuries, more married women saints—some
with children—were canonized than ever before.[3] Whether it was the
"democratization and laicization of religious life," the opportunities
presented by the novel ideals of poverty and service, or the flourishing
of mystical experience, the later Middle Ages gave rise to a religious
culture within which mothers, it would seem, had finally found a place.[4]

What these historical facts obfuscate, however, is that the Church's
willingness to recognize the sanctity of a handful of holy mothers in no
way meant an appreciation of motherhood itself as an avenue toward sanctity. Apart from the Virgin Mary, her mother, Anne, and Monica (the
long-suffering mother of St. Augustine), very few—if any—mothers in
Christian history have merited the admiration of their hagiographers
on account of having performed their maternal duties to a heroic degree.
In contrast to the legions of holy queens, abbesses, and humanitarians venerated for their excellence *as* queens, abbesses, and humanitarians, those
rare "saints who were mothers . . . were honored at the altar despite rather
than because of their children."[5] In the lives of the saints, motherhood was
not an opportunity for sanctity, but an obstacle that stood in the way. Pat-
ent proof that the holy woman had failed to preserve her virginal integrity, motherhood was a fact—uncomfortable and inconvenient—to be

disposed of as quickly and neatly as possible in favor of a focus on the saint's admirable service to the sick and the needy or compassionate authority as sovereign or superior. Even within the context of a late medieval Europe which "rediscovered" a certain "compatibility of holiness and physical maternity," motherhood remained, at best, only marginal to Christian conceptions of sanctity.[6]

With one exception. For holy women with aspirations to sanctity, motherhood offered a unique advantage over a life of dedicated virginity—an unmatched opportunity for renunciation in imitation of Christ. In the lives of holy mothers, from Perpetua to Paula to Ivetta of Huy to Birgitta of Sweden, the renunciation of children plays a key role in the construction of female sanctity. While in some cases the hagiographer gives but passing reference to the holy woman's decision to relinquish her children in favor of religious life, in other cases the renunciation of children carries significant narrative weight as evidence of the heroic virtue required of the saints.[7]

I am not the first to notice the theme of the renunciation of children in hagiographic narrative. In *From Virile Woman to WomanChrist*, Barbara Newman examines the paradigm of the "maternal martyr" in Christian hagiography and secular romance. The maternal martyr, Newman writes, was "a virgin manquée who married for the sake of obedience; took little or no pleasure in sex; bore children to fulfill her conjugal duty; raised them with detachment; cared more for their souls than for their bodies; accepted their deaths with equanimity or abandoned them willingly, if not without grief; took advantage of her widowhood to serve God single-mindedly; and only then displayed her truly 'maternal' character in compassion for the infant Christ, loving service to the poor, and zealous care for her spiritual sons and daughters."[8] Within the context of hagiographic narrative, Newman argues that the maternal martyr paradigm functions alternately as evidence of the woman's triumph over her female sex, as proof of the woman's willingness to follow Christ, as atonement for the loss of her virginity, as a form of holy poverty, and as a means of identifying "with the grief of Mary at the Cross."[9]

The theme of the renunciation of children is indeed, as Newman suggests, polyvalent in the stories of the saints. In what follows, however, I contend that in the last instance (and in each instance) a holy woman's relinquishment of her children submits to the hagiographic mandate of *imitatio Christi*. In the first part of this chapter, I draw on *The Passion of Perpetua and Felicity*, Jerome's letter of Eustochium, Guibert of Nogent's *Monodies*, and the lives of St. Margaret of Cortona and St. Birgitta of Sweden, as well as the latter's own *Revelations*, to argue that in the writings about and by holy mothers, the renunciation of children testifies to the presence of heroic virtue—variously modulated according to historical context, but always modeled on the paradigmatic heroism of Christ's own sacrifice. Whether illustrative of the holy woman's laudable virility, unconditional love for God, admirable faith, or commitment to the ideal of evangelical poverty, the renunciation of children within the context of hagiographic narrative operates as a proxy for the painful renunciation of self in the image of the crucified Christ.

Marie de l'Incarnation's decision to abandon her son, Claude, in favor of religious life—and her representation of that decision—was informed, no doubt, by this distinctive hagiographic tradition. But there was more than that to the narrative that was waiting for Marie. In the second part of this chapter, I argue that at least as much as it was informed by the hagiographic tradition, Marie's decision to leave Claude for the Ursulines was inflected by her particular location within the context of a seventeenth-century French Catholicism saturated with spiritualities of abandonment. Rendered by Charles de Condren as annihilation, by Pierre de Bérulle as abnegation, by François Fénelon as holy indifference, the notion of abandonment implied the total cession of the self to God. In imitation of Christ, the abandoned soul offered itself up before God, sacrificing its own will entirely to divine providence and God's good pleasure, such that even in the course of trials and tribulations it was but a "tool . . . in the hands of a worker."[10] Within this spiritual milieu, then, Marie's relinquishment of her maternal responsibilities vis-à-vis Claude was hardly neutral. It was, instead, pregnant with theological meaning as an act performed in imitation of Christ's own sacrifice, against her personal inclinations, and in complete submission to the will of the omnipotent God.

In 203 under the rule of the Roman Emperor Septimus Severus, a twenty-two-year-old married woman named Vibia Perpetua, "having a father and mother and two brothers . . . and a son, a child at the breast," found herself imprisoned together with four fellow catechumens.[11] It was dark in the prison and very hot, and Perpetua, involuntarily separated from her newborn son, was "tormented there by care for the child." Soon enough, however, thanks to the machinations of "Tertius and Pomponius, the blessed deacons who ministered to us," Perpetua was reunited with her son, who was delivered to her in prison. "I suckled my child," Perpetua writes, "that was now faint with hunger. And being careful for him, I spoke to my mother and strengthened my brother and commended my son unto them . . . I obtained that the child should abide with me in prison; and straightway I became well and was lightened of my labour and care for the child; and suddenly the prison was made a palace for me, so that I would sooner be there than anywhere else." But Perpetua's father—who had long opposed her attraction to Christianity—could not let matters rest where they lay. He "returned from the city spent with weariness," pleading with his daughter to renounce her faith. Invoking her mother, her mother's sister, her brothers, and his own "grey hairs," Perpetua's father begged his daughter to have pity on her kin and, last of all, on "your son, who will not endure to live after you." Some days later, Perpetua's father again appeared, this time before the tribunal and together with his grandson, of whose custody he had somehow gained control in the interim. "Perform the sacrifice," Perpetua's father urged his daughter, "have mercy on the child." Hilarian the procurator, too, sought to persuade Perpetua to apostatize by appealing to her roles as both daughter and mother: "Spare your father's grey hairs; spare the infancy of the boy." But Perpetua stood firm. Neither filial duty nor maternal sentiment could dissuade Perpetua from her resolution to suffer a martyr's death.

Sentenced by Hilarian and condemned to the beasts, Perpetua went "cheerfully . . . down to the dungeon" with her fellow catechumens. Then, "because my child had been used to being breastfed and to staying with me in the prison," Perpetua asked for her son from her father. "But my father would not give him. And as God willed, no longer did he need to be suckled, nor did I take fever; that I might not be tormented by care for the child and by the pain of my breasts." At this point Perpetua's son disappears from the narrative, presumably to be raised a pagan among her father's family. *The Passion* concludes with Perpetua's death in a Carthaginian amphitheater, not as her persecutors intended, by the teeth of the "most savage cow, prepared . . . [in order to] mock [her] sex," but by her own hand, for "so great a woman could not else have been slain . . . had she not herself so willed it."

The Passion of Perpetua and Felicity is a useful place to begin an inquiry into the hagiographic theme of the renunciation of children, in part because of its antiquity and in part because of the way it so aptly illustrates how the dynamic between a mother and her rejected child operates in the context of hagiographic narrative as testimony to the presence of heroic virtue. In *The Passion of Perpetua and Felicity*, Perpetua's repudiation of her newborn son illumines her super-human (or, at least, super-feminine) resolve and the contours of her triumphant virility. Early Christian martyrs, Stephanie Cobb points out, did not "wholly reject the culture and world around them," but rather "embraced . . . Roman definitions of honor, strength, and reason," displaying to the witnessing public what it meant to live a "good and honorable Roman life."[12]

Even the female martyrs represented in the passion texts of the early Church embody the Roman virtues of courage, self-control, and apatheia, the dimensions of which loom all the larger in their stories on account of the (presumed) natural weakness of their feminine sex. Preaching on the subject of Perpetua and Felicity on the occasion of their feast day sometime in the early fifth century, Augustine insisted that these two martyred women deserved "[a] crown more glorious" because "towards these women a manly courage did work a marvel, when beneath so great a burden their womanly weakness failed not."[13] There were, Augustine reminds his audience, "men too who were martyrs, very brave men who conquered by their sufferings on the same day; and yet they haven't stamped their names on this day." The reason why, Augustine is at pains to make clear, is "that it was a greater miracle for women in their weakness to overcome the ancient enemy." In conquering their feminine fragility, women like Perpetua and Felicity—and their contemporaries Agathonike, Blandina, and others—succeeded in becoming men, a transformation made explicit by Perpetua's reported vision in which she "was stripped naked, and . . . became a man."[14] Indeed, Augustine affirmed, over the course of her passion, Perpetua "did run *towards the perfect man, to the measure of the age of the ful[l]ness of Christ.*"[15]

Within this narrative context, Perpetua's interactions with and ultimate renunciation of her newborn son operate as an index of her progressive (and heroic) masculinization. As the text unfolds, Stephanie Cobb argues, Perpetua's "escalating . . . masculinity" contrasts with her father's escalating femininity.[16] While her father rages in anger, "kissing my hands and groveling at my feet," Perpetua remains a model of masculine stoicism throughout the story, crying out only at the end as she is "pierced between the bones." Perpetua's father even goes so far as to "pluck out his beard"—the beard being a symbol of masculinity in second-century Rome—"throw[ing] it on the ground and . . . fall[ing] on his face." The transformation (and transferal!) of genders is complete midway through Perpetua's narrative when she ceases to lactate (no longer "tormented by care for the child and by the pain of my breasts") and willingly cedes the care of her infant son to her distraught father.[17] If, for Augustine, a woman's triumph over the natural weakness of her sex gave evidence of heroic virtue, a mother's conquest of her maternal affections merited all the more admiration. Commenting on Perpetua's "strength of character," Augustine marvels that she "was a mother likewise, that unto the frailty of her sex might be added a more importunate love." Assimilating maternal affections to the temptations of the devil, Augustine continues: thus "the Enemy assailing them at all points and hoping they should not bear the bitter and heavy burden of persecution, might think they should straightaway yield themselves up to him and be soon his own."[18] Perpetua's father and Hilarian the procurator seem to have assumed the same.[19] This is not, of course, the way things turned out. Perpetua—much as the crucified Christ in Matthew 27 resisted the temptation to save himself—"with the prudent and valiant strength of the inward man did blunt his devices every one and break his assault."[20]

In contrast to *The Passion of Perpetua*, in which expressions of maternal emotion are virtually absent, Jerome's letter to Eustochium highlights Paula's (his spiritual companion and Eustochium's own mother) emotionally charged separation from her children, who were "eager by their demonstrations of affection to overcome their loving mother."[21] The way Jerome tells the story, Paula, nobly born and honorably wedded, "bore five children; Blaesilla . . . Paulina . . . [the virgin] Eustochium, Rufina, whose untimely end overcame the affectionate heart of her mother; and Toxotius, after whom she had no more children." You can thus see, Jerome declares, "that it was not her wish to fulfill a wife's duty, but that she only complied with her husband's longing to have male offspring." When her husband died, Paula grieved—so much so "that she nearly died herself." For Paula, however, as for Marie de l'Incarnation, her husband's death was an opportunity to "give herself to the service of the Lord." Paula dedicated herself to ministering to the poor, showing "great consideration . . . to all . . . even to those whom she had never seen." Indeed, "so lavish was her charity that she robbed her children; and, when her relatives remonstrated with her for doing so, she declared that she was leaving to them a better inheritance in the mercy of Christ." Finally, inflamed by the virtues of two visiting bishops, Paula resolved to leave behind "her house, her children, her servants, her property, and in a word everything connected with the world." When "at last . . . the winter was over and the sea was open, and when the bishops were returning to their churches," Paula sailed with them. She "went down to Portus accompanied by her brother, her kinsfolk and above all her own children eager by their demonstrations of affection to overcome their loving mother. At last the sails were set and the strokes of the rowers carried the vessel into the deep. On the shore the little Toxotius stretched forth his hands in entreaty, while Rufina, now grown up, with silent sobs besought her mother to wait till she should be married." The pleas of her children, however, fell on deaf ears. Paula's eyes, Jerome writes, "were dry as she turned them heavenwards; and she overcame her love for her children by her love for God."[22]

For Jerome, at stake in Paula's renunciation of her children was not, as it was for Perpetua and other early Christian martyrs in the Roman world, the holy woman's triumph over her fragile and frivolous femininity, but her triumph over her immoderate (and unconscionable) love for her children. There is no hint of Paula's virilization in Jerome's letter. The way Jerome would have it, Paula does not leave her children behind as proof of her masculinization in the model of the disciplined and dispassionate Roman man, but rather as a testament to her preferential love of God. Jerome repeats himself later in the letter: "Overcoming her love for her children by her greater love for God, she concentrated herself quietly upon Eustochium alone," who accompanied her mother with the intention of joining her in religious life.[23] Paula did, indeed, love her children (a conclusion the reader of Perpetua's passion is left to reach, or not, on her own).

But she loved God more. For Jerome (and perhaps for Paula, too), a life of Christian sanctity could not accommodate both love of God and love of children together. Rather, the one conflicted with, distracted from, and compromised the other, leaving the holy mother to choose—and choose rightly—between them.

———————————

You can't do it all, my friend Megan had told me. Something has to suffer. This was not an ad hominem (or feminam) remark. We were having a more abstract conversation about working and mothering and her own decision to step back from professional life while her three children were still young. But I knew what she meant. And it rankled me. On the one hand, I agreed with Megan. Of course you couldn't have it all. You couldn't be at the same time a professional basketball player and a best-selling novelist and a professor of astrophysics and an international financier and Martha Stewart and the mayor of St. Louis. Of course you couldn't have it *all*. But I wasn't trying to have it *all*. I was only trying to have *some* of it all. I was only trying to both mother my children to the best of my abilities and have a moderately successful academic career. I was only trying to have two things. And were there even two things? After all, the boundary between my work life and my family life was porous, so porous that it would have been better to think of them as braided strands of a single life—which indeed they were. This book would never have been written were it not for the influence of my children and my accumulated experiences in raising them. The conversations in my classrooms would not circle back, again and again, to the place of the family in the Christian tradition were it not for the lived reality of my daily life as a wife and mother of four. But in a very real sense, what Megan said was true. There are, in fact, only twenty-four hours in a day and time's finitude forces us to choose between this, that, and the other (because there are, of course, more than just two things). Do I stay for the whole faculty meeting or do I duck out early to pick Bobby up from school myself and ask about his day? Do I attend the Newman Convocation and the reception afterward or do I stay home to fix dinner for my children, bathe them, and put them to bed? Do I make a point of traveling to conferences and presenting my work or do I make a point, instead, of being reliably, entirely, unconditionally available to my children who learn how to love, John Bowlby claims, at the feet of the *magistra materna*? At any given moment, there is time for just one thing.

————————

Allusions to maternal love—and, indeed, to the mutual exclusivity between love of God and love of children—are present in the life and writings of Birgitta of Sweden, as well. The daughter of Lord Birger of Upper Sweden and Lady Ingeborg (who were "noble according to the flesh . . . but more noble according to God"), Birgitta was born in 1302 or 1303. At the age of thirteen, she married Lord Ulf of Ulvåsa, prince of Närke, with whom she "lived in virginity for one year, devoutly asking God that if they ought to come together, he . . . would from them create an offspring that would be at his service."[24] Eventually Birgitta gave birth to a total of eight children (assisted in her labor and delivery by the "Blessed Virgin . . . who mitigated the labors, the pains, and the peril of her handmaid"). Birgitta educated and nurtured her sons and daughters "with great concern and diligence, handing them over to teachers by whom they were instructed in discipline and good behavior . . . [and weeping] daily over [their] sins, fearing they would offend their God."[25] When her husband died, Birgitta—like Paula before her and Marie de l'Incarnation after—divested herself of her personal property and devoted herself to religious pursuits. Inspired by the revelations she received from God, Birgitta embarked on a career of spiritual activism, prophesying on the subject of the papal schism, establishing a new religious community, and performing acts of charity in the service of the poor and the needy. Birgitta, too, embarked on a number of pilgrimages over the course of her lifetime—to Compostela, to the Holy Land, and ultimately to Rome, where she died in 1373.

The collection of writings about Birgitta "frequently refer to her concern for her children's souls and care for their religious training," but it is in the saint's own *Revelations* that the subject of motherhood appears with a greater degree of detail and regularity.[26] In the *Revelations*, Birgitta reveals not only her abiding concern for the fates of her children (from which not even her religious vocation could distract her), but also her suspicion that a mother's love for her children interfered with the cultivation of an even greater love for God. Love for Birgitta, as it was for Paula, was something of a limited resource. Too much love for one's children meant not enough love for God, a point the Virgin Mary made clear to Birgitta in the course of a vision in which she described how Christ's betrothed ought to prepare for her wedding day. First, Mary advised Birgitta, "you should be ready for the wedding of my divinity wherein there is no carnal desire but only the most sweet spiritual pleasure, the kind that is appropriate for God to have with a chaste soul. In this way, neither the love for your children nor for temporal goods nor for your relatives should drag you away from my love."[27] Indeed, Jesus asked Birgitta in another vision, "What is my will but that you should want to love me above all things and want nothing but me?"[28]

In contrast to Perpetua, whose separation from her newborn son seems not to have struck any sort of maternal nerve, it was not easy for Birgitta (as it hadn't been for Paula) to leave her children behind. On the eve of her first sojourn to Rome where "Our Lord Jesus Christ" had commanded his bride to go as his mouthpiece before "the supreme pontiff and the emperor there," Birgitta hesitated on account of her sons and daughters, who would be "bereft of maternal advice" and in danger of "audaciously offend[ing] God in some way."[29] Birgitta's anxiety about her imminent departure found expression in a vision of a demon blowing on the coals in a jar "placed above a fire . . . so that the jar was engulfed in flames." Birgitta asked the demon, " 'Why do you try to enflame it thus, so that the jar is set on fire?' The [demon] responded, 'So that your love for your sons will be more ignited and inflamed in you.' " Then Birgitta, "understanding such inordinate love existed in her heart for her sons, straightaway corrected herself, so that she would place nothing before her love of Christ."[30]

As hard as it was, Christ promised to Birgitta in exchange for substituting her love for her children an even greater love for God, "a most precious and delightful reward."[31] It was not just a superior love for God that animated her decision to leave behind her children in pursuit of religious life, then, but a confident faith that her sacrifice—like the sacrifice of Christ—would be recompensed. The calculation that is only implicit in Jerome's account of Paula's abandonment of her own children is made explicit in Birgitta's *Revelations*: the cost of renouncing one's children does not match the benefit of its eternal reward. Like the little woman who gave God her only goose, Birgitta "surrendered to [God] the one living thing she had, that is, the love of the world and of her children." For that, God would "provide for [Birgitta] in [his] kindness."[32]

Like Paula and Birgitta, Margaret of Cortona (1247–97) seems to have presumed the incompatibility between mothering the fruit of her own womb and a life of Christian discipleship. Born in the small village of Laviano to parents of humble origins, Margaret did not have a particularly happy childhood. When she was just seven years old, her mother died and her father remarried, to a woman with whom Margaret did not get along. At the age of seventeen, Margaret ran away with a young nobleman with whom she eventually had a son. Although the two never married, they lived together openly until the nobleman was found murdered. Whether this dramatic event provoked Margaret's religious conversion or whether her attraction to religious life had, in fact, been growing for some time, shortly after her lover's death she adopted the habit of the Franciscan tertiaries and took up residence in a cell next to the convent of St. Francis in Cortona, where she lived together with her son until he began his noviotiate among the Franciscan friars at Arezzo.

It is, admittedly, almost painful to read Fra Giunta Bevegnati's account of Margaret's interactions with her son during the time that they lived together in the cell in Cortona. Margaret, Fra Giunta writes, "was detached from any worldly concerns which could hinder her spiritual progress; she lacked maternal affection, as if she were not of this world, a world of which she had only horror." It was as if, Fra Giunta declares, "she had never given birth to her son."[33] Like Paula and Birgitta who subordinated their love for their children to their love for God, Margaret "preferred the eternal Love to the son of her womb." Indeed, so much so did Margaret love God above her own child that she "did not want to cook anything for him lest it interrupt her time for prayer."[34] In fact, Fra Giunta continues, "she rarely spoke to her son, except to say, 'My son, when you return to the cell take whatever raw food you find and eat it in silence, since I find in you no reason for interrupting the divine praises.'"[35]

In *The Life and Miracles of Saint Margaret*, the saint's conviction in the mutual exclusivity between love for God and love for children is expressed, more particularly, in her dogged service to the poor at the expense of her own son. In contrast to her near-criminal neglect of her own son, Margaret had a "maternal piety" for the needy, feeding "the poor by the work of her own hands" and giving them "shirts, knives, belts, bowls, glasses, firewood, clothes, and blankets. When these things were gone, she cut off the sleeves of her dress and gave them the veil off her head, her belt, her prayer bench, the beams of her roof, even her little jug of holy water." In short, Fra Giunta states, "Margaret gave whatever she could, but concerning her own son, she acted as if she had forgotten maternal concern."[36]

As in Jerome's letter to Eustochium and Birgitta's *Revelations*, the motif of the renunciation of children in Fra Giunta Bevegnati's *Life and Miracles of Saint Margaret of Cortona* testifies to the holy women's love of God above all else. The *Life and Miracles of Saint Margaret*, however, bears the unmistakable imprint of the Franciscan ideals of poverty and an active apostolate of Christian charity. In this text, Margaret's fraught relationship with and ultimate rejection of her only son serves as an index of her love of God refracted through her commitment to evangelical poverty and the Franciscan ideal of service to the poor. As Fra Giunta would have it, Margaret's repudiation of her own child was an act of voluntary impoverishment.[37] It was, at the same time, a prerequisite to Margaret's service to the poor. Margaret, Fra Giunta concludes, "thoroughly fulfilled the Gospel message, when on account of love for her beloved spouse Jesus she expelled her only son, preferring, out of love for Christ, pilgrims, the poor, the notorious."[38]

Whether conceived as proof of the holy woman's triumph over her pathetic femininity, her expansive love for God, her faith in divine recompense, or her dedication to a life of poverty and Christian service (or, indeed, some combination of any number of these), the renunciation of children in the lives of the saints characteristically involved some degree of maternal suffering.[39] Paula, for example, emerges from the lines of Jerome's letter as almost a caricature of maternal sentiment. Her dry eyes notwithstanding, upon leaving her children behind in Rome Paula's "heart was rent within her, and she wrestled with her grief, as though she were being forcibly separated from parts of herself."[40] Jacobus de Voragine's rendition of Paula's departure in the *Legenda Aurea* only amplifies the description of her maternal anguish: "As she fought her grief, her entrails were twisted in pain as if being torn from her body." But in the end, "her full faith made her bear this suffering; more than that, her heart clung to it joyfully, and for love of God she put aside love of sons and daughters." Nonetheless, once the ship "put to sea . . . while all her fellow passengers were looking back to the shore, Paula looked away so as not to see what she could not see without pain."[41]

In his *Monodies* (which, though not technically an instance of Christian hagiography, reads in large part as a hagiographic paean to his mother), the late eleventh-century Benedictine Guibert of Nogent records in dramatic detail the emotional event of his own mother's entry into religious life when he was just twelve years old. As it had been for Paula, it was not easy for Guibert's mother to forsake her favorite son. "When she was moving to the monastery," Guibert recounts, "her heart was so torn that she was unable to bear the pain of looking at the house [where her son lived]. She felt the most bitter pangs of melancholy when she thought of what she was leaving behind." She must have felt, Guibert continues in harmony with Jerome's description of Paula, "as if her own limbs were being torn from her body." To make matters worse, Guibert's mother's sufferings upon separating herself from her son were amplified by her own sense of maternal guilt. Much as Marie de l'Incarnation would, several centuries later, accuse herself of being "the cruelest of all mothers," Guibert's mother "considered herself, and heard others call her, a heartless, cruel woman" for leaving her son "utterly without support."[42] But ultimately, Guibert confirms, like Paula before her and Birgitta after, Guibert's mother "broke with those things she had loved before" by the strength of her intense and uncompromising love for God.[43]

In the writings about holy women, these descriptions of maternal suffering brought about by the renunciation of children invoke the paradigmatic suffering of Christ and raise to the level of saintly heroism the virtues illuminated by the act of renunciation.[44] Just as Christ suffered, so the holy mothers who renounced their children in favor of religious life suffered, too. Within the context of a hagiographic economy that measured holiness against the rule of Christ, the graphically physical descriptions of the sufferings of holy women like Paula and Guibert's mother were anything but gratuitous. Instead, they were vivid and evocative references to Christ's tortured body hanging on the cross, tightening the connection between instances of maternal suffering and the suffering of the crucified Christ—a connection that depended on the very intensity of the affective relationship between a mother and her children. The renunciation of children was meaningful in the lives of holy mothers because it was hard. As Jerome explains with regard to Paula, "The greatness of the affection [for her children that] she had to overcome made all admire her victory the more . . . Though it is against the laws of nature, she endured this trial with unabated faith." No mother, Jerome avers, "ever loved her children so dearly."[45] Like Christ's sacrificial gift of self, a mother's renunciation of her children—whether motivated by a greater love for God, a confident faith in his providence, or a commitment to the ideal of evangelical poverty—was nothing short of heroic.

The sufferings of mothers who relinquished their children in favor of religious life functioned within the context of hagiographic narrative not only to illuminate the heroism of the act of renunciation but also its salvific dimensions. Just as Christ suffered in order to bring about the salvation of humankind, so the holy mothers who renounced their children did so in the interests of saving themselves and others, including the children they renounced. Guibert's mother, for example, overcame her resistance to leaving her son out of concern for her personal salvation. "Softness of heart," Guibert explains, "would most certainly have been her ruin if she had put us ahead of her own salvation and, if neglecting God because of us, had turned her attention to worldly things."[46] In many cases, the holy woman's decision to leave behind her sons and daughters provoked those children themselves to enter religious life. Paula's daughter Eustochium, for example, accompanied her mother to the Holy Land, where she lived as a virgin vowed to religious life. Birgitta's daughter Catherine (canonized as St. Catherine of Sweden in 1484) likewise served as the companion to her holy mother, later becoming abbess of the Brigittine convent at Vadstena. Even Margaret of Cortona exerted a salvific influence over the son she had so badly mistreated—he eventually became a Franciscan friar. The influence of Ivetta of Huy extended even further—not only did both sons (first the eldest and, eventually, the youngest) join the Cistercians, but her father did as well, no doubt inspired by the example of his devout daughter. Others, like Adelheid of Rheinfelden and Rilindis of Bissegg whose religious careers are briefly chronicled in the fourteenth-century *Vitae Sororum* from Unterlinden, stimulated the conversions of not only the children they left behind, but also their abandoned husbands.[47]

———————

Many of the themes that mark the narratives of maternal renunciation discussed above characterize Marie de l'Incarnation's own account of her decision to abandon Claude in favor of religious life. As it did for holy women like Paula and Birgitta, Marie's separation from Claude gave proof

of her love of God above all things. Just as Paula and Birgitta had overcome their love for their children by their greater love for God, so Marie
testifies to having "abandoned [Claude] for [God's] love at a time when according to all human reasons you needed me most."[48] Marie's relinquishment of Claude was also, as it was for Margaret of Cortona, an expression
of her commitment to evangelical poverty. Understood within the context
of her personal vow of poverty (undertaken in 1624), Marie's determination to renounce her son was but a radical instance of a more general
determination to renounce all worldly material goods and possessions.
And, as it was for the host of other holy mothers who renounced their children in favor of religious life, Marie de l'Incarnation's abandonment of
Claude was a sacrifice in imitation of Christ.[49] While the sacrificial over-
tones of the renunciation of children is only implicit in the narratives discussed above, it is this theme (as we have seen) that dominates Marie's
explication of the event of Claude's abandonment. Just as the act of maternal renunciation had provoked the suffering of mothers like Paula and
Birgitta, so Marie's decision to leave Claude for a vocation among the
Ursulines had not been easy. Marie had abandoned her son only "with
strange convulsions," suffering so acutely that "it seemed to me that my
bones were breaking apart and becoming disjointed, because of the pain
that my natural sentiments felt on account of this abandonment."[50] But as
it had for Paula, Birgitta, Ivetta, and others, Marie's maternal sacrifice
had redounded to the salvific benefit of her abandoned son. Attributing
Claude's spiritual success as a professed Benedictine to her own act of renunciation, Marie reminds Claude in a letter dated August 16, 1664, that
"it is assuredly because I abandoned you out of love for him" that God "fa-
vored you . . . , granting you the great and inestimable happiness of the
religious profession . . . [and giving you] such honorable charges and such
dazzling occupations."[51]

———————

I wish I knew how to save my own children. I wish I knew what would
assuredly lead to their inestimable happiness and their dazzling success. I
wish I knew the right answer—and I wish there *was* a right answer. Parenting, as every mother and father can attest, is a fraught enterprise, involving
doubt and uncertainty, trial and error, constant calculations, reevalua-
tions, and second thoughts. Am I doing enough for my children? Am I

doing the right things? Should I play with them more? Should I play with them less? Should I demand the best? Or praise the effort? When should I worry? When should I not? And if the stakes in the parenting game are high with regard to Bobby, Frankie, and Johnny (which they are), they are that much higher with regard to Aggie. Realistically, I know that Bobby, Frankie, and Johnny will be fine. They will all go on to honorable charges and dazzling occupations of some sort, regardless of my maternal interventions at the margins. But Aggie? Hers is a situation—at least I think it is—of urgent proportions. I can make her. Or I can break her. Am I doing enough to save her? Am I doing the rights things? There are days when she's not interested in stacking blocks or crawling through her nylon tunnel, and there are days when I forget to use her balance beam or work through her consonant cue cards. And I worry—irrationally, I know, but I worry anyway—that these missed opportunities will set her back. Sometimes, though, I catch myself and I wonder if it wouldn't just be best for Aggie (and, indeed, for her development) to go about her early years together with her brothers, as one of the gang, pushed to keep up with her boisterous and quick-witted peers. If only I knew what would assuredly lead to Aggie's happiness and her own dazzling success.

———————

The meanings "embodied, expressed, and available" to Marie were, however, more than just these. The narrative waiting for Marie within the historical context of seventeenth-century French Catholicism was not just a hagiographic one that recognized in the renunciation of children proof of the heroic virtue demanded of the saints, but also a spiritual one that rendered abandonment itself chief among the spiritual virtues.[52] It is this distinctive spiritual milieu that informed not only Marie's decision to relinquish her maternal responsibilities vis-à-vis Claude, but also her representation of that decision as one, particularly, of "abandonment."

Indeed, unique to Marie's account of her own act of maternal renunciation is the conspicuous and repetitive terminology of "abandonment"—terminology that is altogether absent from the hagiographic narratives discussed above. Marie's recourse to the vocabulary of abandonment bears consideration not only for the ways in which it distinguishes her narrative from those of her holy predecessors, but also for the ways in which it—ironically—draws attention to the qualitative difference between

Marie's conduct toward Claude and the historical phenomenon of child abandonment in medieval and early modern Europe. As we have seen, the circumstances of Marie's relinquishment of maternal responsibility over Claude were nothing like those of the host of medieval and early modern parents who simply exposed their children, unwilling or unable to cope with the burdens of raising them to adulthood. Marie saw to it that Claude was cared for by her sister and brother-in-law, made arrangements for his education, and even maintained regular and intimate contact with him well after she left France for the New World. By any account, this was a far cry from abandonment as it was understood and prosecuted in early modern French law.[53] Why, then, does the terminology of abandonment loom so large in both the *Relations* and Marie's letters, as well as in Claude's *Vie de la Vénérable Mère Marie de l'Incarnation*?

"One would have to be a foreigner in France," declared Bishop Jean-Pierre Camus in 1640, "to be unfamiliar with" the spiritual implications of the notion of abandonment.[54] Indeed, comments Gabriel Joppin, "the entire seventeenth century spoke of annihilation, of death, of disappropriation," not to mention abnegation, indifference, and abandonment. Pierre de Bérulle, for example, developed the themes of holy indifference and self-renunciation in his *Bref discours de l'abnegation interieur*, calling for an annihilation (*anéantissement*) of self that would leave room for the activity of Christ alone. Charles de Condren, similarly, laid much emphasis on the ideals of holy indifference and total abandonment to divine providence, recommending to the spiritually ambitious self-immolation following the model of Christ. Jean-Jacques Olier, too, insisted that only through concerted effort toward self-annihilation might the human person participate in the life of Christ and achieve regeneration by the grace of God. And Jean Eudes, whose theology bears the mark of a distinctive devotion to the heart of Jesus, likewise called for a death to self and commitment to servitude, concluding that "the greatest of all practices . . . the greatest of all devotions . . . is to be detached from all practices . . . and to surrender to the Spirit of Jesus."[55] The litany of exemplars of seventeenth-century French spiritualities of annihilation, abnegation, and indifference is virtually endless.

Although one could—and perhaps should—trace the roots of the spirituality of abandonment adumbrated in seventeenth-century France and elaborated by the likes of Bérulle, de Condren, Olier, and Eudes to the

Alumbrados of late-fifteenth- and sixteenth-century Spain, it is in the work of Francis de Sales that the spirituality of abandonment finds its most direct antecedent.[56] Central to Salesian spirituality is the notion of holy indifference, which de Sales likens to a "perfect submission of spirit and heart" to divine providence.[57] For de Sales, implicit in the act of perfect submission to God's "good pleasure" is the abandonment of one's own will, so "entirely and without reserve" that it "is totally annihilated in itself and is converted into God's will."[58]

French theologians like Jacques-Bénigne Bossuet and others would pick up and elaborate on the themes of self-renunciation and mystical union implicit in the Salesian understanding of abandonment. For Bossuet, spiritual perfection needed "only one thing"—the individual's abandonment of himself entirely to God, "his soul, his body in general and in particular, all his thoughts, all his sentiments, all his desires, all his members, all his veins, with all their blood, all his nerves up to his least ligaments, all his bones, both up to the interior and up to the marrow, all his entrails, all that is inside and outside."[59] In ceding everything to God, Bossuet, like de Sales, anticipated the relinquishment of his own free will to divine providence. In its stead, Bossuet demanded "a pure heart, a docile and obedient heart"—a heart, in other words, that was no longer his own but God's. Bossuet put it bluntly: "I abandon myself to you, O my God, to your unity, in order to be made one with you . . . in order to lose myself and to forget myself . . . to be governed according to your plans and not according to my own thoughts . . . to be always under your hand [and] . . . your paternal bounty."[60]

Oddly enough (since Bossuet would later lead the charge in condemning her writings as heretical), Jeanne-Marie Bouvier de la Mothe Guyon understood abandonment in much the same way. For Guyon, abandonment was "an ongoing process of purification that leads gradually toward increasingly perfect union with God in the higher stages of prayer."[61] The "key to inner life," abandonment "is giving up all care for ourselves in order to leave ourselves entirely to God's way." It involves a "total surrendering and putting of your life into God's hands, forgetting yourself and thinking only of God."[62] Sounding a note in harmony with de Sales, Guyon advised her reader "to make yourself indifferent and desire only what God has desired from the beginning of time. Be indifferent to all things, whether for the body or for temporal and eternal goods."[63]

If, for Bossuet and Guyon, the state of abandonment was best understood as one of union with God, for the anonymous author of *L'abandon à la providence divine* the indifference of the abandoned soul was comparable to the posture of a devoted servant vis-à-vis his master.[64] In the act of abandonment, the author explains, "one finds oneself belonging to God by a total and complete surrender of all one's rights over oneself: over one's words, actions, one's thoughts, one's movements, over the use of one's time and over all its possibilities."[65] Under these circumstances, the abandoned soul has only a single desire—and that is "to have its eyes fixed on the master to whom it has given itself, and to keep its ears always open to discover and hear his will and to execute it immediately."[66]

Paradoxically, however, as both the author of *L'abandon à la providence divine* and Madame Guyon alike suggested, there is freedom in the sort of submission entailed by the act of abandonment. The heart entirely surrendered to divine providence "remains always free, joyous, and detached."[67] The only rule, after all, "is the present moment." There, the author of *L'abandon* explained, the soul is "as light as a feather, as fluid as water, as simple as a child."[68] Forgetting itself, the abandoned soul "eternally occupies itself with loving [God] and obeying him without the fears, reflections, hesitations, and worries that arise from a preoccupation with one's salvation and its proper perfection."[69] The abandoned soul is unconditionally submitted "to the order of God according to the nature of the present moment," concerned neither with "what came before nor with what must follow after."[70]

The day I found out Aggie needed glasses, I called Bobby on the phone to tell him the news. And I cried. "I won't be able to see her pretty eyes, and," I had spat over the receiver, "I hate accessories!" Bobby did as Bobby does—comforted me in the midst of my heartache and assured me that Aggie would look adorable with her glasses (which, indeed, she does). "What bothers you most about Aggie's situation?" Bobby had asked me later that day. That was an easy one. "It's the not knowing," I had said. "It's the not knowing whether she will talk or how well, the not knowing what kind of school she'll go to, how well she'll do math, how well she'll read, how well she'll run, or draw, or dance. It's the not knowing whether she'll get married or not, whether she'll have children, whether she'll

work, and live on her own, whether she'll be blissfully, capably independent or whether she'll need care and support and some sort of custo-
dian." The not knowing is, of course, also the beauty of Aggie's situation.
So unchartered is the medical territory of her genetic difference that
Aggie's possibilities really are endless. There are no known limits, there
is no known ceiling. And although I wouldn't have it any other way, it is
hard to not know. It makes me anxious and I grind my teeth in the night
worrying about Aggie's future.

———————

The state of abandonment implicated by the ideal of holy indifference, suggested de Sales, is one of spiritual passivity. Whereas for Ignatius Loyola
indifference had meant actively disposing oneself to determine just what
God's good pleasure was at any given moment, for Francis de Sales indifference meant "the simple and general state of waiting."[71] To wait, de
Sales explained, "is neither to do nor to act, but only to remain subject to
some event . . . It is not an action, but rather a simple disposition to receive
whatever shall happen."[72] The author of *L'abandon à la providence divine*
agreed: abandonment involves "a simple and passive submission to the im-
pressions of the good pleasure of God."[73] This, for de Sales, is what differentiated indifference from resignation (which "is practiced by way of effort
and submission") and, for the author of *L'abandon*, abandonment from
obedience.[74] Obedience requires "vigilance . . . care . . . prudence . . .
discretion . . . [and] ordinary efforts." Abandonment, in contrast, involves
nothing of the self, "beyond an attitude of general good will that wants
everything and nothing, being like a tool . . . in the hands of a worker."[75]
    Abandonment, Bossuet affirmed, "is the most perfect and simplest of
all acts; for it is not an effort made by a man who wants to act by himself,
but a letting oneself go to be moved and pushed by the Spirit of God."[76]
For Bossuet, however, the abandoned soul was hardly an inactive or idle
one. Against the Quietists, who insisted that the abandoned soul was
under no obligation to act virtuously, Bossuet pointed out that "we are the
more active when we are more pushed, more moved, more animated by
the Holy Spirit."[77] Fénelon, too, was at pains to distinguish the tempered
passivity implicated by the state of abandonment from the extreme passivity advocated by the Quietists. Passive contemplation properly understood, explained Fénelon, does not "exclude real action: actions positive,

deliberate, and meritorious of free will, or the real and successive acts that we must repeat at each moment." Rather, it "is called passive only to exclude . . . [the] eager, harried and discursive acts" of Christians anxious about their own salvation.[78] The author of *L'abandon* puts it this way: the abandoned soul "is active as regards that which the present moment demands, but passive . . . as regards all the rest." Lest his reader misunderstand the implications of the passivity of the abandoned soul, the author confirms that in the state of abandonment, "one loves God, one satisfies one's Christian obligations, one frequents the sacraments, one carries out the exterior acts of religion to which the whole world is obliged, one obeys one's superiors, the needs of the state are met, one constantly resists the movements of the flesh and the blood and the devil, for no one is more attentive and more vigilant than these [abandoned] souls about acquitting themselves of all their obligations."[79] Even Madame Guyon was careful to insist that "when the soul has reached complete abandonment to God in the highest stages of mystical contemplation, exterior activity in service of God's will in the world never ceases."[80] In fact, she continued, "those who surrender completely to God in their interior depths become completely free to act virtuously in the world precisely because their own desires have been conquered."[81]

Central to the spirituality of abandonment elaborated by seventeenth-century French Catholic theologians was an emphasis on suffering. The soul entirely submitted to divine providence, explained de Sales, loves even suffering and affliction out of love for God, for "love reaches its most exalted state when we accept afflictions not only easily and patiently, but even cherish, like, and embrace them because of that divine good pleasure from which they come."[82] Indeed, averred Fénelon, the cultivation of the disinterested love that marks the summit of Christian perfection involves a process of interior purification. As understood by Guyon, this process of purification is painful because it requires the obliteration of the individual's "fallen and selfish" human nature and its transformation into divine nature.[83] In the background of seventeenth-century elaborations on the suffering implicated in the act of abandonment was the model of the crucified Christ, who voluntarily suffered, died, and rose again for the sake of a sinful humanity. Bossuet, for one, found the inspiration to abandon himself "to [God's] inexorable rigors" in Jesus Christ, "who abandoned himself to them for me, in order to deliver me from them."[84] Jean-Baptiste de la Salle, similarly, insisted that it was in suffering in the model of Jesus Christ that abandonment found its most perfect expression. Try to find your consolation in suffering, de la Salle advised, "because there you will find God most purely."[85]

While we know that Marie de l'Incarnation was familiar with the work of Francis de Sales (she had read, she testifies in the *Relation* of 1654, his *Introduction à la vie dévote*), evidence for the direct influence of Bérulle, Olier, and others on the formation of her spirituality is lacking. If the writings of Bossuet, Fénelon, Guyon, and the anonymous author of *L'abandon à la providence divine* are any indication, however, the seventeenth-century France within which Marie conceived, bore, and forsook Claude was one fairly saturated with the spirituality of abandonment. Within this religious context—which predicated spiritual perfection absolutely and unconditionally on the renunciation of self and submission to God's good pleasure (whatever that might be at any given moment)—Marie's relinquishment of Claude was pregnant with theological meaning. Carried out against her own inclinations and in imitation of Christ's own sacrificial subordination to the will of God the Father, Marie's renunciation of Claude was nothing short of abandonment, the "only thing necessary," the "most perfect and simplest" of all Christian acts.[86]

Virginity, Jerome declared, "is to marriage what fruit is to the tree . . . Although the one-hundred-fold, the sixty-fold, and the thirty-fold sprang from one earth . . . yet there is a great difference in respect of number. The thirty-fold has reference to marriage . . . the sixty-fold applies to widows . . . [and the] one hundred-fold expresses the crown of virginity."[87] Physically corrupted, guilty of concupiscence, and bound to the things of this world by the fetters of their children, mothers were—at least by Jerome's calculation—at best second-class citizens in the world of Western European Christianity. Although "something happened" in late medieval Europe with respect to sanctity and motherhood, it wasn't much. Despite the language of affective piety and the ideal of spiritual motherhood, mothers—real flesh and blood mothers of real flesh and blood children—remained peripheral to the Christian tradition. Even Birgitta of Sweden, the mother of eight and a saint in her own right, had to admit that virginity was better than marriage and motherhood: "Virginity merits a crown; widowhood comes near to God; marriage is not excluded from heaven."[88] That was the best she could do.

All its liabilities and handicaps aside, however, motherhood had one inalienable, incontrovertible advantage over virginity. Mothers, bound passionately and intimately to the children they loved as much as themselves, could renounce these children—heroically, virtuously, painfully, and in imitation of the crucified Christ. In the stories of holy women like Perpetua, Paula, Birgitta, Margaret of Cortona, Ivetta of Huy, and others, the renunciation of children was heroic. And it was hard. It was hard because there was nothing dearer or more precious to a mother "in all the world" than her own children, and the harder it was, the more closely the act of maternal renunciation replicated the virtuous heroism of Christ on the cross.[89] Within the context of a Christian tradition that recognized Christ's own crucifixion as the paradigmatic instance of suffering transformed and redeemed, the painful sacrifices made by mothers who loved their children and then renounced them were heavily freighted with sacred meaning. In this limited sense, then, as Atkinson puts it, motherhood did not block access to the sacred, but "made it available through sorrow and suffering, permitting women to share the tears of Mary and the pains of Christ."[90]

By Marie de l'Incarnation's time, so central had the renunciation of children become to the construction of maternal sanctity that Jeanne de Chantal's own son could not resist dramatizing his mother's entry into religious life as a renunciation of motherhood—and this despite the evidence that the seventeenth-century dévote had, in fact, managed to pursue a mitigated spiritual regimen while discharging her maternal duties. When Jeanne left home to found the Congregation of the Visitation, her youngest son, Celse-Bénigne, was already fifteen years old and attending school away from home. Nonetheless, this teenage son threw himself upon the ground in an attempt to prevent his mother's departure, saying, "Well, mother, I am too weak and unlucky to hold you back but at least it will be said that you trampled your own child underfoot!"[91] Even if—or perhaps especially if—Celse-Bénigne's reaction to his mother's leave-taking was nothing more than a staged performance of emotional extravagance (as some scholars suggest), the weight of this episode in the biography of

Jeanne de Chantal testifies to the enduring significance of the renunciation of children in hagiographic narrative.[92]

Within the context of a seventeenth-century France marked by shifting ideologies of motherhood, the hagiographic significance of the renunciation of children could only have increased. The conviction that the business of raising children required "passionate, single-minded maternal devotion" could only have made more impossible the conjunction of Christian discipleship and actual maternal practice; the growing appreciation for children as the objects of their mothers' intense (and natural) affections could only have augmented the sacrificial dimensions of their renunciation.[93] In an emerging domestic world in which mothers were expected, as we saw in Chapter 2, to love their children tenderly, inwardly, and affectionately, the renunciation of children was harder than ever before.

But it was, at the same time, more meaningful than ever before. A mother's decision to renounce her children was one of profound theological significance, readily assimilated within the spiritual context of seventeenth-century France to an act of abandonment on the order of Christ's paradigmatic sacrifice on the cross. Like Christ who had relinquished his own life in submission to God the Father and in the interests of the salvation of others, those holy mothers who gave up their children in favor of religious life proved themselves the exemplars of holy indifference, of self-abnegation, of perfect, disinterested abandonment to the good pleasure of the omnipotent God.

These, then, were the meanings "embodied, expressed, and available" in the Christian tradition, meanings that shaped Marie's decision to abandon Claude in favor of religious life and her representation of that decision as a sacrifice performed in imitation of Christ and in submission to the uncompromising will of God.[94] To suggest, however, that the Christian tradition informed and inflected Marie's decision to abandon Claude and her representation of that decision is not to suggest that the Christian tradition compelled either. It is, instead, to illuminate the ways in which Marie's agency with regard to the abandonment was constrained within the boundaries of what was possible and probable within the context of her seventeenth-century French Catholic world.

It is worth considering, as Newman does in the case of the medieval "maternal martyrs," to what extent interests of a more profane nature might have influenced Marie's decision to abandon Claude for religious life.[95] In actual fact, speculates Newman, "the maternal martyr paradigm might have covered many types of women, including some who wished good riddance on children they had never wanted in the first place, others who consoled themselves for their youngsters' deaths in the conviction that God had willed it so, and perhaps still more who believed, as their culture so loudly proclaimed, that it was impossible to combine the careers of motherhood and sainthood."[96] Margaret of Cortona's shocking neglect of her only son, for example, might have been motivated more by her acute sense of shame about his illegitimate origins than by any sort of radical commitment to evangelical poverty. Perhaps Guibert's mother's did not so much feel grief upon relinquishing her favorite son as relief at having divested herself of the child-rearing responsibilities she had never wanted to shoulder in the first place. And affecting Marie's own (long-gestating) decision to abandon Claude in favor of religious life might have been at least as much her traumatic history as a very young widow overwhelmed by the burdens of her newborn son and her husband's troubled business as her desire to imitate Christ and abandon herself to the will of God. We will, of course, never know. "Since we learn of saintly mothers who abandoned their children primarily through their hagiographers," Newman points out, "we cannot know with confidence how they actually felt about this decision."[97]

If the question is one of discerning the motivations of those women who renounced their children in pursuit of religious life, Newman is right to point an accusing finger at their hagiographers. Hagiography is, after all, not history, and the intentions of the hagiographer are not to report "what really happened," but to construct a model of Christian sanctity intended to edify the faithful and honor the admirable.[98] What Bourdieu's analysis adds to the picture, however, is the insight that these holy women themselves—the Paulas, the Birgittas, the Maries—might not have been entirely conscious of their *own* motivations in relinquishing their maternal responsibilities. Operating strategically "outside conscious control and discourse," holy women like Marie knew "without knowing . . . the right thing to do."[99] Within the context of a seventeenth-century French Catholic world which excluded maternal practice from the orbit of Christian discipleship and invested abandonment with a heavy dose of theological capital, the logic of leaving Claude for religious life must have seemed to Marie all but irrefutable. Confined within the boundaries of the possible and limited by the horizon of the probable, Marie, "with a mastery acquired by the experience of the game," made a virtue of necessity.[100]

———————

In a twist of events almost too poetic to be true, some fifty years after his own mother abandoned him for a vocation among the Uruslines, Claude Martin pressed Madame Guyon—who, we recall, was one of the most vocal exponents of the spirituality of abandonment in seventeenth-century France—to leave her four children to pursue a religious calling in Geneva. While in Paris on business, Madame Guyon had found herself engaged in conversation with a priest who had mysteriously (since she had not shared her inclinations to religious life with him) urged her to "do what the Lord has made known to you." Madame Guyon had protested that she was a widow with little children: "What else could God require of me, but to take due care of them in their education?" But the priest had replied, "You know that if God manifests to you that he requires something of you; there is nothing in the world which ought to hinder you from doing his will. One may have to leave one's children to do that."[101]

Unsettled by this exchange, Madame Guyon "went to consult Father Claude Martin." Claude promised to "pray about it," vowing to "write to me what should appear to him to be the will of God concerning me."[102] Some time later, Claude did write to Madame Guyon. After many prayers God had revealed to him "that he required me at Geneva, and to make a free sacrifice of everything to Him."[103] Reluctant to part with her children whom "I loved very much, having great satisfaction in being with them," Madame Guyon hesitated, suggesting to Claude that perhaps God "required of me nothing more than a sum of money to assist in founding an institution which was going to be established there."[104] But Claude insisted that God "had made him know that he wanted not my worldly substance but myself."[105]

"As soon as I became fully convinced of its being the will of the Lord, and saw nothing on earth capable of detaining me," Madame Guyon admits, "my senses had some pain about leaving my children. And upon reflecting thereon a doubt seized my mind."[106] Trusting, however, that God "would furnish the means necessary for the education of my children," she "resolved then to go."[107] She "put everything by degrees in order, the Lord alone being my guide," and left.[108]

5 Motherhood Refigured: Kristeva, Maternal Sacrifice, and the Imitation of Christ

To his critics, Bourdieu's understanding of human agency (upon which I have relied to loosely structure my explanation of the abandonment) amounts to nothing more than a sophisticated version of social determinism.[1] Although Bourdieu's intention had been to articulate a way of thinking about why people do what they do that transcended the reductive binaries of domination and resistance, his critics have consistently accused him of proposing a model of agency that condemns human actors to the reproduction of their own histories. And it is easy to see upon what logical grounds such accusations rest. For Bourdieu, after all, social practice is the result of the interaction between an individual's habitus ("structured structures predisposed to function as structuring structures") and the objective environment that structures those structured and structuring structures. The cacophony of cognate terminology is deliberate here, gesturing toward the apparent circularity of Bourdieu's understanding of human agency. If it is the objective environment that gives rise to habitus which, in turn, generates social practice in conformity with what is probable or possible within that environment, then what room is there for theorizing social change?

In an interview with Loïc Wacquant given in 1989, Bourdieu addressed these charges directly.[2] Faulting his critics for having attended more to the titles of his works (like 1977's *Reproduction in Education, Society, and Culture*) than to their content, Bourdieu contends that the possibility—indeed, the inevitability—of social change is implicit in his analyses of human practice. The conditions of the objective environment are not, after all, static. Changes in the objective environment drive changes in the relations both between positions within a particular social field and between multiple social fields, forcing the adjustment of individual habitus and making way for creative expressions of human agency. Taking the student uprisings of May 1968 as an example, Bourdieu demonstrates how the bigger crisis of the university was the consequence of the collision of two smaller independent crises—the one a crisis among the faculty, whose swelling ranks caused heightened tensions between its junior and senior members; and the other a crisis among the students, whose degrees lost value as a result of an oversupply of graduates. These two crises converged, Bourdieu explains in *Homo Academicus*, and exploded outward into other social fields, prompting similar conflicts between the old guard and the "new contenders."[3] We are not, Bourdieu insists, doomed to repeat the past—well, not exactly, anyway. Despite Bourdieu's description of the habitus as "a present past that tends to perpetuate itself," the past as it is carried forward in the habitus is never quite the same. Times change. People change. And habitus changes, too. There is, therefore, always room for social change and the possibility of creative action.

I have argued that Marie de l'Incarnation understood her decision to abandon Claude in favor of religious life as a sacrifice in imitation of Christ and in submission to the will of God; that in leaving Claude with no means of support Marie resisted the norms of seventeenth-century French family life; that the abandonment is, nonetheless, best understood not as an instance of domination or resistance but instead as a more subtle form of human agency located somewhere between these binary poles. I have argued, taking Bourdieu's understanding of social practice as my starting point, that Marie's decision to abandon Claude was informed (but not coerced) by a hagiographical tradition that honored the renunciation of children, and inflected (but not determined) by a seventeenth-century French Catholicism saturated with spiritualities of abandonment. Following Bourdieu, who stubbornly refuses to relinquish his faith in human agency (no matter how cramped the objective environment or how crabbed an individual's habitus), I have argued that Marie's hand was not forced. But, in truth, it might as well have been. In the tight spaces of a Christian tradition that marginalized the practices of conceiving, bearing, and mothering actual biological children, what choice did Marie have but to abandon Claude in favor of religious life and to have made a virtue of this necessity?

Not much of one. We can't—or, at least, ought not to—condemn Marie for the abandonment. It is hard, after all, to see how she could have done things differently. Called—badgered, even—by God to a religious vocation as a cloistered nun (first in France, and then in New France),

Marie could not stay in the world to shepherd Claude through to adult-hood. Marie's lively mystical life and career in the service of the indige-nous girls of Canada left scant space for maternal ministrations toward her young son. Or maybe the truth is that her husband's untimely death and her fragile economic situation just left Marie too overwhelmed to carry out her obligations toward Claude. Maybe it wasn't so much that Marie felt herself called beyond a shadow of a doubt to the convent but that she found in religious life a socially legitimate shelter against the hazards of life as a widow in seventeenth-century France. There is, in the end, more than one way to tell Marie's story.

But whatever the case, Marie de l'Incarnation's decision to abandon the eleven-year-old Claude made sense—not perfect sense, but enough sense—to Marie, in her time and in her place. It has been my attempt in this book to make the abandonment make enough sense to us, too—to myself and to my readers for whom the abandonment is, I suspect, "'bi-zarre,' 'strange' . . . 'deranged,'" unthinkable.[4] Few of us would have made the decision Marie did. But we are not Marie. We are not mystics in a seventeenth-century France still reeling from the wars of religion. Most of us are, instead, ordinary women and men living in a contemporary Western society in which traditional Christianity (including its hagio-graphic legends and its various spiritualities) is simply one among many possible "ways of being in the world."[5] We are, to borrow Bourdieu's ter-minology, living in a contemporary Western society in which the relations between the various social fields—and the relations between the people within those fields—have changed, and changed quite a bit. This makes it possible for us to think creatively about just how Marie might have, in a different time and place, found a way of imagining flesh and blood motherhood as central to the Christian tradition and actual maternal practice as compatible with a Christian way of life.

In what follows, I bend away from the historical and sociological and toward the theological, proposing that we think about motherhood itself—and not its renunciation—as sacrifice in imitation of Christ.[6] Draw-ing on the work of Julia Kristeva, I argue that maternal subjectivity is a sacrificial subjectivity that finds its closest analogue (and ultimate model) in Jesus Christ. Like the subjectivity of Jesus Christ, which is an ineffable coalescence of humanity and divinity, vulnerability and omnipotence, mortality and eternity, death and life, maternal subjectivity is a "strange fold" between nature and culture, the Symbolic and the semiotic, meaning and affect, self and other.[7] Like the subjectivity of Jesus Christ, too, maternal subjectivity is a sacrificial subjectivity distinguished by a mother's "willingness to give herself up" and motivated by the force of love.[8]

I am well aware of the very real dangers posed by a theology of sacrifice to the actual men and women who live their lives in its shadow. Indeed, I can think of no more eloquent testimony to just how damaging Christian narratives of sacrificial suffering can be than Orsi's chapter on Gemma and his grandmother Giulia (titled, tellingly, "Two Aspects of One Life: Saint Gemma Galgani and My Grandmother in the Wound between Devotion and History, the Natural and the Supernatural"). Juxtaposing "hagiographical lore" about Gemma, which makes much of the intensity of the saint's emotional and physical pain, with stories about his own grandmother who suffered cruelly at the hands of her youngest son, Orsi makes the point that these narratives are "mutually constitutive."[9] The story of St. Gemma Galgani at once grew out of and at the same time sustained, justified, and enabled not only a late-nineteenth-century Tuscan "family culture in which love and pain were inevitably paired and in which love was demonstrated, expected, and expressed often enough in the language of suffering," but also the particular pathos of a specific Italian American family—Orsi's own.[10] Both "called by men to victim lives of sacrificial suffering," Gemma and Giulia alike "took pain as a destiny and endurance as a virtue," encouraged no doubt by the gospel narrative of the bloodied and humiliated Christ who for us and for our salvation was crucified under Pontius Pilate, suffered death, and was buried.[11]

Although he doesn't say so explicitly, I suspect that one of the dangers Orsi perceives in a Christian theology of sacrifice is the potential for legitimating and even encouraging the victimization of some (especially women) by others. I suspect, although he doesn't say so explicitly, that Orsi sees in a Christian theology of sacrifice the source of much of his grandmother's suffering and the reason why she never broke the dusty bottle of vermouth that her son vowed to drink in celebration of her death, choosing instead to tolerate the bottle's menacing presence "on the top shelf of the cabinet, for many, many years."[12] I suspect, too, that Orsi sees in a Christian theology of sacrifice yet one more instance of the sort of totalizing search for meaning (with its own long history in the field of religious studies) which occludes the painful realities and disorienting ambiguities of individual lives. The movement, Orsi reminds us, "between life and meaning . . . is not a straightforward one . . . and the meeting of the two often enough deepens pain, becomes the occasion for cruelty, catches persons and communities in stories that are made against them . . . , that may alienate them from their own lives, and that bear within them the power to undermine them and make them and the people around them miserable and confused."[13] Attention to the end product (meaning) rather than to the process of meaning-making, Orsi insists, distracts us from the wound that marks the juncture between the sacred and the secular, Gemma's story and Giulia's, heaven and earth.

Despite the liabilities of a theology of sacrifice (to which I will return below), I think it is worth attempting to retrieve and, indeed, to rehabilitate, given the centrality of the sacrificial narrative to the Christian tradition generally, and to Marie's own experience in particular. In what follows, I argue that Kristeva's rendering of maternal subjectivity creates an opening for a reconsideration of sacrifice that has nothing to do with victimization and nothing to do with the occlusion of the ambiguous complexities of individual lives. Indeed, if Kristeva's sacrificial maternal subject stands anywhere it stands in *between*, in the midst of that wound betwixt life and meaning to which Orsi urges us to attend. In what follows, I argue that if we attend carefully to Kristeva's rendering of maternal subjectivity (which I do in the first part of this chapter), we can appreciate the ways in which for Kristeva maternal sacrifice does not implicate the immolation of the mother at the altar of the Other but rather the immolation of the idol of fixed and bounded identity that would maintain (without success) the hard and fast difference between the mother and the Other. Only "the most obvious example" of a general and universal human subjectivity positioned between culture and nature, love and the Law, "the 'other' and the 'same,'" the maternal body illuminates the inadequacy of "fundamental notions of identity and difference."[14] Like the paradigmatic sacrifice of Christ which did not fortify but rather obliterated the boundaries between human and divine, earth and heaven, finitude and eternity, maternal sacrifice thus conceived is informed not by a logic of exclusion, but one of inclusion.

Thinking about maternal practice as a sacrifice in imitation of Christ compels a reconsideration of conventional notions of agapic love—again, a point to which I will return below. Critical of traditional notions of *agape* that stress the disinterested and self-sacrificial qualities of divine love, feminist theologians like Valerie Saiving Goldstein, Christine Gudorf, and Sally Purvis have turned to maternal experience to propose a reformulation of *agape* as intensely interested, mutual, and not altogether distinguishable from *eros*. Just as, for Kristeva, the willingness of the mother to give herself up is motivated by the "mother's love for [her] child, which is a love for herself," so for these feminist theologians, Christ's own sacrifice is not as disinterested as traditional theology supposes.[15] At the root of all sacrifice—whether maternal or Christian—is not just a love for the other (*agape*), but a love for the self (*eros*) with which, given the nature of subjectivity (whether maternal or Christian), *agape* is impossibly entangled.

———

Julia Kristeva was born in Bulgaria in 1941. At the age of twenty-five, she moved to Paris to begin her career as a linguist. By 1974, she had already published three books (*Le Texte du Roman*, *Séméiotiké*, and *La Révolution du langage poétique*) and a number of essays in journals like *Critique*, *Langages*, and *Tel Quel*. One of Europe's most productive and influential theorists, Kristeva has effectively challenged the hegemony of structuralist understandings of language and human subjectivity, insisting on the dynamic and embodied qualities of signification and the mobility and heterogeneity of the subject-in-process. Over the course of the past five decades, Kristeva's work has ranged broadly from linguistics to psychoanalysis to literature, philosophy, and (most recently) fiction. A common thread that weaves these disparate projects together, however, is Kristeva's attention to the persistent presence of otherness—to, in other words, the ubiquity of alterity, the survival of the semiotic, the return of the abject, and the realness of the maternal.

Kristeva's understanding of human subjectivity and the development of language owes a heavy debt to the model of mid-century French psychoanalyst Jacques Lacan. Simply (and perhaps crudely) put, for Lacan the process of the formation of the human subject begins in the "mirror stage," when the infant recognizes his own image in the mirror.[16] At this point, the infant begins to develop a sense of himself as an independent and autonomous "I," separate and distinct from his mother with whom he had, until now, merged indistinctly, dependent on her for the identification and fulfillment of his physical needs. According to Lacan, the infant delights in recognizing himself the mirror. Over and against his infantile experience of himself as a fragmented body driven by a diversity of chaotic demands, the image in the mirror permits the infant to perceive himself as a unified and stable subject. At the same time, however, Lacan insists that the infant's recognition of himself in the mirror is ultimately self-alienating, exposing the "I" as an object (an Other) that can be perceived rather than as a subject (a Self) that really exists.

For Lacan, the process of identity formation which begins in the mirror stage retains the decentered quality made apparent by the disconnect between the ideal "I" in the mirror and the chaos and fragmentation of human materiality. Founded on a deliberate misrecognition (*méconnaissance*) of the imaginary (the unified, stable mirror-image) as the Real (the chaotic, fragmented body), identity continues to unfold aided by the acquisition of language in the early years of a child's life. The acquisition of language marks, for Lacan, the child's entry into the symbolic order, the social world within which human beings relate to one another according to the rules of signification and the conventions of culture. Entry into the symbolic order, however, only exaggerates the object-position of the "I." An "empty signifier" whose content is determined by its relationship to other signifiers in the symbolic (paternal) order, the "I" is characterized by what is lacks and its estrangement from the (maternal) Real.[17]

Following Lacan, Kristeva proposes a model of psychosocial development that conditions the emergence of the subject on its separation from the pre-social maternal order (what Kristeva calls the semiotic *chora*) and its entry into the Symbolic paternal order, marked by the acquisition and use of language.[18] Central to Kristeva's understanding of human subjectivity is the idea of the abject. Simultaneously attractive and repulsive, the abject exists on the borderline between meaning and nonsense, Self and Other, (paternal) culture and (maternal) nature, at once constituting and threatening the boundaries of subjectivity. Examples of the abject include vomit, waste, "that skin on the surface of milk"—realities that harry human subjects "as radically separate, loathsome. Not me. Not that. But not nothing, either. A 'something' that" exists on "the edge of non-existence and hallucination" and that threatens to annihilate the subject.[19] It is through the process of abjection, which amounts to a violent separation from and exclusion of that uncanny "something," that human subjects draw the boundaries of their identities. For Kristeva, the original and paradigmatic instance of abjection is birth. At the moment of birth, the infant abjects the maternal body, entering into the social world as a unique being, separate and distinct from his mother. As for Lacan, for Kristeva psychosocial development depends on the repudiation of the maternal as a precondition for the acceptance of the paternal and for the subject's integration within the social and Symbolic order. Matricide, as Kristeva puts it, "is our vital necessity."[20]

Where Lacan, however, supposes that the child enters into the Symbolic order out of fear of castration, Kristeva argues that it is, in fact, pleasure that entices the child to abject his mother and acquiesce to the Law of the Father. For Kristeva, paternal threats alone are not sufficient to account for the child's accession to the Symbolic order. As Kelly Oliver puts it, "If what motivates the move to signification are threats and the pain of separation" then more people would choose to "remain in the safe haven of the maternal body and refuse the social realm."[21] More people would, in short, "be psychotic."[22] In lieu of the stern, punishing father of Lacan and Freud, Kristeva posits the imaginary father whose identity as the object of his mother's love permits the child to "negotiate the passage between the maternal body and the Symbolic order."[23] A placeholder for maternal desire, the imaginary father permits the child to identify with his mother's desire and therefore with "the paternal function as it *already exists* in the mother."[24] The presence of the imaginary father thus eases the passage to the Symbolic order, making it possible for the child to substitute his pre-social identification with the maternal body with an imaginary identification with maternal desire, "which is a move into the Symbolic order."[25]

As the above account of the imaginary father suggests, Kristeva—against Lacan—does not maintain such a hard and fast separation between the maternal (semiotic) and paternal (Symbolic) orders. Indeed, as Oliver understands it, as a function of maternal desire, Kristeva's imaginary father "can be read as a metaphorical or imaginary reunion with the maternal body."[26] For Kristeva, the Symbolic order, governed by the Law of the Father and characterized by the acquisition and use of language, does not absolutely exclude elements of the semiotic and maternal. Rather, the semiotic persists in the midst of the Symbolic, organizing bodily drives in language and revealing itself in the "echolalias, rhythms, and silences that comprise material aspects of language and their maternal mark-ings."[27] At the same time, the "logic of signification," which is the logic of abjection that marks the boundaries of the Symbolic, is "already operat-ing in the body," structuring the time and space of the maternal *chora* and the experience of the autoerotic infant.[28] Beginning at the moment of birth, the logic of abjection (which forcibly draws the lines between the "me" and "not me," the "that" and "not that," the self and the other) oper-ates to constitute the infant as a social being whose boundaries are marked by what goes in (and is included within the self) and what comes out (and is excluded from the self). For Kristeva, in short, the semiotic is not an alternative to the Symbolic but instead both precedes and exists within the Symbolic as "traces of alterity and heterogeneity."[29] It is "the dialectic oscillation" between the semiotic elements of language (rhythms and tones) and the symbolic elements of language (syntax and grammar) that "makes signification possible," for without the symbolic, signification lacks sense and without the semiotic signification lacks affect.[30]

Like language (by means of which the subject constitutes itself), the human subject is a subject-in-process, constantly "oscillati[ng] between in-stability and stability or negativity and stasis."[31] Just as the semiotic per-sists in the Symbolic, "show[ing] itself in breaks, nonsense, and puns that display a subversion of language by the imagination," so the abject haunts the subject, "creat[ing] a fading or instability in the arrangements under-taken by the subject in an attempt to secure its being, showing them as ruse."[32] The abject—death, filth, disease—lingers at the borders of human subjectivity, mocking our fragile identities and threatening to undo what we have labored to construct. And so, if to become subjects we must kill our mothers, then to maintain our subjectivity we must kill our mothers (so to speak) over and over again. We must, in other words, repeat the ritual of abjection in an endless chain of mimetic matricidal acts, constituting ourselves as subjects over and against the maternal "matrix that threatens to subsume" us.[33] We can't, in short, live with the abject. But we can't live without it, either. "Through abjection," Noëlle McAfee explains, "the I is formed and renewed."[34] Human subjectivity (founded on the logic of negativity—not me, not that) depends on the abject and the perpetual process of abjection. At once the "vandal and the policeman of the self," the abject simultaneously threatens to dissolve the subject and at the same time marks its boundaries ever more darkly.[35]

Even as Kristeva maps the trajectory of psychosocial development, she recognizes the gendered liabilities of the process in Western patriarchal culture. Although Kristeva confirms that human subjectivity does, indeed, demand the child's abjection of the maternal body, she laments that because Western culture conflates the maternal function with women as a group, women at large "bear [the] marks" of the abject and are therefore at increased risk for the sacrificial violence upon which the maintenance of the boundaries of the Symbolic order depends.[36] The social contract, Kristeva confirms, "is an essentially sacrificial relationship" for women.[37]

It was as a first step toward developing a new discourse on maternity—one that would permit the child to abject the maternal body without abjecting the mother or, indeed, women as a group—that Kristeva published "Stabat Mater" in 1976. Extending her critique of the prevailing cultural discourses on motherhood first articulated in her 1975 essay "Motherhood According to Giovanni Bellini," Kristeva contends that the figure of the Virgin Mary (whose mythology, until recently, monopolized the maternal ideology of the European West) can no longer manage the threat of "feminine paranoia."[38] Kristeva's analysis exposes the Virgin Mary as a "refined symbolic construct" that alienates women from their own embodied subjectivity.[39] Impregnated with the Word, the Virgin Mary—whose conception by the Holy Spirit precludes any experience of sexual pleasure or *jouissance*—is incorporated wholesale into the Symbolic order. The Virgin Mary of the Christian tradition is thus, as Oliver puts it, "a paternal mother," a mother abstracted from the rhythmic and heterogeneous reality of maternal experience and settled "permanently in the spirit."[40] A "paradigm of the violent erasure of difference in patriarchy and the ascent of phallic truth," the Virgin Mary offers to women a maternal identity that makes scant room for the semiotic and the abject—for, in other words, the real maternal experience of the infolding of otherness in the self.[41]

If the Christian tradition is no longer capable of furnishing an adequate discourse on maternity, neither are science and feminism. Science, Kristeva contends, "is not concerned with the subject, the mother as site of her proceedings."[42] Whether understood as subject *to* or master *of* the biological, pre-social processes of conception and gestation, the mother has no identity as a speaking subject within a scientific discourse. Feminism, for its part, tends to accept cultural representations of motherhood that equate maternity with femininity. Anxious to save women from abjection, feminists tend to reject maternity altogether rather than turning a critical gaze on cultural constructions of motherhood and laboring to articulate new conceptions of motherhood that maintain a distinction between woman and mother.[43]

In the absence of a tenable cultural discourse on maternity, Kristeva proposes in "Stabat Mater" a new way of thinking about motherhood that attempts to capture "the real experience that fantasy overshadows."[44] The real experience of motherhood is, for Kristeva, a fundamentally heterological one. The mother, Kristeva insists, is a split subject, undecidable between "I, and he," self and other, the semiotic and the Symbolic. She is the "very embodiment of alterity-within," confounding the categories of identity and difference and illuminating the irrefutable heterogeneity at the heart of the self.[45] Written in two registers—the one consisting of the logical prose of academic analysis and the other of the lyrical language of maternal experience—"Stabat Mater" itself reads as a vivid expression of the heterogeneity that founds maternal experience. The essay itself is, like the maternal body, a "site of infolding of the 'other' and the 'same.'"[46] The conjunction of the two parallel columns (the one representing the Symbolic and the other the semiotic) that constitute "Stabat Mater" make, admittedly, for a disorienting reading experience. But that is precisely Kristeva's point: "Trying to think through that abyss [of heterogeneous subjectivity]: staggering vertigo."[47] The truth about maternal subjectivity—signified by the way in which the semiotic and lyrical column representing (Kristeva's own) lived experience of embodied motherhood repeatedly interrupts its Symbolic and analytical counterpart—"would restore [the mother] as cut in half, alien to its other."[48] This, Kristeva confirms, "is a ground favorable to delirium."[49] The maternal body blurs the lines between self and other, subject and object, the Symbolic and the semiotic, revealing the infolding of difference in every sort of claim to identity. For Kristeva, the mother is not an exception to the rule of human subjectivity but rather "the most obvious example of a subject-in-process."[50] We are all, as the title of Kristeva's 1994 book suggests, strangers to ourselves.[51]

For Kristeva, too, the mother is a prototype for a new kind of ethical subject, one that "honors difference and does not violently assimilate it to itself."[52] In "Stabat Mater," Kristeva takes the maternal subject as the starting point for a new kind of ethics, an outlaw ethics, what Kristeva calls a herethics. Founded on the ambiguity between subject and object most dramatically embodied by the pregnant mother, Kristeva's herethics challenges the Cartesian fantasy of the autonomous self, separate and distinct from the others around him. Kristeva's new kind of ethical subject is one fractured, interrupted, and constituted by others with whom the subject deals through love as opposed to the Law. This new kind of ethical subject does not "love the other as himself," but instead "love[s] the other in herself."[53] In Kristeva's herethical scheme, there is no need for the Law of the Father to set the rules of social relations, for (as Oliver puts it), "the social relation is inherent in the subject."[54]

Rooted in the reality of maternal experience, Kristeva's model of human subjectivity and the attendant (her)ethical program grants women a place within the Symbolic order while preserving their heterogeneity as embodied beings. No longer compelled to play "the part of the phallic castrated mother within the Law of the Father, or subversive mother on the margins, outside the symbolic order, trapped in the semiotic *chora*," the maternal subject is mainstreamed within Kristeva's herethical scheme as the paradigmatic subject-in-process.[55] Within Kristeva's herethical scheme, matricide is no longer our vital necessity. The maternal (the abject, the semiotic, the other, difference) no longer stands for that which we must exclude in order to declare ourselves subjects, but that which we must acknowledge within ourselves in order to realize the truth about our subjectivity—which, it turns out, is "not completely exhausted by the Law of the Father."[56]

It is true, as I said earlier, that what bothers me most about Aggie's diagnosis is the "not knowing." I don't know if she'll go to a normal school (or not), if she'll have cognitive deficits (or not), if she'll have a learning disability (or not). I don't know if she'll play sports (or not), go to sleepovers (or not), kiss her boyfriend (or not). And, as I said earlier, this worries me. I can't, of course, predict the futures of Bobby, Frankie, and Johnny either, but somehow I operate according to the fiction that I can—more or less, at least. I presume that Bobby, Frankie, and Johnny will end up, more or less, just like their dad and me because they are, more or less, just like us. Thirteen months ago, however, when we received the results of Aggie's chromosomal microarray we were told in no uncertain terms that Aggie was different. She is not like your other children, we were told. She is not like you.

But she is. Every bit of Aggie's genetic material came from Bobby and me. She is, in fact, *just like us*, except for a few missing genes somewhere on the long arm of her seventeenth chromosome. I see it in her dark black eyes, her wide Dunn grin, and her impish sense of humor. I don't know what will become of Aggie. But, the truth is, I don't know what will become of any of her brothers either. The truth is, neither Bobby, Frankie, nor Johnny are *just* like their dad or me. They are all different from one another and other than us. And they are all my children.

So what does any of this have to do with Marie de l'Incarnation, the abandonment, and motherhood in seventeenth-century France? Let me explain. Filtered through the lens of a Kristevan hermeneutic, the abandonment comes into focus as an instance of abjection, a defensive and exclusionary strategy deployed by Marie in the process of declaring her identity as a mystic united in marriage to Christ. Confined within the boundaries, on the one hand, of a Christian tradition that left little room for actual maternal bodies and real maternal practice and, on the other hand, a seventeenth-century Catholicism that made a theological virtue of abandonment, Marie could not fathom how to draw the boundaries of her mystical subjectivity other than by means of abjecting motherhood itself and Claude, its embodied proof. As it was for holy women like Perpetua, Paula, and Margaret of Cortona, matricide was Marie's vital necessity.

Understanding the abandonment as an instance of abjection illuminates the ways in which Marie's identity as a mystic takes shape through the logic of negativity that orients Kristeva's model of signification and human subjectivity. Not me. Not that. But, as Kristeva reminds us, "not nothing, either."[57] The reality of her maternity and the materiality of her son lingered on "the edge of non-existence and hallucination," threatening to annihilate Marie's mystical subjectivity.[58] Like Kristeva's abject (assimilated to the maternal, the semiotic, the other, difference), Marie's own memories of her *jouissance* in the act of Claude's conception and her personal experience of alterity within haunted her carefully constructed identity as a mystic planted firmly in the Symbolic order. Try as she might, Marie could not abject motherhood once and for all. Instead, if her repeated return to the subject of the abandonment over the course of her thirty-one-year correspondence with Claude is any indication, motherhood persisted as an irritant on the borderline of Marie's subjectivity, compelling her to relive the abandonment—if only discursively—over and over again.

———————

It took a month after that initial encounter with Dr. Inder in the imaging room at Children's Hospital to get the results of Aggie's chromosomal microarray. During the space of that month, Bobby and I visited and revisited the facts we had about Aggie—the opinions of her various doctors, the assessments of her assorted therapists, our own independent observations. Dr. Meyer said her muscle tone was normal, Bobby would say. And Toni noticed that she was very responsive to physical cues, I would add. Dr. Inder, we would remind each other, hadn't even held Aggie in her own arms before she pronounced her confident diagnosis. Had she taken all of Aggie's variables into account? Hadn't she spoken precipitously? On what grounds did she make that judgment? It is possible, we agreed and agreed again, that she might be entirely mistaken. We made ourselves crazy chasing our own thoughts in circles. But what else could we do? There was nothing else to talk about, and nothing else to think about. We were desperate to abject the possibility that there might be something wrong with our daughter. Not her. Not us. Not that.

———————

Central to Marie de l'Incarnation's subjectivity as a mystic deployed in the service of God was, as we have seen, the ideal of sacrifice in imitation of Christ. In the company of the legions of saints whose *vitae* unfold in mimetic variations on Christ's own life, Marie founds her own identity as a holy woman on the imitation of Christ's sacrifice, perhaps the most powerful expression of which within the context of the *Relations* and the letters is the act of the abandonment. For Marie, as we have seen, the abandonment was a sacrifice performed in imitation of Christ and in submission to the will of God. Against her own inclinations and despite her persistent misgivings, Marie gave Claude up to answer the call of a religious vocation among the Ursulines of Tours and, later, Quebec.

It is hard to imagine how Marie might have drawn the lines of her mystical subjectivity other than in imitation of Christ's original sacrifice.

There is, after all, no event more fundamental to the Christian narrative, and no ideal more essential to Christian identity. It is, however, possible to imagine a mystical identity oriented toward sacrifice that makes room for motherhood and maternal practice. It is, in other words, possible to imagine how—in another time and place—Marie might have drawn the boundaries of her identity as a mystic in imitation of Christ to include flesh and blood motherhood and actual maternal practice. It is, in short, possible to imagine motherhood itself and maternal practice as sacrifice in imitation of Christ. In what follows, I contend that Kristeva's maternal subject is, precisely, one constituted by sacrifice in imitation of Christ. Like Christ, the man–God who shatters that most basic binary of human and divine, Kristeva's maternal subject is fractured between self and other, same and different, the Symbolic and the semiotic. Marked by "the willingness to give herself up, to embrace the strangeness within herself in order to love herself," Kristeva's maternal subject is, like Christ himself, a "crossroads being . . . [a] crucified being."[59]

The suggestion that notions of sacrifice might profitably inform our conceptions of who a mother is and what a mother does rubs uncomfortably, I admit, against the fabric of a feminist scholarship that has condemned a sacrificial ideology of motherhood as inapt and detrimental to women.[60] Building on the work of Sara Ruddick, who draws attention to the ways in which a sacrificial model of motherhood proves complicit with the interests of patriarchy and the maintenance of a gendered hierarchy, Bonnie Miller-McLemore rejects an ideal of motherhood premised on the virtue of self-sacrifice (as well as an ideal of fatherhood premised on that of hard work). Miller-McLemore argues that a gendered division of the "burdens and rewards" of work and family both damages families and distorts the gospel. In lieu of the self-destructive ideal of sacrificial love that animates traditional ideologies of motherhood, Miller-McLemore calls for "reclaiming women's experiences of mothering as fresh ground for reflecting on the nature of human fulfillment" and for imposing on both mothers and fathers alike the obligation of self-*giving* (carefully distinguished from the temptation of self-*sacrifice*).[61] Christine Gudorf, for her part, argues that the rhetoric of sacrifice that shapes ideologies of motherhood serves as "cover for gender and generational power imbalances."[62] For Gudorf, sacrificial ideologies of motherhood disguise the extent to which mothers misuse their authority over their children, sublimating "their desire for autonomy in the more socially acceptable domination of children."[63] The relationship between mothers and their children is best understood, Gudorf insists, as "a source of growth and enrichment for both parties."[64] In truth, mothers (and fathers) do not love their children disinterestedly, but in the expectation and the hope that their children will love them back.

Like her feminist counterparts in the fields of philosophy and theology, Martha Reineke finds in ideals (and practices) of sacrifice a source of women's oppression. In her study of the etiology of violence against women in Western culture, Reineke points a finger at the process of abjection so critical to the formation of human subjectivity. Abjection, Reineke contends, is a kind of sacrifice, a "death-work oriented toward matricide" that repeats the subject's original differentiation from his mother at the moment of birth.[65] Within the context of patriarchal culture, this repetitive and mimetic "defensive strategy" makes victims of women at large.[66] "In patriarchy," Reineke explains, women "become victims of sacrifice when, found to bear abject marks, they are made hostage to others' dramatic efforts to repeat individuation from the maternal matrix."[67] Because patriarchy, in other words, conflates women with the maternal, "any woman maybe marked for murder when subjects who struggle to resecure their roles in the Symbolic invest her body with the effects of that abject struggle."[68]

Reineke locates a solution to the cultural problem of violence against women in Kristeva's model of herethics. For Reineke, Kristeva's herethics offers a way out of the sacrificial economy that victimizes women. If the logic of sacrifice is exclusionary, expulsive, and abjecting, then the logic of herethics is inclusionary, incorporative, and receptive. "In the somatic discourse of maternity" which is the basis for Kristeva's herethics, Reineke maintains, "is glimpsed a positive mimesis that emphasizes a 'plenitude of difference in the field of historical existence' rather than a Law of absence."[69] As Reineke understands it, sacrifice is startlingly out of place in Kristeva's brave new herethical world.

But Reineke *mis*understands it. Sacrifice is, in fact, central to Kristeva's rendering of maternal subjectivity and fundamental to the herethical model. The sort of sacrifice implicated in maternal subjectivity as Kristeva would have it, however, is not one that runs the risk of reinforcing and legitimating the victimization of women (and children) within Western

patriarchal culture. As Kristeva would have it, the sort of sacrifice implicated in maternal subjectivity is one that gives up the fantasy of the
bounded, autonomous self (in the model of the likes of Descartes and Leibniz) in favor of the reality of dynamic, heterogeneous identity fractured
between self and other. The sort of sacrifice implicated in maternal subjectivity, in other words, is not one that ends in the depletion of the maternal subject through the *exclusion* of difference but instead one that
celebrates its enrichment through the *infolding* of difference. Productive
of "an acute sense of both identification and separation, . . . pleasure and
pain," maternal sacrifice is oriented toward loving the other as opposed
to obliterating the other.[70] It is, as Kristeva puts it in "Stabat Mater," "undeath [*a-mort*], love [*amour*]."[71] Only the most obvious example of the
subject-in-process, Kristeva's maternal subject is not abjected beyond the
borderline of the Symbolic as a sacrifice to social order, but instead
finds a place squarely within the Symbolic as the paradigm of a universal
human subjectivity constituted by the sacrifice of the autonomous self.

Maternal subjectivity as Kristeva understands it is thus a sacrificial subjectivity that finds its closest analogue and archetype in Jesus Christ. The
"Word [that] became flesh and lived among us," Jesus Christ models a subjectivity that is ineffably inclusive of humanity and divinity, vulnerability
and omnipotence, mortality and eternity, death and life.[72] The Jesus Christ
of the gospel narratives is at once a defenseless baby and a powerful king,
an impoverished Palestinian and the almighty God, a crucified criminal
and the triumphant messiah. He is, indeed, the incarnate Word of the
gospel of John. But he is also at the same time the Jesus of the gospel of
Matthew who raged against the money changers, the Jesus of the gospel
of Luke who snapped at the hemorrhaging woman, the Jesus of the gospel
of Mark who cried out bitterly from the cross, "My God, my God, why have
you forsaken me?"[73] I do not intend to offer a thorough theological analysis of Jesus's rather more human characteristics here (lacking both space
and expertise), but only to suggest two things: first, that in conjunction
with his unassailable divinity these human characteristics expose Jesus
Christ as a subject-in-process, a site of competing discourses that (like the
mother) inhabits the "unruly border" between self and other, identity and
difference; and second, that Christ's rage and anguish operate as traces
of the semiotic within the Symbolic economy of Christianity.[74] Like the
milk and tears of the Virgin Mary—those "privileged signs of the *Mater*

Dolorosa"—the rage and anguish of Jesus Christ "are metaphors of non-speech, of a 'semiotics' that linguistic communication does not account for."[75] At least as much as the milk and tears of the Virgin Mary represent the "return of the repressed" in Christian monotheism, Jesus Christ's rage and anguish—not to mention the blood and sweat shed upon the Via Dolorosa—"reestablish what is nonverbal" and challenge the hegemony of Symbolic Christianity governed by the Word.[76]

Jesus Christ's subjectivity as a "crossroads being" gestures toward and culminates in his crucifixion, rendered in Christian tradition as the ultimate sacrifice of self in the service of others. Like maternal sacrifice as conceived by Kristeva, however, Christ's own sacrifice on the cross did not end with the annihilation of Christ himself in the service of humanity but in Christ's resurrection and restoration, as the Nicene creed puts it, "at the right hand of the Father." The crucifixion, in other words, is not the end of the Christian salvation narrative. It is, instead, only the beginning and the necessary antecedent to the "resurrection of the dead and the life of the world to come" (Amen). Like the sort of sacrifice implicated by Kristeva's notion of maternal subjectivity, Christ's sacrifice on the cross proceeds according to a logic of inclusion, not exclusion, working not to shore up the boundaries that separate human from divine, the mundane from the sacred, heaven from earth, but to efface them altogether. After all, as Christian theology has it, it is the sacrifice of Christ that ultimately redeems humanity and opens up the possibility of eternal life in the beatific presence of God.

Thinking about Christ's subjectivity as a maternal subjectivity complements and extends a traditional Christology that imagines Jesus as mother. I have argued, in Chapter 3, that the relationship between real maternal practices and actual maternal bodies, on the one hand, and the traditions of affective piety and spiritual motherhood, on the other, was mostly a unidirectional one. Mothers and maternal experiences were, for medieval and early modern Christians, useful tools for thinking about the meanings and merits of Christ and the saints. But the meanings and merits of Christ and the saints did not redound to the glory of mothers themselves and their collective maternal experiences. Medieval and early modern Christians could see, in other words, that Christ and the saints were a lot like mothers. Few, if any, however, were willing to invert the equation. Few, if any, could see that *mothers* were like Christ and the saints.

But why not? As far back as patristic times, after all, Christian theologians were in the habit of alluding to the maternal characteristics of Jesus Christ.[77] Augustine of Hippo, for example, likened Jesus to a mother hen who, "affected by [her children's] infirmity," became sick herself, "protecting her children with her wings."[78] Clement of Alexandria described the Word as the "nourishing substance of milk" produced by Christ's "breasts of love" that provides the faithful with "spiritual nutriment."[79] And Ambrose of Milan identified Christ as "the virgin who entered into marriage, carried us in her womb, gave birth to us, and fed us with her own milk."[80]

It is in the medieval period, however, that a maternal Christology finds its most sustained elaboration.[81] For twelfth-century Cistercians (the subjects of Caroline Walker Bynum's *Jesus as Mother*), references to the breasts and womb of Christ served to draw attention to Jesus's maternal compassion, his capacity for nurture, and his receptivity to union with his monastic devotees. Anselm of Canterbury, for example (echoing Augustine), invoked Jesus as "that mother who, like a hen, collects her chickens under her wings" in order to comfort those who hurt and reform the despairing.[82] Bernard of Clairvaux advised those who "feel the stings of temptation" to "suck not so much the wounds as the breasts" of Christ, for "he will be your mother, and you will be his son[s]."[83] And Guerric, abbot of Igny—although equally as eager to illuminate Jesus's paternal characteristics—affirmed that Jesus "is a mother, too, in the mildness of his affection, and as a nurse."[84]

Perhaps the most well-developed expression of a maternal Christology is found in the *Showings* of fourteenth-century English anchoress Julian of Norwich. For Julian, Christ is "our true Mother."[85] Having assumed human nature in order to "reform . . . and restore . . . us" and to unite "us to our substance," Christ performs "all the lovely works and all the sweet and loving offices of beloved motherhood."[86] Like a mother, he bears us (but "for joy and for endless life" rather than "for pain and for death"); he "feeds us with himself" and "sustains us most mercifully and graciously" with "all the sweet sacraments"; he leads "us easily into his blessed breast through his sweet open side"; he "knows and sees" the needs of his children and acts differently according to the circumstances, "but . . . does not change his love."[87]

Julian of Norwich's representation of Christ as the one "out of whom we have all come, in whom we are all enclosed, [and] into whom we shall

all go" is consistent with a Kristevan model of maternal subjectivity that forecloses the possibility of ultimate differentiation between mother and child, self and other, subject and object.[88] Just as, for Kristeva, subjectivity formation is an ongoing process that replicates again and again the original birth event, so for Julian of Norwich we are "endlessly born" in God and yet "out of [him] we shall never come."[89] Similarly (and perhaps more to the point of the argument that I am making here), Julian's representation of Christ's sacrifice as an act motivated by a maternal love and oriented toward an end point beyond death strikes a note in harmony with Kristeva's rendering of maternal sacrifice as at once an act of self-surrender and at the same time one of self-fulfillment. Having died once, Julian explains, Christ "could not die anymore, but he did not want to cease working" on behalf of humanity, for "the precious love of motherhood has made him our debtor."[90] As Patricia Donohue-White puts it, for Julian of Norwich Christ's "dying is not an end in itself nor does it represent the obliteration of" the maternal Christ. Rather, Christ's death is for Julian a "spiritual bringing to birth" which, paradoxically and contrary to expectations, "leads to joy and endless life, not only for the child but for the mother as well."[91]

I know only one person who says she loved motherhood from the very beginning. And I don't believe her. It's not that I think she's lying. I just think she's forgotten what it was really like. To be fair, motherhood does bring pleasure and delight at the outset—there's nothing quite like the soft downiness of a newborn's body, the warmth of a swaddled infant, the awe at having brought forth life itself. But in the beginning, motherhood is much more about labor and fatigue and confusion and uncertainty. There are sleepless nights, there is the awkward discomfort of breast-feeding, there is the frightening responsibility of the baby's utter dependency. From the very beginning, I loved little Bobby with a primal ferocity, but (I'll admit) it took those first smiles and the gradual emergence of a personality to make me really *fall in love*. And then he began to laugh (at me!), and eventually to walk (toward me!) and talk (to me!), and I began to love him even more deeply and more intensely. I began to see, too, that all that unidirectional giving at the beginning of his infancy was worth it. I was getting something back.

Even as my children get older, all the giving I continue to do is done with the expectation that the giving will become reciprocal. I continue to work hard for my children (at the cost of personal, social, and professional opportunities) because I want them to grow up to be happy, successful adults. I want this for their own sakes, I do. But I want it for my own sake, too. The happiness and success of my children will justify my efforts. It will recompense my sacrifice. It will redound to my credit. They made it. I did it.

Consistent with feminist reconsiderations of traditional notions of *agape*, thinking about Kristeva's model of maternal subjectivity as sacrifice in imitation of Christ compels us to attend to the ways in which conventional distinctions between *agapic* and *erotic* love do not hold up. Traditionally imagined as radically impartial, utterly disinterested, and wholly oriented toward the needs of others, *agape* finds its antithesis in *eros*.[92] If, as Anders Nygren put it nearly a century ago, *agape* describes God's love—a love so pure that Christ gave up his own life to save a sinful and undeserving humanity—then *eros* describes human love. Erotic love is ineluctably self-interested and always looking for a yield on its investment. *Agape*, to the contrary, wants nothing in return. Agapic love pays no heed to the needs or wants of the self. It is, as Søren Kierkegaard would have it, most perfectly expressed in a love for the dead who have no way to reciprocate.[93]

As early as 1960, feminist theologians began to challenge such traditional binary readings of *agape* and *eros*. In her widely influential "The Human Situation: A Feminine View," Valerie Saiving Goldstein made the point that the idealization of agapic love as self-sacrifice and its erotic antithesis as self-assertion fails to take into account the lived experience of women.[94] To begin with, Saiving Goldstein argued, women (and, particularly, mothers) know that self-sacrificial love, pure and unadulterated by one's own interests, is not only impossible, but undesirable. A mother's attempt to sustain "a perpetual I–Thou relationship . . . can be deadly. The moments, hours, and days of self-giving must be balanced by moments, hours, and days of withdrawal into, and enrichment of, her individual selfhood if she is to remain a whole person." A woman, Saiving Goldstein insisted, can "give too much of herself so that nothing remains of her own uniqueness; she can become merely an emptiness, almost a zero, without (s).

any value to herself, to her fellow men, or, perhaps, even to God."[95] More-over, Saiving Goldstein continued, a theology that lauds self-sacrificial love as the most perfect kind of love actually works to aggravate women's sin-ful tendencies. As far as men are concerned, traditional theology gets it right in suggesting that sin "is the unjustified concern of the self for its own power and prestige" at the expense of others.[96] But as far as women are concerned, traditional theology gets it very, very wrong. Unlike men, women are not tempted to "pride" and the "will-to-power," but rather to "triviality, distractibility, and diffuseness . . . in short, underdevelopment or negation of the self."[97] What Christian theology needs, Saiving Gold-stein concludes, is a doctrine of love that makes room for both self-giving and self-fulfillment in the interests of the flourishing of both men *and* women.

Extending Saiving Goldstein's critique of the gendered liabilities of ide-alizing *agape* as a love oriented toward self-sacrifice, Christine Gudorf contends that all love—whether agapic or erotic—contains elements of both gift and need. There is no such thing, Gudorf maintains, as a Chris-tian love purified of all traces of self-interest. Nor, she implies, is there such a thing as love that does not demand at least a small gift of self. For Gudorf, all kinds of love both implicate the sacrifice of the self and anticipate the mutual enrichment of both lover and beloved. Taking her own experi-ence of maternal love as a starting point for a reformulation of traditional notions of *agape*, Gudorf does not deny that a mother's love involves ele-ments of sacrifice. But sacrifice is not the whole story of maternal love. In harmony with Kristeva's allusion to the masochistic and narcissistic qualities of maternal love, Gudorf draws attention to the ways in which a mother's love is at least as much self-interested as it is self-sacrificial. Although it might seem as if much of a mother's "early giving" toward her infant is unidirectional, because "children [are] considered extensions" of their parents, these efforts in fact "rebound" to the mother's credit. And, Gudorf adds, parents expect "that the giving [will] become more mu-tual."[98] All love, Gudorf insists, "is directed at mutuality."[99] Even Christ's paradigmatic sacrifice on the cross is but a moment "in a process de-signed to end in mutual love."[100] All of us, even Christ himself, love others because we want—and expect—to be loved back.

Like Gudorf, Sally Purvis takes maternal love as a model for Christian *agape*. But if Gudorf trains her critical lens on the sacrificial implications of traditional notions of *agape*, Purvis takes issue with the representation of agapic love as disinterested. Following Sallie McFague, who disparages the traditional take on *agape* as "a sterile and unattractive view of divine love," Purvis dismisses a disinterested model of agape as not only untenable but also undesirable.[101] In lieu of a disinterested paradigm of agapic love, Purvis proposes an "intensely involved" and "other-directed" sort of love.[102] This love, exemplified by a mother's love for her children, is "fully mindful of the concrete realities of persons"—"extravagant," even—and at the same time inclusive and unconditional.[103] Purvis's conception of agapic love, which takes the "'special relations' in our lives, the relationships in which we care most deeply and love most strongly, . . . as guides and models for the movement outward into concern for all human beings," is consistent with a Kristevan understanding of heterogeneous human subjectivity.[104] As Purvis re-works and re-presents it, *agape* does not demand a loosening of the ties that bind one unique individual to another in pursuit of an ideal of benevolent disinterest, but to the contrary, a tightening of those ties and their extension beyond "the parochialism of the biological family."[105] Like Kristeva's herethics which take the mother as the model for a new kind of ethical subject marked by an infolding of difference, Purvis's conception of agapic love builds on the intensely interested, responsive, and fundamentally erotic love of a mother for her child. In both cases, it is the mother and maternal love that structure a (Christian) ethics oriented toward inclusion, providing the model for how to live lovingly with the strangers in and among ourselves.

––––––––––

If you asked me now, I would say that I knew from the very beginning of the pregnancy that something wasn't quite right. I was nervous, unsettled. And I made no secret of my qualms. I feel like I'm rolling the dice, I remember telling my friend Nancy. I can't put my finger on it, I confessed to Emma, but I'm just worried about this baby. When I admitted my apprehension to Bobby, he reminded me that I had no good reason to feel that way. Our other children had been born healthy, all in-vitro test results had been reassuring, the fetal heartbeats had been consistently strong. He was right, of course. I had no good reason to feel the way I did. My fears were irrational. They were illogical. But they were still there.

If things had turned out differently, I might have forgotten altogether about these feelings. And if I hadn't yet forgotten about them altogether, I might have explained them away as the by-products of a mature awareness of the dangers and risks of pregnancy and childbirth. After all, by the time I was pregnant with Aggie at age thirty-five, I had heard enough stories of babies born with swelling in their brains, holes in their hearts, extra chromosomes, or missing limbs. I had heard enough stories of suffering and loss, agony and grief—that dark underbelly of the "baby joy" so monochromatically depicted in the media—that I was arguably just more attuned to the range of possible outcomes than I had been when I had my first child six years earlier.

If you asked me now, though, I would say that my unreasonable, irrational, illogical, nonsensical sense of unease was an instance of the irruption of the semiotic into the Symbolic order within which I had believed myself to be firmly situated. It was a kind of knowing that had no place in the universe of science and reason, logic and language. But it was very, very real. I did know.

Jeffrey Kripal calls the kind of knowing I'm describing here as gnostic. At once "beyond belief" and "beyond reason," Kripal's gnostic epistemology depends on "the body, and in particular . . . the erotic body, as a source of wisdom and delight and as the fundamental ground of its comparative theorizing."[106] Not unlike Kristeva, who insists that there is more to social experience than the Symbolic order alone, Kripal contends that there is more to human experience, generally, than what can be "reconciled with the claims of any past or present religious tradition . . . whose common radical dualisms and consistent rejections of the body, sexuality, and the physical world render any simplistic mimicking of these elaborate mythological systems quite impossible and hardly desirable."[107] Sometimes you just know what you know without knowing *why* you know what you know. But you do know.

This has been my experience. And I suspect that it was Marie's, too. Though she might not have been able to see it, I suspect that motherhood for Marie was a rich source of inspiration and information that inflected her mystical experience. Though she might not have been able to see it, I suspect that Marie's mystical subjectivity—oriented toward the ultimate (re)union of human and divine—was actually profoundly dependent on her maternal subjectivity, defined by the infolding of mother and child, self and other, subject and object. Marie's identity as a mystic was not, as she seems to have presumed, conditional upon the *abjection* of motherhood, but on the *experience* of motherhood which anticipated and echoed the dynamic play between self and other, human and divine, at the heart of Christian mysticism. Besides, Marie never could abject motherhood once and for all anyway. For, as Kristeva puts it, "you may close your eyes, cover up your ears, teach courses, run errands, tidy up the house, think about objects, subjects. But a mother is always" a mother, "branded by [the] pain" of heterogeneity's indwelling.[108]

Conceived as a sacrifice in imitation of Christ animated by mutual love and oriented toward inclusion, motherhood takes shape no longer in opposition to mysticism (as it did for Marie), but in harmony with mysticism. Indeed, motherhood—marked by the inexorable infolding of difference—becomes a kind of mystical experience itself, which, as Kripal reminds us, seeks to push "beyond every sort of dualism or Two into a realm of being . . . that simply cannot be captured by normal our binary ways of thinking."[109] To suggest that embodied motherhood is itself a kind of mystical experience is not to sentimentalize motherhood (even a passing familiarity with the sometimes brutal history of Christian mysticism would preclude as much), nor is it to exoticize maternal practice. It is, instead, to draw attention to the ways in which the erotics of motherhood can be a locus for the holy, the "abundant events" that "transform objects, persons, [and] places."[110] It is surely no accident that Christian mystics from Bernard of Clairvaux to Teresa of Avila to Marie de l'Incarnation herself turned to the erotic language of human sexuality to express the excesses of mystical experience. What Marie overlooked—to the detriment of Claude—however, was that the potency of the erotic as a *metaphor* for mystical experience hinges on the *reality* of the mystical dimensions of erotic experience. What Marie overlooked, in other words, was that it only makes sense to express the mystical in the terms of the erotic because, as Kripal puts it, mystical experience "is a kind of mathematics that finds its most obvious and probably most ancient experiential base in the phenomenology of sexuality: the Two who unite ecstatically to produce a Third"—or, might I suggest, in the phenomenology of motherhood.[111]

Afterword/Afterward

So, what happened afterward? What became of the abandoned son? We know that Marie went on to enjoy a vibrant mystical life and an active occupation among the indigenous girls of the New World. But what about Claude? How does his story end?

After completing his education with the Jesuits of Orléans, Claude went on to become a Benedictine monk in the Congregation of St. Maur. Over the course of his five-decade-long monastic career, Claude held a diversity of administrative positions, serving as prior at various monasteries and eventually as assistant to the superior general of the Maurists. He published a number of written works, including a book of *Meditations*, several manuals geared toward the instruction of novices, and a critical edition of the works of Augustine of Hippo. He also, and perhaps most famously, took command of his mother's legacy after her death, establishing himself as her sole conservator and the exclusive editor of her written record. By any account, Claude's adult life was, indeed, one ornamented with "honorable charges and . . . dazzling occupations."[1]

And what about Aggie? How does her story end? I don't know, of course. It's too soon to say. But I can tell you this: she has managed—in some cases by the skin of her (four) teeth, but managed nonetheless—to make nearly every one of her developmental milestones. She has consistently defied her doctors' expectations, baffled her therapists, and astounded her parents (though, delightfully, not her brothers, who never seem to have doubted what Aggie could do). Based on the data available at the time of her diagnosis, Bobby and I would have been fools to have expected Aggie to be where she is now. But Aggie has done the impossible.

I know Kripal didn't quite have Aggie in mind when he made a plea for a "more expansive, imaginative, and attractive vision of what it means to be human."[2] But he might as well have, for Aggie proves the point that the term "human potential . . . suggests that human nature is fundamentally open, instinctually plastic, and that it might be more, much more, than we typically imagine it to be in our premature foreclosures."[3] Will Aggie continue to grow and develop, succeed and achieve beyond anyone's wildest dreams? Maybe she will and maybe she won't. That's not what matters most anyway.

When Aggie was first diagnosed, I prayed daily, with as much faith and fervency as I could muster, for a miracle. I'm not really sure who I was praying to or what I was praying for. But I know I wanted two things: I wanted Aggie to get better and I wanted to get better, too. I wanted to stop agonizing, to cease speculating, to reorganize, regroup, and move on. I wanted to learn how to live comfortably—joyfully, even—with the difference that Aggie had brought into my world. I don't ask for a miracle much anymore. This is, in part, because I think I have already witnessed one. Aggie has gotten better. Way better. But it is also because I no longer think that the miraculous is always something that breaks through from the outside with a *grand éclat* and an unambiguous finality. Sometimes it is, instead, something that takes shape slowly and subtly through the dynamic interplay between self and other, subject and object, through (in other words) the "dance of sameness and difference . . . that . . . produces a genuine transfiguration of being."[4]

I am not the same person I was when I began work on this book four years ago. Too much has happened for that. I don't know how Aggie's story will end. And I don't know how my own story will end, either. But I do know that Aggie and I—together with Bobby and our three boys—will dance our way to the very last page in a rhythm that is "far more fantastic, amazing, incredible, and uncanny" than we could possibly have imagined.[5]

Notes

Introduction

1. Marie de l'Incarnation, "Lettre CIX," in *Marie de l'Incarnation: Correspondance*, ed. Dom Guy-Marie Oury (Sablé-sur-Sarthe, France: Solesmes, 1971), 316.

2. For a full-length English-language biography of Marie de l'Incarnation, see Dom Guy-Marie Oury, *Marie Guyart (1599–1672)*, trans. Miriam Thompson (Sablé-sur-Sarthe, France: Solesmes, 1978).

3. Claude Martin, *La Vie de la Vénénerable Mère Marie de l'Incarnation* (Sablé-sur-Sarthe, France: Solesmes, 1981), 2. I have relied primarily on Claude's *Vie* for the biographical information provided in this section; his work is itself based on Marie's *Relation* of 1633 and 1654, the *Supplément* to the *Relation* of 1654, and Claude's own commentary. The erotically charged dimensions of Marie's relationship with God are unexceptional within the history of Christian mysticism. Similar themes characterize the writings of Origen, Bernard of Clairvaux, Hadewijch, Marguerite Porete, and others. For analyses of the erotic imagery at work in the records of mystical experience, see Bernard McGinn, "Mystical Consciousness: A Modest Proposal," *Spiritus* 8, no. 1 (2008): 44–63; Amy Hollywood, *Sensible Ecstasy: Sexual Difference and the Demands of History* (Chicago: University of Chicago Press, 2002); Steven Katz, "Mysticism and the Interpretation of Sacred Scripture," in Steven Katz, ed., *Mysticism and Sacred Scripture* (New York: Oxford University Press, 2000), 7–67.

4. Marie de l'Incarnation, *Relation de 1654*, in *Marie de l'Incarnation: Écrits spirituels et historiques*, ed. Dom Albert Jamet, vol. 2 (Paris: Desclée-de Brouwer, 1929), 161.

5. Martin, *Vie*, 9.

6. Ibid., 10.

7. Ibid., 25, 12.

8. Ibid., 15.

9. Ibid., 14

10. Neither Marie de l'Incarnation nor her son reveals the direct cause of Claude Martin's business problems. Based on allusions in the *Vie*, however,

Guy-Marie Oury suggests that the problems might have been instigated by a woman who had been infatuated with but rebuffed by Marie's husband. Oury, *Marie Guyart*, 28–29.

11. Marie de l'Incarnation, *Relation de 1654*, 172.

12. Ibid., 173.

13. Estimations of the proportion of newborn children given over to the care of hired wet nurses vary widely. While Steven Ozment suggests that no more than 4 percent of the infant population in early modern Europe was breastfed by hired help at any one time, Alain Bideau and colleagues contend that the rate was much higher in Normandy and in and around Paris, where as many as 20–25 percent of newborns were given over to the care of others. Steven Ozment, *Ancestors: The Loving Family in Old Europe* (Cambridge, Mass.: Harvard University Press, 2001), 67; Alain Bideau et al., "La mort quantifiée," in Jacques Dupâquier, ed., *Histoire de la population française*, vol. 2 (Paris: Presses Universitaires de France, 1988), 222–42.

14. Whatever the actual extent of the wet-nursing business in early modern Europe, it was a deadly one for the infants involved. Statistics available for the eighteenth century (when wet-nursing reached its apex in France) suggest that in some regions in France 62–75 percent of babies given over to the care of wet nurses did not survive to return to their families. The infant mortality rate of infants nursed by their own mothers in the same period was much lower. In late-eighteenth-century Rouen, for example (where a full 91 percent of infants breastfed by wet nurses died within the first year of life), fewer than 19 percent died at the hands of their own mothers. See Jean-Louis Flandrin, *Families in Former Times: Kinship, Household, and Sexuality*, trans. Richard Southern (Cambridge: Cambridge University Press, 1979), 204. See also Bideau et al., "La mort quantifiée."

15. Martin, *Vie*, 182.

16. Marie de l'Incarnation, *Relation de 1654*, 281.

17. Martin, *Vie*, 178.

18. Ibid., 41, 43.

19. Ibid., 55.

20. Ibid.

21. Marie de l'Incarnation, *Relation de 1654*, 484–85.

22. Oury, *Marie Guyart*, 82.

23. Martin, *Vie*, 161.

24. Ibid., 168.

25. Ibid., 174–75. Curiously, Marie explains the motivation for Claude's flight differently. In her *Relation* of 1654, Marie attests that Claude ran away from home in order to follow a Feuillant priest to Paris with the intention of entering religious life. As Marie would have it, it was not she who had

abandoned Claude, but Claude who had abandoned her for religious life. Whatever Marie had done in leaving Claude for religious life, Claude had done first.

26. Marie de l'Incarnation, *Relation de 1633*, in *Marie de l'Incarnation: Écrits spirituels et historiques*, ed. Dom Albert Jamet, vol. 1 (Paris: Desclée-de Brouwer, 1929), 276-77

27. Marie de l'Incarnation, *Relation de 1654*, 290.

28. Marie de l'Incarnation, "Lettre CCXLVII," in Oury, *Correspondance*, 837.

29. Martin, *Vie*, 186. Or perhaps his uncle sought out the assistance of Claude. Paul Buisson, after all, no doubt felt the loss of his able and hardworking sister-in-law keenly.

30. Marie de l'Incarnation, "Lettre CCXLVII," in Oury, *Correspondance*, 837.

31. Martin, *Vie*, 187.

32. Martin, *Vie*, 229-30.

33. Oury, *Marie Guyart*, 268, 270.

34. Marie de l'Incarnation, "Lettre CLV," in Oury, *Correspondance*, 525.

35. Ibid.

36. Ibid., 526.

37. Marie de l'Incarnation, "Lettre CLXII," in Oury, *Correspondance*, 548.

38. Martin, *Vie*, xvii.

39. In the process of compiling his mother's correspondence, Claude separated the letters he considered historical from those he considered spiritual, in some cases even splitting a single letter into multiple portions. Consistent with his editorial style in the *Vie*, Claude also amended his mother's prose, not only modernizing Marie's archaisms, but going so far as to rearrange certain paragraphs and even rewrite some passages.

40. To date, the only available version of the *Relation* of 1633 is that embedded in the *Vie*. A different book, motivated by a different set of questions and oriented toward a different set of objectives, might have given more attention to the abandoned son himself. Without a doubt, Claude's influence on the shape of both Marie's own interpretation of the abandonment and its later representation in his *Vie* and edited versions of his mother's works was profound. An extended inquiry into Claude's role in this narrative is, however, beyond the scope of this particular book.

41. Marie de l'Incarnation, "Lettre CCXLVII," in Oury, *Correspondance*, 837.

42. Sharon Hays, *The Cultural Contradictions of Motherhood* (New Haven, Conn.: Yale University Press, 1996), 8-9.

43. In alluding here to the hardworking woman who keeps my family's house clean and organized, I am very much aware of the thorny issues of race, class, and opportunity that complicate the possibility of a shared ideology and experience of motherhood. For a discussion on point, see Patricia Hill Collins,

"Shifting the Center: Race, Class, and Feminist Theorizing about Motherhood," in Donna Bassin, Margaret Honey, and Meryle Mahrer Kaplan, eds., *Representations of Motherhood* (New Haven, Conn.: Yale University Press, 1994), 56–74.

44. Robert Orsi, "2+2=5, or the Quest for an Abundant Empiricism," *Spiritus: A Journal of Christian Spirituality* 6, no. 1 (2006): 116.

45. Ibid., 118.

46. Wayne Proudfoot, *Religious Experience* (Berkeley: University of California Press, 1985), 180.

47. Gananath Obeyesekere, *The Work of Culture: Symbolic Transformation in Psychoanalysis and Anthropology* (Chicago: University of Chicago Press, 1990), 224. See also Bruce Lincoln, *Gods and Demons, Priests and Scholars: Critical Explorations in the History of Religions* (Chicago: University of Chicago Press, 2012), 3, arguing that "when one permits those whom one studies to define the terms in which they will be understood . . . one has ceased to function as a historian or scholar. In that moment, a variety of roles are available: some perfectly respectable (amanuensis, collector, friend and advocate), and some less appealing (cheerleader, voyeur, retailer of imported goods). None, however, should be confused with scholarship."

48. Proudfoot, *Religious Experience*, 74.

49. Marie de l'Incarnation, *Relation de 1633*, 271.

50. Pierre Bourdieu, *The Logic of Practice* (Cambridge: Polity Press, 1990), 69–70.

51. Ibid., 54.

52. Ibid.

53. Ibid.

54. Kelly Oliver, "Introduction: Julia Kristeva's Outlaw Ethics," in Kelly Oliver, ed., *Ethics, Politics, and Difference in Julia Kristeva's Writing* (New York: Routledge, 1993), 4; Julia Kristeva, "Stabat Mater," in *Tales of Love*, trans. Leon S. Roudiez (New York: Columbia University Press, 1987), 259.

55. Kelly Oliver, ed., *The Portable Kristeva* (New York: Columbia University Press, 2002), 298; Kelly Oliver, *Reading Kristeva: Unraveling the Double-Bind* (Bloomington: Indiana University Press, 1993), 65.

56. Jonathan Z. Smith, *Relating Religion: Essays in the Study of Religion* (Chicago: University of Chicago Press, 2004), 241–42. See also Smith, *Imagining Religion: From Babylon to Jonestown* (Chicago: University of Chicago Press, 1982), 102–20.

57. Ibid., 112.

58. Ibid.

59. Robert Orsi, ed., *The Cambridge Companion to Religious Studies* (Cambridge: Cambridge University Press, 2011), 13.

60. Michael Jackson, "The Witch as a Category and as a Person," in Russell T. McCutcheon, ed., *The Insider/Outsider Problem in the Study of Religion: A Reader* (London: Continuum, 2005), 326.

61. See Jonathan Z. Smith, *Map Is Not Territory: Studies in the History of Religion* (Leiden: Brill, 1978). See also Tyler Roberts, "All Work and No Play: Chaos, Incongruity, and *Différance* in the Study of Religion," *Journal of the American Academy of Religion* 77, no. 1 (2009): 81–104; and Sam Gill, "No Place to Stand: Jonathan Z. Smith as *Homo Ludens*, the Academic Study of Religion *Sub Specie Ludi*," *Journal of the American Academy of Religion* 66, no. 2 (1998): 283–312.

62. Gill, "No Place to Stand," 284.

63. In a very real sense, I could not do otherwise anyway. We are always and ineluctably juxtaposing our own circumstances with those of our subjects. Whether we admit to it or not, we scholars can't help but reflect on our subjects of study through the lenses of our own experiences. In the same way, we likewise can't help but reflect *back* on our own experiences through the lenses of our subjects of study. Juxtaposition, whether self-conscious or not, is (as Smith insists) at the heart of the enterprise of religious studies.

64. Robert Orsi, *Between Heaven and Earth: The Religious Worlds People Make and the Scholars Who Study Them* (Princeton, N.J.: Princeton University Press, 2005), 198.

65. See Mark Muesse, "Religious Studies and 'Heaven's Gate': Making the Strange Familiar and the Familiar Strange," in McCutcheon, *Insider/Outsider*, 390–94.

66. Manuel A. Vásquez, *More That Belief: A Materialist Theory of Religion* (New York: Oxford University Press, 2011), 321.

67. Orsi, "2+2=5," 119.

68. Ibid.

69. Constance M. Furey, "Body, Society, and Subjectivity in Religious Studies," *Journal of the American Academy of Religion* 80, no. 1 (2012): 10.

70. Brenna Moore, "Friendship and the Cultivation of Religious Sensibilities," *Journal of the American Academy of Religion*, forthcoming.

71. Orsi, "2+2=5," 120.

72. Adrienne Rich, *Of Woman Born: Motherhood as Experience and Institution* (New York: Norton, 1976), 54.

73. Russell McCutcheon, *Manufacturing Religion: The Discourse on Sui Generis Religion and the Politics of Nostalgia* (New York: Oxford University Press, 1997), 209.

74. For an overview of the history of critical scholarship on religion, see Orsi, *Between Heaven and Earth*, 177–204.

75. Brad S. Gregory, *The Unintended Reformation: How a Religious Revolution Secularized Society* (Cambridge, Mass.: Belknap Press, 2012), 358.

76. Orsi, *Between Heaven and Earth*, 198.

77. Ibid., 196.

78. Ibid., 198.

79. Ibid., 204.

80. Marie de l'Incarnation, "Lettre CLV," in Oury, *Correspondance*, 526.

1. Explication: Representations of the Abandonment in the *Relations*, the Letters, and the *Vie*

1. Paul Ricoeur, *Oneself as Another*, trans. Kathleen Blamey (Chicago: University of Chicago Press, 1992).

2. Ibid., 147.

3. Ibid.

4. Ibid., 148.

5. Marya Schechtman, *The Constitution of Selves* (Ithaca, N.Y.: Cornell University Press, 1996), 94.

6. Ibid., 95.

7. Ibid.

8. Ibid.

9. Steven T. Katz, "Language, Epistemology, and Mysticism," in Steven T. Katz, ed., *Mysticism and Philosophical Analysis* (Oxford: Oxford University Press, 1978), 26. See also Wayne Proudfoot, *Religious Experience* (Berkeley: University of California Press, 1985), arguing for the ways in which religious experiences depend on the availability of concepts already there.

10. Katz, "Language," 26.

11. Ricoeur, *Oneself*, 147.

12. Kate Greenspan, "The Autohagiographical Tradition in Medieval Women's Devotional Writing," *A/B: Auto/Biographical Studies* 6 (1991): 158; Kathleen Meyers, ed., *Word from New Spain: The Spiritual Autobiography of Madre Marie de San Jose (1656–1719)* (Liverpool: Liverpool University Press, 1993); Jane Turner, *Choice Experiences of the Kind Dealings of God before, in, and after Conversion* (1653).

13. Greenspan, "Autohagiographical Tradition," 158.

14. Ibid., 157.

15. Ibid., 159. Many spiritual autobiographies penned by seventeenth-century women in particular found inspiration in the sixteenth-century *Life of Teresa of Avila*. For women "seeking legitimacy for their own spiritual experiences"—particularly within the context of a post-Reformation Catholic Church wary of religious innovation—Teresa's autobiography provided an apt

template for the crafting of their own life stories. Andrew W. Kiett, *Inventing the Sacred: Imposture, Inquisition, and the Boundaries of the Supernatural in Golden Age Spain* (Leiden: Brill, 2005), 114–15. Although Marie did not explicitly invoke Teresa in her *Relations*, Claude did in the context of his *Vie de la Vénérable Mère Marie de l'Incarnation*. For Claude, his mother was "a second Teresa," a holy woman who shared with her Spanish predecessor both the experience of mystical marriage and the status of spiritual autobiographer. Claude Martin, *La Vie de la Vénérable Mère Marie de l'Incarnation* (Sablé-sur-Sarthe, France: Solesmes, 1981), xix.

16. Martin, *Vie*, 1.

17. Marie de l'Incarnation, *Relation de 1654*, in *Marie de l'Incarnation: Écrits spirituels et historiques*, ed. Dom Albert Jamet, vol. 2 (Paris: Desclée-de Brouwer, 1929), 159.

18. See, respectively, Alison Weber, *Teresa of Avila and the Rhetoric of Femininity* (Princeton, N.J.: Princeton University Press, 1990), arguing that the remarkable transformation of Teresa of Avila from an object of Inquisition inquiry to a candidate for sanctity depended in part on her deliberate exploitation of the stereotypes of female ignorance, timidity, weakness, modesty, and incompetence; Gillian Ahlgren, *Teresa of Avila and the Politics of Sanctity* (Ithaca, N.Y.: Cornell University Press, 1996), arguing that Teresa deliberately employed strategies of humility and obedience in her writings as a means of navigating Christian orthodoxy within the context of Counter-Reformation Spain; and Patricia Pender, *Early Modern Women's Writing and the Rhetoric of Modesty* (New York: Palgrave Macmillan, 2012).

19. Pender, *Early Modern Women's Writing*, 24.

20. Marie de l'Incarnation, "Lettre CLV," in *Marie de l'Incarnation: Correspondance*, ed. Dom Guy-Marie Oury (Sablé-sur-Sarthe, France: Solesmes, 1971), 526.

21. Marie de l'Incarnation, "Lettre CLXII," in ibid., 548.

22. Ibid.

23. Ibid.

24. Pender, *Early Modern Women's Writing*, 3. Commenting on the rhetorical strategy of Madame de Sévigné, Michèle Longino Farrell makes a similar point: "By asserting the willfulness of her at once unruly and pathetic pen . . . [Madame de Sévigné] frees herself of accountability for what she produces in writing and attests thereby to the inevitable, since uncontrollable, sincerity of her writing." In the correspondence of Madame de Sévigné, "negligence represents the aestheticization of a prerogative of class: the valorization of the idle life as the idyllic life." Michèle Longino Farrell, *Performing Motherhood: The Sévigné Correspondence* (Hanover, N.H.: University Press of New England, 1991), 65–66.

25. Pender, *Early Modern Women's Writing*, 122.

26. Marie de l'Incarnation, "Lettre CCLXVII," in Oury, *Correspondance*, 897.

27. Pender, *Early Modern Women's Writing*, 28, citing Harry Berger, Jr., *The Absence of Grace: Sprezzatura and Suspicion in Two Renaissance Courtesy Books* (Stanford, Calif.: Stanford University Press, 2000), 10–11.

28. Until recently, readers of the *Vie de la Vénérable Mère Marie de l'Incarnation* tended to confirm Claude's assessment of the insignificance of his editorial influence. Within the last few decades, however, scholars like Guy-Marie Oury and Natalie Zemon Davis have refused to take Claude at his word and have subjected the *Vie* to a more critical inquiry in order to determine just how far and in what directions Claude's additions, explanations, clarifications, and refinements prod the *Relation* of 1654. See Guy-Marie Oury, *Dom Claude Martin: Le Fils de Marie de l'Incarnation* (Sablé-sur-Sarthe, France: Solesmes, 1983), 182; and Natalie Zemon Davis, *Women on the Margins: Three Seventeenth-Century Lives* (Cambridge, Mass.: Harvard University Press, 1995), 128–38. See also Mary Dunn, " 'But an Echo'?: Claude Martin, Marie de l'Incarnation, and Female Religious Identity in Seventeenth-Century New France," *Catholic Historical Review* 100, no. 3 (2014): 459–85.

29. To be fair, within the context of seventeenth-century France where the phenomenon of collaborative authorship was a key feature of the literary culture of the salons, Claude's liberal manipulation of his mother's writings was hardly unusual. See Joan E. DeJean, *Tender Geographies: Women and the Origins of the Novel in France* (New York: Columbia University Press, 1991), 94–126, for a discussion of the early modern culture of the salon within which writing was a collaborative and public effort. See also Pender, *Early Modern Women's Writing*, 92–121. Indeed, in rendering himself at once the conservator and the editor of his mother's written work, Claude (according to Elizabeth Goldsmith) "sets up a model for publishing a woman's voice that we will find repeated in the editorial history of female autobiographies and letters through the seventeenth and eighteenth centuries"—one that manages to sustain both "the reader's belief in that author's modesty or reserve, and in the male hegemony over the printed text." Elizabeth C. Goldsmith, *Publishing Women's Life Stories in France, 1647–1720: From Voice to Print* (Aldershot: Ashgate, 2001), 36.

30. Martin, *Vie*, 26–27.

31. Ibid., 156.

32. Ibid., 162–63.

33. Marie de l'Incarnation, *Relation de 1633*, in *Marie de l'Incarnation: Écrits spirituels et historiques*, ed. Dom Albert Jamet, vol. 1 (Paris: Desclée-de-Brouwer, 1929), 268; Nicholas D. Paige, *Being Interior: Autobiography and the Contradiction of Modernity in Seventeenth-Century France* (Philadelphia: University of Pennsylvania Press, 2000), 18.

34. Marie de l'Incarnation, *Relation de 1633*, 268.
35. Ibid., 269.
36. Marie de l'Incarnation, *Relation de 1654*, 274.
37. Marie de l'Incarnation, *Relation de 1633*, 270.
38. Ibid.
39. Ibid.
40. Marie de l'Incarnation, *Relation de 1654*, 274; Marie de l'Incarnation, *Relation de 1633*, 270.
41. Matthew 10:37.
42. Marie de l'Incarnation, *Relation de 1633*, 271.
43. Ibid., 276; Marie de l'Incarnation, *Relation de 1654*, 275.
44. Marie de l'Incarnation, "Lettre CCXLVII," in Oury, *Correspondance*, 837.
45. Marie de l'Incarnation, *Relation de 1633*, 271.
46. Martin, *Vie*, 171–72.
47. Marie de l'Incarnation, *Relation de 1633*, 288.
48. Marie de l'Incarnation, *Relation de 1654*, 279.
49. Ibid., 280.
50. Ibid., 280–81.
51. Martin, *Vie*, 185.
52. Ibid.
53. Ibid., 186.
54. Ibid.
55. Marie de l'Incarnation, "Lettre CCXLVII," in Oury, *Correspondance*, 837.
56. Marie de l'Incarnation, *Relation de 1654*, 280; Marie de l'Incarnation, *Relation de 1633*, 288.
57. Martin, *Vie*, 186.
58. Ibid., 186–87.
59. Marie de l'Incarnation, *Relation de 1633*, 289.
60. Marie de l'Incarnation, "Lettre CCXLVII," in Oury, *Correspondance*, 837.
61. Marie de l'Incarnation, *Relation de 1633*, 291. See also, Marie de l'Incarnation, *Relation de 1654*, 281; and Marie de l'Incarnation, "Lettre CCXLVII," in Oury, *Correspondance*, 837.
62. Marie de l'Incarnation, *Relation de 1633*, 291.
63. Ibid., 270.
64. Ibid., 272.
65. Marie de l'Incarnation, *Relation de 1654*, 272.
66. Ibid.
67. Marie de l'Incarnation, *Relation de 1633*, 292.
68. Marie de l'Incarnation, "Lettre CCLXVII," in Oury, *Correspondance*, 898.
69. Marie de l'Incarnation, "Lettre LVI," in ibid., 130.
70. Marie de l'Incarnation, "Lettre CLV," in ibid., 527.

71. Marie de l'Incarnation, "Lettre CIX," in ibid., 316.

72. Marie de l'Incarnation, "Lettre LVI," in ibid., 131.

73. Marie de l'Incarnation, *Relation de 1633*, 271.

74. Ibid., 292–93. There is also a scene in the *Relation* of 1633 that, tellingly, evokes the gospel accounts of Jesus in the garden of Gethsemane on the eve of his crucifixion. In the days leading up to her entry into religious life Marie found herself so consumed by prayer "that even at night I could not rest." Over the course of those few days, Marie wrestled with the question of the abandonment, pleading with God to make his will concerning Claude known to her and resigning herself to yield to whatever it was that God wanted. Ibid., 272.

75. Marie de l'Incarnation, "Lettre LVI," in Oury, *Correspondance*, 130.

76. Marie de l'Incarnation, "Lettre CLV," in ibid., 527.

77. Marie de l'Incarnation, "Lettre CCXI," in ibid., 725.

78. Marie de l'Incarnation, *Relation de 1654*, 273.

79. Ibid.

80. Marie de l'Incarnation, "Lettre CCXLVII," in Oury, *Correspondance*, 836; Marie de l'Incarnation, "Lettre CCXI," in ibid., 725.

81. Marie de l'Incarnation, "Lettre CLV," in ibid., 526–27.

82. Ibid., 527.

83. Martin, *Vie*, 170.

84. Ibid., 171.

85. Ibid., 186.

86. Ibid., 187.

87. For biblical references to Jesus as the paschal lamb, see John 1:29 and 1:36.

88. Marie de l'Incarnation, "Lettre CIX," in Oury, *Correspondance*, 316. See also Matthew 10:34–37.

89. Marie de l'Incarnation, "Lettre CIX," in Oury, *Correspondance*, 316; Marie de l'Incarnation, "Lettre CCXLVII," in ibid., 836.

90. In his *Vie*, Claude carries the theme of mutuality between mother and son—which undergirds the sacrificial interpretation of the abandonment—one step further. Recounting a speech his mother delivered to him on the eve of her entry into religious life (which Guy-Marie Oury concludes is almost certainly a fabrication), Claude remembers his mother asking for his consent. "I did not want to [leave you]," Claude recalls his mother saying, "without telling you and begging you to find it good." Marie goes on to explain to Claude that the abandonment is God's will, that God has given her a "great honor in having chosen [her] to serve him," that she "will pray to him for you day and night." "That being the case," she concludes, "don't you therefore want very much that I obey God, who commands me to separate myself from you?" After securing his mother's promises that she would be able to see him and talk to him regularly, Claude consented: "I do want it very much." Martin, *Vie*,

176–78. Initially resistant to the abandonment and aggrieved over the separation, Claude—like Marie—ultimately assents to the will of God.

91. Marie de l'Incarnation, "Lettre CCXLVII," in Oury, *Correspondance*, 836.

92. Ibid. In his *Vie de la Vénérable Mère Marie de l'Incarnation*, Claude expands on his mother's point, eager (it would seem) to eliminate any ambiguity about the depth of his mother's affections for him. "She did not leave," Claude avers, "on account of inconsideration or hardness or with the intention of unburdening herself of him." She had, Claude confirms, "a very sensible love for him, and the only goodness of her nature in regard to the whole world, made known what might be her maternal sentiments toward her own son. In such a manner that during all the time when she was planning to leave him, whenever she cast her eyes upon him it was with a compassion that tore apart her insides; but the force of grace carried her off and whatever love she had for him, she had infinitely more for the one who commanded her to leave him." Martin, *Vie*, 171.

93. Marie de l'Incarnation, "Lettre XLIX," in Oury, *Correspondance*, 115.

94. Robert Orsi, *Between Heaven and Earth: The Religious Worlds People Make and the Scholars Who Study Them* (Princeton, N.J.: Princeton University Press, 2005), 113.

95. Ibid., 144.

96. Ibid., 145.

97. Ibid.

98. My argument here owes a debt to Judith Butler's understanding of gender identity, which is, in Butler's estimation, never quite fixed and never quite finished. For Butler, gender identity is ongoing process of "becoming" and "constructing" through the repetition of stylized acts that, far from expressing a pre-given sexual identity, expose just how unstable notions of gender identity really are. Judith Butler, *Gender Trouble: Feminism and the Subversion of Identity* (New York: Routledge, 1990), 43. See also Sophie Houdard, "Le cri public du fils abandonné ou l'inexprimable secret de la cruauté d'une mère," *Littératures classiques* 68 (Summer 2009): 273–84, arguing that the meaning of the abandonment remains contested for both Marie and Claude.

2. Explanation: Contextualizing the Abandonment within Seventeenth-Century French Family Life

1. In her *Relation* of 1654, Marie tells the story of Claude's flight from home on the eve of her entry into religious life with the addition of one significant detail that has much the same effect. Claude ran away from home, Marie contends in the *Relation* of 1654, with the intention of going to Paris "to

become a religious with a good Feuillant father whom he knew." Marie de l'Incarnation, *Relation de 1654*, in *Marie de l'Incarnation: Écrits spirituels et historiques*, ed. Dom Albert Jamet, vol. 2 (Paris: Desclée-de Brouwer, 1929), 274. Altogether absent from the *Relation* of 1633 and explicitly contradicted by Claude himself in the *Vie* (who admits that he ran away from home because he had fallen into a "profound melancholy . . . which was like a presentiment and a prediction of the misfortune that was about to befall him"), Marie's claim that Claude ran away from home to enter religious life operates within the context of the *Relation* of 1654 to anticipate—and, indeed, preempt—Marie's own decision to abandon Claude in favor of religious life. Claude Martin, *La Vie de la Vénénerable Mère Marie de l'Incarnation* (Sablé-sur-Sarthe, France: Solesmes, 1981), 174. If Marie had left Claude to pursue a religious vocation, Claude had done it first. Thus understood, the abandonment was not an original act conceived and executed by Marie, but one repeated by Marie in imitation of her son whose idea it had been in the first place to leave his mother for religious life.

2. R. Marie Griffith, *God's Daughters: Evangelical Women and the Power of Submission* (Berkeley: University of California Press, 1997), 212.

3. Ibid., 137.

4. Ibid., 14.

5. Ibid., 14, 16.

6. Ibid., 175.

7. Griffith, *God's Daughters*, 173–74.

8. Marie de l'Incarnation, *Relation de 1633*, in *Marie de l'Incarnation: Écrits spirituels et historiques*, ed. Dom Albert Jamet, vol. 1 (Paris: Desclée-de Brouwer, 1929), 271.

9. Marie de l'Incarnation, "Lettre LVI," in *Marie de l'Incarnation: Correspondance*, ed. Dom Guy-Marie Oury (Sablé-sur-Sarthe, France: Solesmes, 1971), 130.

10. Marie de l'Incarnation, *Relation de 1633*, 271.

11. It is worth considering the ways in which the abandonment not only registered as an act of resistance against the norms of seventeenth-century family life, but also functioned as the means by which Marie could seize the opportunity presented to her by widowhood. For seventeenth-century women, widowhood opened a host of possibilities—possibilities of vulnerability and marginalization, but also possibilities of independence and reinvention. For Marie in particular, widowhood was an opportunity to realize the religious vocation toward which she had been strongly inclined since childhood and which was, after her husband's death, delayed "only on account of my son." Marie de l'Incarnation, *Relation de 1654*, 267. It was, paradoxically, in abandoning Claude in submission to the will of God that Marie gained the freedom to

respond to the spiritual vocation she had deferred in obedience to the wishes of her parents and the cultural expectations of marriage and motherhood.

12. To be sure, Marie's renunciation of Claude in favor of religious life and her representation of this renunciation as, specifically, abandonment was heavily freighted with theological significance within the context of seventeenth-century France—a point to which I will return and on which I will elaborate in Chapter 4.

13. See John Boswell, *The Kindness of Strangers: The Abandonment of Children in Western Europe from Late Antiquity to the Renaissance* (New York: Pantheon Books, 1988). See also Joel Harrington, *The Unwanted Child: The Fate of Foundlings, Orphans, and Juvenile Criminals in Early Modern Germany* (Chicago: University of Chicago Press, 2009), who argues that "far from representing an anomaly or system failure, informal child circulation in various forms was in fact one of the core mechanisms that held together [Western European] communities and thus society as a whole" (278).

14. Boswell, *Kindness of Strangers*, 357.

15. Ibid, 322.

16. Ibid., 394, 335.

17. Antoine Furetière, *Dictionaire Universel* (1690).

18. Philippe Ariès, *Centuries of Childhood: A Social History of Family Life*, trans. Robert Baldick (New York: Vintage Books, 1962).

19. Steven Ozment agrees and attributes the emotional aridity of the medieval family to three factors: a high rate of child mortality, a tendency toward the integration of home life and work life, and a relative lack of privacy within the home. See Steven E. Ozment, *Ancestors: the Loving Family in Old Europe* (Cambridge, Mass.: Harvard University Press, 2001), 11.

20. David Herlihy, *Medieval Households* (Cambridge, Mass.: Harvard University Press, 1985), 112.

21. David Hunt, *Parents and Children in History: The Psychology of Family Life in Early Modern France* (New York: Basic Books, 1970), 34.

22. See Lloyd DeMause, *The History of Childhood* (New York: Harper & Row, 1975); Edward Shorter, *The Making of the Modern Family* (New York: Basic Books, 1977); and Lawrence Stone, *The Family, Sex and Marriage in England, 1500–1800* (London: Weidenfeld & Nicolson, 1977).

23. For a helpful review of the historiography of childhood and the family in Western Europe, see Hugh Cunningham, *Children and Childhood in Western Society since 1500* (London: Longman, 1995), 1–18.

24. Linda Pollock, "Parent–Child Relations," in David Kertzer and Marzio Barbagli, eds., *Family Life in Early Modern Times, 1500–1789* (New Haven, Conn.: Yale University Press, 2001), 192. See also Pollock, *Forgotten Children: Parent–Child Relations from 1500 to 1900* (New York: Cambridge University Press, 1983).

25. Shulamith Shahar, *Childhood in the Middle Ages* (London: Routledge, 1990), 1.

26. See André Burguière and Françoise Lebrun, "Priest, Prince, and Family," in André Burguière, Christiane Klapisch-Zuber, Martine Segalen, and Françoise Zonabend, eds., *Histoire de la Famille* (Paris: A. Colin, 1986), 146–58; Hunt, *Parents and Children*, 118–32; and Shahar, *Childhood*, 9–11.

27. Cunningham, *Children and Childhood*, 35.

28. Ozment, *Ancestors*, 79.

29. Pollock, "Parent–Child Relations," 201.

30. Yvonne Knibiehler and Catherine Fouquet, *L'histoire des mères, du moyen-âge à nos jours* (Paris: Montalba, 1980), 12–14.

31. Herlihy, *Medieval Households*, 125–26.

32. Ibid., 129.

33. Among the better-known instances of a saint's conflict with his family of origin is the story of Francis of Assisi, who famously renounced his inheritance and the paternal authority of his own father.

34. Herlihy, *Medieval Households*, 115.

35. See, for example, Karin Lee Fishbeck Calvert, *Children in the House: The Material Culture of Early Childhood, 1600–1900* (Boston: Northeastern University Press, 1992), 12, arguing that the question is not whether medieval parents loved their children but how medieval parents treated the children they loved. See also Pollock, "Parent–Child Relations," 219, urging scholars not to search "for the existence or absence of love in the past" but to "investigate what love meant in a given culture and era, and how it was expressed."

36. Hunt, *Parents and Children*, 121.

37. Jean-Louis Flandrin, *Families in Former Times: Kinship, Household, and Sexuality*, trans. Richard Southern (Cambridge: Cambridge University Press, 1979), 137–56.

38. Ibid., 154–56.

39. Ibid., 154–55.

40. Ibid., 155.

41. Ibid., 159.

42. Ibid., 160.

43. Ibid., 158–61. For a discussion of the emerging ideal of conjugal love and its impact on the relationship between parents and their children, see Burguière and Lebrun, "Priest, Prince, and Family," 138–46.

44. Ernest Watson Burgess, Harvey James Locke, and Mary Margaret Thomes, *The Family, from Institution to Companionship* (New York: American Book Co., 1963), vii.

45. Phyllis Gaffney, *Constructions of Childhood and Youth in Old French Narrative* (Burlington, Vt.: Ashgate, 2011), 185. David Herlihy, for his part, sees

the twelfth-century popularity of the cult of the child Jesus as evidence of a growth in sentiment with regard to children. The enthusiasm of medieval Christians toward the child Jesus implies, argues Herlihy, "that urban households had themselves come to be oriented in significant measure toward children." David Herlihy, "The Making of the Medieval Family: Symmetry, Structure, and Sentiment," *Journal of Family History* 8 (1983): 127.

46. Gaffney, *Constructions of Childhood*, 126.

47. Protestants, Jeffrey R. Watt argues "were undeniably placing more emphasis on child-rearing than ever before." Jeffrey R. Watt, "The Impact of the Reformation and Counter-Reformation," in David Kertzer and Marzio Barbagli, eds., *Family Life in Early Modern Times, 1500–1789* (New Haven, Conn.: Yale University Press, 2001), 145.

48. Calvert, *Children in the House*, 52.

49. David Herlihy, *Women, Family, and Society in Medieval Europe*, ed. A. Molho (Providence, R.I.: Berghahn Books, 1995), 148, citing Caterina da Siena, *Epistolario*, vol. 2, ed. D. U. Meattini (Siena, 1966), 46.

50. For a study of the ways in which the correspondence of Madame de Sévigné "enact[ed] and inscrib[ed] the maternal figure and the relational posture prescribed for women by male authorities in manuals on 'feminine' comportment and 'feminine' writing during her time," see Michèle Longino Farrell, *Performing Motherhood: The Sévigné Correspondence* (Hanover, N.H.: University Press of New England, 1991).

51. Burguière and Lebrun, "Priest, Prince, and Family," 105.

52. Ibid.

53. Emile Mâle, *L'art religiuex de la fin du XVIe siècle, du XVIIe siècle et du XVIIIe siècle* (Paris: A. Colin, 1951), 301.

54. Pollock, "Parent–Child Relations," 205; and Knibiehler and Fouquet, *L'histoire des mères*, 113.

55. Indeed, it is entirely possible that treatises and manuals passed over the subject of parental love in relative silence *not* because love had no place in the premodern family, but because love had such a natural place that parents and children needed no prompting to cultivate affection for one another.

56. Christopher Corley, "Gender, Kin, and Guardianship in Early Modern Burgundy," in , Suzanne Desan and Jeffrey Merrick, eds., *Family, Gender, and Law in Early Modern France* (University Park: Pennsylvania State University Press, 2009), 198.

57. The literature on the phenomenon of wet-nursing in early modern France is extensive. See, for example, Flandrin, *Families in Former Times*, 203–12; Alain Bideau et al., "La mort quantifiée," in Jacques Dupâquier, ed., *Histoire de la population française*, vol. 2 (Paris: Presses Universitaires de France, 1988), 222–42; Pollock, "Parent–Child Relations," 193–95; Olwen

Hufton, "Le travail and la famille: La maternité," in Georges Duby and Michelle Perrot, eds., *Histoire des femmes en occident* (Paris: Plon, 2002), 50–63. See also George Sussman, "The End of the Wet Nursing Business in France, 1874–1914," in Robert Wheaton and Tamara K. Hareven, eds., *Family and Sexuality in French History* (Philadelphia: University of Pennsylvania Press, 1980), 224–52; Shahar, *Childhood*, 53–76.

58. In the *Relation* of 1654, Marie confesses on the eve of the abandonment that she "foresaw [Claude] would suffer much, since ordinarily relatives do not have the tenderness of a mother, nor a child such confident recourse." Marie de l'Incarnation, *Relation de 1654*, 281. Marie, too, was aware that her refusal to caress her son "as one does children" was outside the norm. Ibid. It had been a good ten years "that I mortified him," Marie explains in the *Relation* of 1633, "not permitting him to caress me at all, just as I did not caress him, so that he would not be attached to me when Our Lord commanded me to leave him." Marie de l'Incarnation, *Relation de 1633*, 271. Marie's reserve toward her son did not, however, have the intended effect: "All that did not prevent him from having a great resentment toward my departure." Ibid., 271–72.

59. Marie de l'Incarnation, "Lettre CIX," in Oury, *Correspondance*, 316; "Lettre LVI," in ibid., 130; and Marie de l'Incarnation, *Relation de 1654*, 275.

60. Marie de l'Incarnation, "Lettre LVI," in Oury, *Correspondance*, 130.

61. Marie de l'Incarnation, *Relation de 1633*, 292.

62. Ibid.

63. Martin, *Vie*, 218.

64. Marie de l'Incarnation, "Lettre CCXLVII," in Oury, *Correspondance*, 836.

65. Marie de l'Incarnation, *Relation de 1633*, 321.

66. Ibid.

67. Marie de l'Incarnation, "Lettre CCLXVII," in Oury, *Correspondance*, 898.

68. Martin, *Vie*, 177.

69. Ibid., 185–87. See also Marie de l'Incarnation, "Lettre CCXLVII," in Oury, *Correspondance*, 836–38.

70. Martin, *Vie*, 187.

71. Julie Hardwick, "Seeking Separations: Gender, Marriages, and Household Economies in Early Modern France," *French Historical Studies* 21, no. 1 (1998): 157–80.

72. Sylvie Perrier, "Logique patrimoniale et relations sociales: Les familles recomposées dans la France d'Ancien Régime," in Agnès Martial and Agnès Fine, eds., *La valeur des liens: Hommes, femmes et comptes familiaux* (Toulouse: Presses Universitaires du Mirail, 2007), 69–90.

73. Nicole Pellegrin and Colette H. Winn, eds., *Veufs, Veuves, et Veuvage dans la France d'ancien régime* (Paris: Champion, 2003), 8; Lyndan Warner, "Widows, Widowers and the Problem of 'Second Marriages' in Sixteenth-

Century France," in Sandra Cavallo and Lyndan Warner, eds., *Widowhood in Medieval and Early Modern Europe* (London: Longman, 1999), 84.

74. Francis de Sales, *Introduction à la vie dévote*, ed. André Ravier with the collaboration of Roger Devos (Paris: Gallimard, 1969), 247 (my emphasis).

75. Marie de l'Incarnation, "Lettre XLIX," in Oury, *Correspondance*, 115. At the same time, however, Marie refused to accept sole responsibility for her son's future, chastising Claude to "push yourself" and "find some courage." Ibid.

76. Marie de l'Incarnation, "Lettre LVI," in ibid., 131.

77. Marie de l'Incarnation, "Lettre CCXI," in ibid., 725.

78. Marie de l'Incarnation, *Relation de 1633*, 271; and *Relation de 1654*, 272.

79. Marie de l'Incarnation, *Relation de 1654*, 272–73.

80. Marie de l'Incarnation, "Lettre CLV," in Oury, *Correspondance*, 527.

81. A comparison—albeit one that trespasses the boundaries of time and place—is instructive here. Christiane Klapisch-Zuber argues that widows in late medieval Florence were considered cruel if they remarried. When a widow's children—who, according to Florentine custom, remained with the family of their deceased father—complained about their mother's cruelty, it was not because they regretted the loss of her affectionate presence but rather because they regretted the loss of her dowry, which their mother was entitled to take with her upon her remarriage. Christiane Klapisch-Zuber, "The 'Cruel Mother': Maternity, Widowhood, and Dowry in Florence in the Fourteenth and Fifteenth Centuries," in *Women, Family, and Ritual in Renaissance Italy* (Chicago: University of Chicago Press, 1985), 117–31.

82. Saba Mahmood, *Politics of Piety: The Islamic Revival and the Feminist Subject* (Princeton, N.J.: Princeton University Press, 2005), 14.

83. Ibid., 8.

84. Ibid., 15.

85. Ibid., 22, 31.

86. Ibid., 14.

87. Martin, *Vie*, 188, citing Marie de l'Incarnation, *Relation de 1633*.

88. Marie de l'Incarnation, "Lettre CIX," in Oury, *Correspondance*, 316; and Martin, *Vie*, 25.

3. Explanation: The Marginalization of Motherhood in the Christian Tradition

1. Martha Beck, *Expecting Adam: A True Story of Birth, Rebirth, and Everyday Magic* (New York: Times Books, 1999), 6.

2. Ibid., 8.

3. Recent studies on the subject of narrative agency include Paul Ricoeur, *Oneself as Another*, trans. Kathleen Blamey (Chicago: University of Chicago

Press, 1992); Catriona Mackenzie and Kim Atkins, eds., *Practical Identity and Narrative Agency* (New York: Routledge, 2008); and Claudia Holler and Martin Klepper, eds., *Rethinking Narrative Identity: Person and Perspective* (Amsterdam: John Benjamins, 2013).

4. Robert Orsi, *Between Heaven and Earth: The Religious Worlds People Make and the Scholars Who Study Them* (Princeton, N.J.: Princeton University Press, 2005), 145.

5. Ibid., 143–44.

6. Luke 14:26.

7. Pierre Bourdieu, *The Logic of Practice* (Cambridge: Polity Press, 1990), 9.

8. Pierre Bourdieu, *Algeria: 1960, the Disenchantment of the World, the Sense of Honor, the Kabyle House or the World Reversed*, trans. Richard Nice (Cambridge: Cambridge University Press, 1979).

9. Richard Jenkins, *Pierre Bourdieu* (London: Routledge, 2002), 32.

10. Ibid.

11. Pierre Bourdieu, *In Other Words: Essays towards a Reflexive Sociology* (Cambridge: Polity Press, 1990), 61.

12. Jenkins, *Pierre Bourdieu*, 72.

13. Bourdieu, *Outline of a Theory of Practice*, trans. Richard Nice (Cambridge: Cambridge University Press, 1977), 95, 72.

14. Jenkins, *Pierre Bourdieu*, 76. It is easy to see how Bourdieu can be (and has been) accused of social determinism. For Bourdieu, after all, the schemes and dispositions which constitute the habitus are the products of individual and collective history which, in turn, generate more history. History, then, would seem to repeat itself. Bourdieu, however, insists that his conceptualization of social practice accommodates the possibility of radical change. See Loïc J. D. Wacquant, "Toward a Reflexive Sociology: A Workshop with Pierre Bourdieu," *Sociological Theory* 7, no. 1 (1989): 36–37; and Francois Collet, "Does Habitus Matter? A Comparative Review of Bourdieu's Habitus and Simon's Bounded Rationality with Some Implications for Economic Sociology," *Sociological Theory* 27, no. 4 (2009): 419–34.

15. Bourdieu, *Logic of Practice*, 54.

16. Ibid., 59.

17. Wacquant, "Toward a Reflexive Sociology," 39.

18. Jenkins, *Pierre Bourdieu*, 78. See also Bourdieu, *Logic of Practice*, 52–65; and Pierre Bourdieu, *Language and Symbolic Power*, ed. John B. Thompson and trans. Gino Raymond and Matthew Adamson (Cambridge: Polity Press, 1991), 37–42.

19. Wacquant, "Toward a Reflexive Sociology," 54.

20. Clarissa Atkinson, *The Oldest Vocation: Christian Motherhood in the Middle Ages* (Ithaca, N.Y.: Cornell University Press, 1991); Dyan Elliot, *Spiritual*

Marriage: Sexual Abstinence in Medieval Wedlock (Princeton, N.J.: Princeton University Press, 1993); Anneke B. Mulder-Bakker, ed., *Sanctity and Mother-hood: Essays on Holy Mothers in the Middle Ages* (New York: Garland, 1995); Jane Tibbets Schulenburg, *Forgetful of Their Sex: Female Sanctity and Society, ca. 500–1100* (Chicago: University of Chicago Press, 1998); Shulamith Shahar, *Childhood in the Middle Ages* (London: Routledge, 1990), 1–20.

21. Atkinson, *Oldest Vocation*, 23–30. See also Grace Jantzen, *Power, Gender, and Christian Mysticism* (Cambridge: Cambridge University Press, 1995), 32–35.

22. Schulenburg, *Forgetful of Their Sex*, 127–76.

23. Luke 14:26. See also Mark 3:31–35 and 13:12; Luke 8:19–21 and 12:51–53; Matthew 10:34–37 and 12:46–50.

24. See Peter Brown, *Body and Society: Men, Women, and Sexual Renunciation in Early Christianity* (New York: Columbia University Press, 1988), 39. For a discussion of sexual ethics in the writings of Paul, see Elaine Pagels, *Adam, Eve, and the Serpent* (New York: Random House, 1988), 16–20; and Kathy L. Gaca, *The Making of Fornication: Eros, Ethics, and Political Reform in Greek Philosophy and Early Christianity* (Berkeley: University of California Press, 2003), 119–89.

25. Luke 8:21. See also Mark 3:31–35, Matthew 12:46–50, and Luke 11:27–28.

26. Matthew 10:34–36. See also Luke 12:51–53 and Mark 13:12.

27. For a comprehensive history of sexual renunciation in the early Church, see Brown, *Body and Society*. See also James A. Brundage, *Law, Sex, and Christian Society in Medieval Europe* (Chicago: University of Chicago Press, 1987); Benjamin H. Dunning, *Specters of Paul: Sexual Difference in Early Christian Thought* (Philadelphia: University of Pennsylvania Press, 2011).

28. Brown, *Body and Society*, 86.

29. Ibid., 95.

30. Ibid., 86.

31. Michel Foucault, *The History of Sexuality*, 3 vols., trans. Robert Hurley (New York: Vintage Books, 1990). Few, at this point, would contest Foucault's thesis regarding the continuity between Greek sexual morality and early Christian sexual morality. Kathy Gaca, however, argues that given the diversity of both Greek and Christian thought on sexuality, there was at least as much discontinuity as there was continuity. See, Gaca, *Making of Fornication*.

32. Brown, *Body and Society*, 22.

33. The Pythagoreans took to extremes the ideal of regulating sexual activity within the limits of calendrical and other constraints, restricting reproductive sex to what was permitted by the elaborately complex "nuptial number." See Gaca, *Making of Fornication*, 94–116.

34. Foucault, *Care of the Self*, vol. 3 of *History of Sexuality*, 228.

35. Gaca, *Making of Fornication*, 83.

36. Foucault, *Use of Pleasure*, vol. 2 of *History of Sexuality*, 138.

37. Gaca, *Making of Fornication*, 59–93.

38. For a discussion of the many meanings of sexual renunciation in early Christianity, see Brown, *Body and Society*; Pagels, *Adam, Eve, and the Serpent*; and Andrew Louth, "The Body in Western Catholic Christianity," in Sarah Coakley, ed., *Religion and the Body* (Cambridge: Cambridge University Press, 1997), 111–30.

39. Brown, *Body and Society*, 230. See also Rosemary Radford Ruether, *Christianity and the Making of the Modern Family* (Boston: Beacon Press, 2000), who argues that this wariness of kinship ties would have been "deeply subversive" in light of Roman and Jewish traditions ideas about the family (31).

40. Schulenburg, *Forgetful of Their Sex*, 212, citing Tertullian, "To His Wife," in *Treatises on Marriage and Remarriage*, trans. William P. Le Saint (Westminster, 1951), 17.

41. Jerome, *Letter 54*, trans. W. H. Fremantle, G. Lewis, and W. G. Martley, in Philip Schaff and Henry Wace, eds., *Nicene and Post-Nicene Fathers*, 2nd ser., vol. 6. (Buffalo, N.Y.: Christian Literature Publishing Co., 1893), rev. and ed. for New Advent by Kevin Knight, http://www.newadvent.org/fathers/3001054.htm.

42. Schulenburg, *Forgetful of Their Sex*, 213, citing Jerome, "Against Helvidius," in *St. Jerome: Dogmatic and Polemical Works*, FC 53, trans. John N. Hritzu (Washington, D.C., 1965), 40–41.

43. See Jean-Louis Flandrin, *Families in Former Times: Kinship, Household, and Sexuality*, trans. Richard Southern (Cambridge: Cambridge University Press, 1979), 155–66. For a discussion of maternal affection as the competitor of Christian devotion in the early modern period, see Larry Wolff, "Religious Devotion and Maternal Sentiment in Early Modern Lent: From the Letters of Madame de Sévigné to the Sermons of Père Bourdaloue," *French Historical Studies* 18 (1993): 359–95.

44. Hugh of Floreffe, *The Life of Yvette of Huy*, ed. and trans. Jo Ann McNamara (Toronto: Peregrina, 1999), 53–60.

45. *The Passion of Perpetua and Felicity*, trans. Thomas J. Heffernan (New York: Oxford University Press, 2012); and A. Harnack, *Die Akten des Karpus, des Papylus und der Agathonike: Eine Urkunde aus der Zeit Mark Aurels, Texte und Untersuchungen* 3 (Leipzig, 1888), 3–4.

46. Rosemary Radford Ruether, "Misogyny and Virginal Feminism in the Fathers of the Church," in Rosemary Radford Ruether, ed., *Religion and Sexism: Images of Woman in the Jewish and Christian Tradition* (New York: Simon and Schuster, 1974), 165–66.

47. The persistence of Christianity's dichotomization of women as, alternatively, mothers or virgins finds expression in traditional tendencies to represent the Virgin Mary as a Second Eve. See, for example, Irenaeus, *Against Heresies*, Book 3, Chapter 22; Justine Martyr, *Dialogue with Trypho*, Chapter 100.

48. Luke 20:34–35; Julia O'Faolain and Lauro Martines, eds., *Not in God's Image: Women in History from the Greeks to the Victorians* (New York: Harper & Row, 1973), 138–39, citing Fortunatus, *Opera Poetica*, ed. C. Nisard (Paris, 1887), Book 8, Poem 3.

49. The notion of the changeless resurrection body, developed by certain Church Fathers like Irenaeus and Tertullian, curiously echoes the Neoplatonic ideal of the immutable and enduring world of Forms. See Caroline Walker Bynum, *The Resurrection of the Body in Western Christianity, 200–1336* (New York: Columbia University Press, 1995), 34–43. The possibility that the perceived incompatibility between motherhood and Christian discipleship owes something to the stark contrast between the constantly changing flesh of mothers and the changeless body of the resurrected Christ deserves further study.

50. There were, of course, exceptions. Origen of Alexandria and Ambrose of Milan, for example, tended more than others toward a bifurcation between body and soul.

51. Brown, *Body and Society*, 26.

52. Ibid., 134.

53. To the Gnostics, for example, human beings were (at best) fallen creatures tragically enfleshed in corrupted and corruptible material bodies. Salvation entailed the sloughing off of corporeal fetters and the reacquisition of one's original heavenly fullness; heaven was a place populated by spirits alone and presided over by a fully divine (and utterly unhuman) God. Christian convictions in divine incarnation and bodily resurrection could not, however, tolerate the dualist anthropology and soteriology of the Gnostics, and by the fifth century the heresy in its many variations had been effectively suppressed. Dualist theologies nonetheless continued to erupt sporadically over the course of Christian history. In the twelfth century, most famously, the Cathars posed a serious challenge to orthodox Christianity.

54. Brown, *Body and Society*, 236.

55. Caroline Walker Bynum, *Holy Feast and Holy Fast: The Religious Significance of Food to Medieval Women* (Berkeley: University of California Press, 1987), 294.

56. Brown, *Body and Society*, 88–90.

57. Ibid., 304.

58. Jerome, *Letter 14*, in *Nicene and Post-Nicene Fathers*.

59. The relationship between Christianity and motherhood has not, of course, been a linear one. As Clarissa Atkinson and others have shown, the place of motherhood in the Christian tradition has shifted (and shifted again) over the course of two millennia of Christian history. See Atkinson, *Oldest Vocation*; and Ruether, *Christianity and the Making of the Modern Family*.

60. Anneke Mulder-Bakker, "Introduction," in Mulder-Bakker, ed., *Sanctity and Motherhood*, 24; Schulenburg, *Forgetful of Their Sex*, 216; *The Life of Marie d'Oignies by Jacques de Vitry*, trans. Margot H. King (Saskatoon: Peregrina, 1986), 4.

61. For an overview of the tradition of affective piety in the Middle Ages, see Clarissa Atkinson, *Mystic and Pilgrim: The Book and the World of Margery Kempe* (Ithaca, N.Y.: Cornell University Press, 1983), 129–56.

62. Ulrike Wiethaus, ed., *Maps of Flesh and Light: The Religious Experience of Medieval Women Mystics* (Syracuse, N.Y.: Syracuse University Press, 1993), 126.

63. Caroline Walker Bynum, *Fragmentation and Redemption: Essays on Gender and the Human Body in Medieval Religion* (New York: Zone Books, 1991), 101.

64. Ibid., 158. References to Jesus as mother are also found in the works of Bernard of Clairvaux, William of St. Thierry, Anselm of Canterbury, and the Ancrene Wisse. See Maud Burnett McInerney, "In the Meydens Womb: Julian of Norwich and the Poetics of Enclosure," in John Carmi Parsons and Bonnie Wheeler, eds., *Medieval Mothering* (New York: Garland, 1996), 157–82.

65. Ineke van't Spijker, "Family Ties: Mothers and Virgins in the Ninth Century," in Mulder-Bakker, ed., *Sanctity and Motherhood*, 181.

66. Mulder-Bakker, "Introduction," 11.

67. Ibid., 24.

68. Atkinson, *Oldest Vocation*, 144.

69. *A Legend of Holy Women: A Translation of Osbern Bokenham's Legends of Holy Women*, trans. and intro. Sheila Delany (Notre Dame, Ind.: University of Notre Dame Press, 1992), 185; *Dicta quatuor ancillarum* (January 1235), in Kenneth Baxter Wolf, *The Life and Afterlife of St. Elizabeth of Hungary: Testimony from Her Canonization Hearings* (New York: Oxford University Press, 2011), 200.

70. Anja Petrakopolous, "Sanctity and Motherhood: Elizabeth of Thuringia," in Mulder-Bakker, ed., *Sanctity and Motherhood*, 271, citing Caeasarius von Heisterbach, *Vita Sancte Elyzabeth Lantgravie*, in Albert Huyskens, ed., *Annalen des Historischen Vereins für den Niederrhein* 86 (1908), 40, 50.

71. Anneke Mulder-Bakker, "Ivetta of Huy: Mater et Magistra," in Mulder-Bakker, ed., *Sanctity and Motherhood*, 238, citing Hugh of Floreffe, *Vita B. Juetta Inclusae auctore Hugone Floreffiensi*, in *Acta Sanctorum*, vol. 2, 13 Januarii, 3rd ed. (Brussels, 1863), 162.

72. Jeannette Nieuwland, "Motherhood and Sanctity in the Life of Saint Birgitta of Sweden: an Insoluble Conflict?" in Mulder-Bakker, ed., *Sanctity and Motherhood*, 317, citing Prior Petrus and Magister Petrus, *Vita b. Brigide*, in *Acta et Processus Caonizacionis beate Birgitte*, ed. Isak Collijn (Uppsala: Almqvist & Wiksells Bokmijckeri AB, 1924–31), 78. For a discussion of the ideal of spiritual motherhood more generally, see Atkinson, *Oldest Vocation*, 64–101; and Mulder-Bakker, ed., *Sanctity and Motherhood*.

73. Nieuwland, "Motherhood and Sanctity," 311.

74. Conrad of Marburg, *Summa Vitae* (1232), in Wolf, *Life and Afterlife*, 93.

75. Fra Giunta Bevegnati, *The Life and Miracles of Saint Margaret of Cortona* (1247–1297), trans. and intro. Thomas Renna and ed. Shannon Larson (St. Bonaventure, N.Y.: Franciscan Institute, 2012), 55.

76. See Revelations 1.1.9, 1.2.8, 1.20.7, 1.20.10–12 in *The Revelations of St. Birgitta of Sweden*, 3 vols., trans. Denis Searby and intro. Bridget Morris (New York: Oxford University Press, 2006).

77. Ruether, *Christianity and the Making of the Modern Family*, 58.

78. Bernard McGinn, "The Language of Love in Jewish and Christian Mysticism," in Steven Katz, ed., *Mysticism and Language* (London: Oxford University Press, 1990), 203; Ruether, *Christianity and the Making of the Modern Family*, 59.

79. Jantzen, *Power, Gender, and Christian Mysticism*, 86–156. It is important to note that for Jantzen, there is a different dynamic at play in the writings of female mystics. With the women, argues Jantzen, "there is a direct, highly charged, passionate encounter between Christ and the writer. The sexuality is explicit, and there is no warning that it should not be taken literally. There is no intellectualizing or spiritualizing." Ibid., 133.

80. Ibid., 91.

81. Merry Weisner, *Christianity and Sexuality in the Early Modern World: Regulating Desire, Reforming Practice* (New York: Routledge, 2000), 44.

82. Bynum, *Fragmentation and Redemption*, 134.

83. Ibid., 133.

84. Ibid., 134.

85. Virginia Burrus, *The Sex Lives of Saints: An Erotics of Ancient Hagiography* (Philadelphia: University of Pennsylvania Press, 2004), 1.

86. Ibid., 2, 10.

87. Bynum, *Fragmentation and Redemption*, 182–83.

88. Giselle de Nie, " 'Consciousness Fecund through God': From Male Fighter to Spiritual Bride–Mother in Late Antique Female Sanctity," in Mulder-Bakker, ed., *Sanctity and Motherhood*, 142, citing Fortunatus, *Carmina* 11.3.1–8, ed. *Monumenta Germaniae Historica: Auctores Antiquissimi*, vol. 4/1, 259.

4. Explanation: Maternal Hagiographies and Spiritualities of Abandonment in Seventeenth-Century France

1. Mulder-Bakker, "Introduction," in Anneke B. Mulder-Bakker, ed., *Sanctity and Motherhood: Essays on Holy Mothers in the Middle Ages* (New York: Garland, 1995), 11.

2. Before the twelfth century, saints who were mothers were depicted in their roles as abbess, queen, or woman religious. Of the five mother-saints who

begin to be represented together with their children in the twelfth century, four (mentioned above) are martyrs and all (with the possible exception of Julita) are apocryphal. See ibid., 9–10.

3. For rates of canonization of married women compared to unmarried women from 1000 to 1700, see Donald Weinstein and Rudolph Bell, *Saints and Society: The Two Worlds of Western Christendom, 1000–1700* (Chicago: University of Chicago Press, 1982), 121–37; and André Vauchez, *La sainteté en Occident aux derniers siècles du Moyen Age* (Rome: École française de Rome, 1981), 355–74. Any study of mother–saints is necessarily limited by its very small sample size. Among the 2,610 saints included in his study, for example, Pierre Delooz could identify only sixteen who had been married, of whom only three were mothers. See Pierre Delooz, *Sociologie et canonisations* (Liège: Faculté de droit, 1969), 330–33.

4. Jennifer Carpenter, "Juette of Huy, Recluse and Mother (1158–1228): Children and Mothering in the Saintly Life," in Jennifer Carpenter and Sally-Beth MacLean, eds., *Power of the Weak: Studies on Medieval Women* (Urbana: University of Illinois Press, 1995), 59.

5. Mulder-Bakker, "Introduction," 4.

6. Clarissa Atkinson, *The Oldest Vocation: Christian Motherhood in the Middle Ages* (Ithaca, N.Y.: Cornell University Press, 1991), 144.

7. In Ceasarius of Heisterbach's *Vita Sancte Elyzabeth Lantgravie*, for example, Elizabeth of Thuringia's decision to separate herself from her two children warrants merely a single line. Widowed and rejected by her husband's family, Elizabeth wandered in search of a place to stay, ultimately compelled by her poverty to send her children away to be cared for by relatives. With a similar concision, Catherine of Gueberschwihr describes Adelheid of Rheinfelden's resolution to enter religious life among the Dominicans at Unterlinden: "inspired by divinity," Adelheid abandoned her husband and her two small children who had "scarcely left the cradles of infancy," handing them over to the custody of their nurse. Jeanne Ancelet-Hustache, ed., "Les 'Vitae Sororum' d'Unterlinden," *Archives d'histoire doctrinale et littéraire du moyen âge* 5 (1930): 394. Although Hugh of Floreffe gives a fair amount of attention to Ivetta of Huy's relationship with her two sons prior to devoting herself to religious life (praising the anchoress for fulfilling her responsibilities toward her "house and . . . her sons, whom she educated in the fear of the Lord as carefully as she could"), he, too, passes over in relative silence the event of Ivetta's separation from her two sons (then ages five and nine), whom she left to go live in a leper colony. Hugh of Floreffe, *The Life of Yvette of Huy*, trans. and intro. Jo Ann McNamara (Toronto: Peregrina, 1999), 53–62. While in some cases hagiographic reserve on the subject of maternal leave-taking no doubt owes to the relatively advanced age of the children in question, in other cases

the holy mother's decision to leave her children might have merited little narrative attention on account of its rather unremarkable ordinariness as a characteristic of late medieval life.

8. Barbara Newman, *From Virile Woman to WomanChrist: Studies in Medieval Religion and Literature* (Philadelphia: University of Pennsylvania Press, 1995), 93.

9. Ibid., 10.

10. Jean-Pierre de Caussade, *L'abandon à la providence divine*, ed. Dominique Salin (Paris: Desclée de Brouwer, 2005), 47.

11. This and the following citations from *The Passion of Perpetua and Felicity* are from W. H. Shewring's edition, *The Passion of SS. Perpetua and Felicity*, trans. W. H. Shewring (London: Sheed & Ward, 1931). *The Passion of Perpetua and Felicity*, which comes down to us, incidentally, as one of the earliest examples of writing by a Christian woman, contains not one, but two accounts of a mother's renunciation of her children. In the first instance it is Perpetua herself who relinquishes her newborn son. In the second instance, it is Felicity (one of Perpetua's fellow catechumens) who gives up her infant daughter. Eight months pregnant when arrested, Felicity "was very sorrowful as the day of the games drew near, fearing lest for this cause she should be kept back (for it is not lawful for women that are with child to be brought forth for torment)." But in a fortuitous turn of events (one the redactor attributes to the fervent prayers of her companions), three days before the scheduled execution Felicity "was delivered of a daughter, whom a sister reared up to be her own daughter." Ibid.

12 L. Stephanie Cobb, *Dying to Be Men: Gender and Language in Early Christian Martyr Texts* (New York: Columbia University Press, 2008), 2.

13. Augustine, *The Sermons of S. Augustine upon the Feast of SS. Perpetua and Felicity*, trans. Edmund Hill and ed. John E. Rotelle (Hyde Park, N.Y.: New City Press, 1994), 52.

14. *Passion of SS. Perpetua and Felicity*, 31.

15. Augustine, *Sermons*, 52.

16. Cobb, *Dying to Be Men*, 97.

17. *Passion of SS. Perpetua and Felicity*, 28.

18. Augustine, *Sermons*, 56.

19. The crowd witnessing the trial of the second-century martyr Agathonike likewise tried (but failed) to persuade this young mother to renounce her Christian faith out of concern for her children. See *Martyrdom of Carpus, Papylus, and Agathonike* discussed in Cobb, *Dying to Be Men*, 116–23.

20. Augustine, *Sermons*, 56.

21. Jerome, *Letter 108*, trans. W. H. Fremantle, G. Lewis, and W. G. Martley, in Philip Schaff and Henry Wace, eds., *Nicene and Post-Nicene Fathers*, 2nd ser., vol. 6. (Buffalo, N.Y.: Christian Literature Publishing Co., 1893), rev.

and ed. for New Advent by Kevin Knight, http://www.newadvent.org/fathers
/3001108.htm.

22. Ibid.

23. Ibid.

24. *The Life of Blessed Birgitta by Prior Peter and Master Peter*, in *Birgitta of Sweden: Life and Selected Revelations*, ed. Marguerite Tjader Harris, trans. Albert Ryle Kezel, and intro. Tore Nyberg (New York: Paulist Press, 1990), 71, 74.

25. Ibid., 76.

26. See Atkinson, *Oldest Vocation*, 173–84. For a discussion of motherhood in Birgitta of Sweden's writings, see Claire Sahlin, *Birgitta of Sweden and the Voice of Prophecy* (Rochester, N.Y.: Boydell Press, 2001), 34–107.

27. Revelation 1.20.10–12, in *Revelations of St. Birgitta of Sweden*, vol. 1, 84–85.

28. Revelation 1.2.8, ibid., vol. 1, 55–56.

29. *Life of Blessed Birgitta*, 92; Birgitta of Sweden, *Den Heliga Birgitta Revelaciones Extravagantes*, ed. Lennart Hollman (Uppsala: Almqvist & Wiksells, 1967), Extrav. 95.

30. Atkinson, *Oldest Vocation*, 175–76, citing Extrav. 95. If the demonic vision helped Birgitta to correct her "excessive and misdirected" love for her children, so too did her contemplation of the example provided by the Virgin Mary. Ibid. In a revelation on the subject of Christ's passion, Birgitta spared no ink in detailing the vicarious suffering of the mother of God, who "could hardly stand on my feet due to my grief." Witnessing Christ on the cross, Mary's "whole body shook with the bitter pain of my heart." It seemed to me, Mary tells Birgitta, "that my own heart had been pierced when I saw my beloved Son's heart pierced." In the end, however, Mary subordinated her maternal emotion in deference to the will of God. I was consoled, Mary concludes, "realizing that this was the way he wanted it and so it was the right way, and I conformed all my will to his." Revelation 1.10, in *Revelations of St. Birgitta of Sweden*, vol. 1, 65–70.

31. Revelation 1.2.8, in *Revelations of St. Birgitta of Sweden*, vol. 1, 55–56.

32. Revelation 4.11, in ibid., vol. 2, 46–47.

33. Fra Giunta Bevegnati, *The Life and Miracles of Saint Margaret of Cortona (1247–1297)*, trans. and intro. Thomas Renna and ed. Shannon Larson (St. Bonaventure, N.Y.: Franciscan Institute, 2012), 61.

34. Ibid., 56.

35. Ibid.

36. Ibid., 55–56.

37. In writings about Elizabeth of Thuringia (also, like Margaret of Cortona, associated with the Third Order of Saint Francis), a similar connection is made between the renunciation of children, love of God, and the ideal of evangelical poverty. Rutebeuf's thirteenth-century versified life of

Elizabeth, for example, praises the saint for cultivating a "love of God . . . so deep / That she renounced all [the goods of the world] . . . and succeeded / In forgetting her children and wealth, / Honors and marital bonds." Brigitte Cazelles, *The Lady as Saint: A Collection of French Hagiographic Romances of the Thirteenth Century* (Philadelphia: University of Pennsylvania Press, 1991), 164.

38. Bevegnati, *Life and Miracles*, 55.

39. For a discussion of the theme of maternal suffering in the lives of the saints, see Atkinson, *Oldest Vocation*, 144–93.

40. Jerome, *Letter 108*.

41. Jacobus de Voragine, *The Golden Legend*, vol. 2, trans. William Granger Ryan (Princeton, N.J.: Princeton University Press, 1993), 122.

42. Guibert of Nogent, *A Monk's Confession: The Memoirs of Guibert of Nogent*, trans. and intro. Paul J. Archambault (University Park: Pennsylvania State University Press, 1996), 45; Marie de l'Incarnation, "Lettre CIX," in *Marie de l'Incarnation: Correspondance*, ed. Dom Guy-Marie Oury (Sablé-sur-Sarthe, France: Solesmes, 1971), 316. The parallels between Guibert's account of his mother's departure and Marie's account of her own leave-taking are striking. In both cases, the abandoned son was around twelve years old when his mother left, and in both cases the mother had long felt herself inclined toward religious life. In both cases, too, the mother testifies to having worried upon leaving her son that he would suffer from a lack of maternal affection. The way Guibert puts it, "[My mother] knew I would henceforth be an orphan and that I could no longer count on anybody's support . . . Though I would not be in want of food and clothing, I would suffer from the lack of affection that is indispensable to children at that tender age and that only women can give." Guibert of Nogent, *Monk's Confession*, 45. Marie, for her part, admits in the *Relation* of 1654 that she "conversed ceaselessly with his Goodness, pleading him to have compassion on this poor abandoned boy who was not yet twelve years old. I foresaw that he would suffer much, since ordinarily relatives do not have the tenderness of a mother, nor a child such confident recourse." Marie de l'Incarnation, *Relation de 1654*, in *Marie de l'Incarnation: Écrits spirituels et historiques*, ed. Dom Albert Jamet, vol. 2 (Paris: Desclée-de Brouwer, 1929), 279–81. In both cases, of course, the mother overcame her love for her son by her greater love for God and entered religious life against the pull of her natural affections. So similar are these two accounts of maternal leave-taking that it is worth considering whether Marie or Claude might have taken inspiration from Guibert's *Monodies*, which was first translated into French from Latin by a Maurist Benedictine in 1651.

43. Guibert of Nogent, *Monk's Confession*, 45.

44. For Atkinson, the sufferings of holy mothers invoked not so much the experience of Christ on the cross as the experience of Mary at the foot of the

cross. By the late medieval period, representations of the Virgin Mary in Western Europe tended to depict the mother of God as the grieving mother at Golgotha. "The appeal of the Pietà and of the Mater Dolorosa," Atkinson contends, "arose from Mary's symbolization of the pain and sorrow believed to be characteristic of all maternity." By the end of the Middle Ages, "maternal anguish had become the emotional center of Marian piety." Atkinson, *Oldest Vocation*, 162.

45. Jerome, *Letter 108*.

46. Guibert of Nogent, *Monk's Confession*, 45.

47. Ancelet-Hustache, "Les 'Vitae Sororum' d'Unterlinden," 394, 460.

48. Marie de l'Incarnation, "Lettre CLV," in Oury, *Correspondance*, 527.

49. It is also possible to read Marie's abandonment of Claude—as Newman does other instances of a holy woman's relinquishment of her children—as atonement for her lost virginity. Newman, *From Virile Woman*, 10. Like Paula and Ivetta and countless other holy women, Marie had married only out of a "respectful fear" for her parents and a desire to "obey them in all things." Claude Martin, *La Vie de la Vénénerable Mère Marie de l'Incarnation* (Sablé-sur-Sarthe, France: Solesmes, 1981), 9. The death of her husband gave Marie the opportunity—as it had for Paula, Ivetta, and others—to make things right, to refuse remarriage, to realize her religious vocation, and to recover her virginal status by means of renouncing the fruit of her womb and the telltale proof of her sinful concupiscence.

50. Marie de l'Incarnation, "Lettre CCXI," in Oury, *Correspondance*, 725.

51. Ibid.

52. Sophie Houdard has written on the relationship between Marie's abandonment of Claude and the spiritual culture of abandonment in seventeenth-century France. See Sophie Houdard, "Le cri public du fils abandonné ou l'inexprimable secret de la cruauté d'une mère," *Littératures classiques* 68 (Summer 2009): 273–84.

53. For a discussion of *ancien régime* laws and regulations concerning abandoned children, see Matthew Gerber, *Bastards: Politics, Family, and Law in Early Modern France* (Oxford: Oxford University Press, 2012), 3–48.

54. Mino Bergamo, *La science des saints: Le discours mystique au XVIIe siècle en France*, ed. Jacques Le Brun (Grenoble: Millon, 1992), 16. For an overview of the spirituality of abandonment in seventeenth-century France, see Louis Cognet, *Post-Reformation Spirituality*, trans. P. Hepburne Scott (New York: Hawthorne Books, 1959), 56–115. See also Bergamo, *La science des saints*, 15–59; M. Olphe-Galliard, "L'abandon a la providence divine et la tradition salesian," *Revue d'Ascétique et de Mystique* 38 (1962): 324–53; and A. Rayez, "La spiritualité d'abandon chez saint Jean-Baptiste de la Salle," *Revue d'Ascétique et de Mystique* 121 (1955): 47–76.

55. Gabriel Joppin, *Fénelon et la mystique du pur amour* (Paris: Beauchesne, 1938), 20; Pierre de Bérulle, *Bref discours de l'abnegation interieur*, ed. F. Nef, *Le Nouveau Commerce* 79–80 (1991): 91–133; Jean Eudes, *Vie et royaume de Jésus* 6 (Paris, 1924), 452. Devotion to the heart of Jesus, though typical to the seventeenth-century French school generally, is richly developed in the theology of Jean Eudes. See Paul Milcent, *Saint Jean Eudes* (Paris: Bloud & Gay, 1964), 48–51. For a summary of spiritualities of abandonment, including those of Charles de Condren and Jean-Jacques Olier, see Henri Brémond, *Histoire littéraire du sentiment religieux en France depuis la fin des guerres de religion jusqu'à nos jours* (Grenoble: J. Millon, 2006), vol. 11, 1313–39; and John Abruzzese, *The Theology of the Hearts in the Writings of St. Francis de Sales* (Rome: Institute of Spirituality, Pontifical University of St. Thomas Aquinas, 1985).

56. For a discussion of the influence of the Alumbrados on the development of the spirituality of abandonment, see Cognet, *Post-Reformation Spirituality*, 26–55. For a discussion de Sales's influence, see Olphe-Galliard, "L'abandon a la providence divine."

57. Olphe-Galliard, "L'abandon a la providence divine," 329.

58. Francis de Sales, *On the Love of God*, vol. 2, trans. and intro. John K. Ryan (Garden City, N.Y.: Image Books, 1963), 130–31.

59. Jacques-Bénigne Bossuet, *Oeuvres Complètes de Bossuet, évêque de Meaux*, vol. 3 (Paris: Lefèvre, 1856), 508.

60. Ibid., 509.

61. Jeanne Guyon, *Selected Writings*, trans. and ed. Dianne Guenin-Lelle and Ronney Mourad (New York: Paulist Press, 2012), 37.

62. Ibid., 65.

63. Ibid., 66.

64. One of the most accessible elaborations of the spirituality of abandonment in seventeenth-century France is *L'abandon à la providence divine*, attributed to Jean-Pierre de Caussade. Discovered in the archives of the Dames de Nazareth at Monmirail, *L'abandon à la providence divine* is a collection of letters written by an ecclesiastical superior to the superior of a religious community. First published in 1861 by Henri Ramière, who took at face value the attribution to de Caussade written on the cover of the letters, *L'abandon à la providence divine* remains of anonymous authorship. It is, nonetheless, of considerable importance to an inquiry into the meaning and significance of the notion of abandonment within the context of seventeenth-century French spirituality.

65. De Caussade, *L'abandon*, 45.

66. Ibid.

67. Guyon, *Selected Writings*, 65.

68. De Caussade, *L'abandon*, 64.

69. Ibid., 69–70.

70. Ibid., 42, 110, 53.

71. De Sales, *On the Love of God*, 136.

72. Ibid.

73. De Caussade, *L'abandon*, 110.

74. De Sales, *On the Love of God*, 104.

75. De Caussade, *L'abandon*, 47–48.

76. Bossuet, *Oeuvres Complètes*, 510.

77. Ibid., 110. For a brief overview of the Quietist controversy in seventeenth-century France, see the introduction to Fénelon, *Selected Writings*, ed. Chad Helms (Mahwah, N.J.: Paulist Press, 2006), 84–111.

78. Fénelon, *Selected Writings*, 275.

79. De Caussade, *L'abandon*, 49.

80. Guyon, *Selected Writings*, 40.

81. Ibid.

82. De Sales, *On the Love of God*, 103.

83. Guyon, *Selected Writings*, 34.

84. Bossuet, *Oeuvres Complètes*, 509.

85. Rayez, "La spiritualité d'abandon," 71.

86. Bossuet, *Oeuvres Complètes*, 508–9.

87. Jerome, *Against Jovinian*, Book 1.3, in Schaff and Wace, eds., *Nicene and Post-Nicene Fathers*.

88. Sahlin, *Birgitta of Sweden*, 49, citing Extrav. 96.

89. Marie de l'Incarnation, "Lettre CLV," in Oury, *Correspondance*, 527.

90. Atkinson, *Oldest Vocation*, 192.

91. Wendy Wright, *Bond of Perfection: Jeanne de Chantal and François de Sales* (New York: Paulist Press, 1985), 100, citing Ste. Jeanne-Françoise Frémyot de Chantal, *Sa vie et ses oeuvres*, vol. 1 (Paris: Plon, 1874), 129.

92. For an argument that Celse-Bénigne's reaction to his mother's departure was exaggerated, see Elizabeth Stopp, *Madame de Chantal: Portrait of a Saint* (Westminster, Md.: Newman Press, 1963), 111.

93. Atkinson, *Oldest Vocation*, 229.

94. Robert Orsi, *Between Heaven and Earth: The Religious Worlds People Make and the Scholars Who Study Them* (Princeton, N.J.: Princeton University Press, 2005), 145.

95. Newman, *From Virile Woman*, 93–96.

96. Ibid., 93.

97. Ibid., 84.

98. For a classic argument about the constructed nature of sanctity, see Pierre Delooz, "Toward a Sociological Study of Canonized Sainthood in the Catholic Church," trans. Jane Hodgkin, in *Saints and Their Cults: Studies in*

Religious Sociology, Folklore, and History, ed. Stephen Wilson (Cambridge: Cambridge University Press, 1985), 189–216.

99. Richard Jenkins, *Pierre Bourdieu* (London: Routledge, 2002), 72.

100. Pierre Bourdieu, *In Other Words: Essays towards a Reflexive Sociology* (Cambridge: Polity Press, 1990), 61.

101. Madam Guyon, *Autobiography of Madame Guyon* (Chicago: Moody Press, 1960), 197.

102. Ibid., 200.

103. Ibid., 203.

104. Ibid., 201, 203.

105. Ibid., 203.

106. Ibid.

107. Ibid., 204, 203.

108. Ibid., 204.

5. Motherhood Refigured: Kristeva, Maternal Sacrifice, and the Imitation of Christ

1. See, for example, Randall Collins, "Cultural Capitalism and Symbolic Violence," in *Sociology since Midcentury: Essays in Theory Cumulation* (New York: Academic Press, 1981), 173–82; Richard Jenkins, "Pierre Bourdieu and the Reproduction of Determinism," *Sociology* 16, no. 2 (1982): 270–81; Pekka Sulkunen, "Society Made Visible: On the Cultural Sociology of Pierre Bourdieu," *Acta Sociologica* 25, no. 2 (1982): 103–15; and Judith Butler, *Excitable Speech: A Politics of the Performative* (New York: Routledge: 1997).

2. Loïc J. D. Wacquant, "Toward a Reflexive Sociology: A Workshop with Pierre Bourdieu," *Sociological Theory* 7, no. 1 (1989): 26–63.

3. Ibid., 37; Pierre Bourdieu, *Homo Academicus*, trans. Peter Collier (Stanford, Calif.: Stanford University Press, 1988).

4. Robert Orsi, "2+2=5, or the Quest for an Abundant Empiricism," *Spiritus: A Journal of Christian Spirituality* 6, no. 1 (2006): 116.

5. Robert Orsi, *Between Heaven and Earth: The Religious Worlds People Make and the Scholars Who Study Them* (Princeton, N.J.: Princeton University Press, 2005), 174.

6. One might well ask, as did one of my colleagues, why it is important to preserve the element of sacrifice

7. Julia Kristeva, "Stabat Mater," in *Tales of Love*, trans. Leon S. Roudiez (New York: Columbia University Press, 1987), 259. Kristeva uses the term "symbolic" to refer to both culture, on the one hand, and the syntax and grammar of language, on the other. I have followed Oliver in distinguishing between the former and the latter by capitalizing the "Symbolic" when

referring to culture and using the lowercase "symbolic" when referring to elements of language.

8. Kelly Oliver, "Introduction: Julia Kristeva's Outlaw Ethics," in Kelly Oliver, ed., *Ethics, Politics, and Difference in Julia Kristeva's Writing* (New York: Routledge, 1993), 6.

9. Orsi, *Between Heaven and Earth*, 113, 140.

10. Ibid., 140.

11. Ibid., 139.

12. Ibid., 118.

13. Ibid., 144.

14. Kelly Oliver, ed., *The Portable Kristeva* (New York: Columbia University Press, 2002), 298; Ewa Ziarek, "At the Limits of Discourse: Heterogeneity, Alterity, and the Maternal Body in Kristeva's Thought," *Hypatia* 7, no. 2 (1992): 102.

15. Oliver, "Introduction," 5.

16. Jacques Lacan, "The Mirror Stage as Formative of the Function of the I as Revealed in Psychoanalytic Experience," in *Écrits: A Selection*, trans. Alan Sheridan (New York: Norton, 1977).

17. Slavoj Žižek, *Jacques Lacan: Society, Politics, Ideology* (London: Routledge, 2003), 305.

18. For an overview of Kristeva's mode of psychosocial development, see Kelly Oliver, *Reading Kristeva: Unraveling the Double-Bind* (Bloomington: Indiana University Press, 1993).

19. Julia Kristeva, *Powers of Horror: An Essay on Abjection*, trans. Leon S. Roudiez (New York: Columbia University Press, 1982), 2.

20. Julia Kristeva, *Black Sun: Depression and Melancholia*, trans. Leon S. Roudiez (New York: Columbia University Press, 1989), 27. For a critique of Kristeva's idea of matricide, see Alison Stone, "Against Matricide: Rethinking Subjectivity and the Maternal Body," *Hypatia* 27, no. 1 (2012): 118–38.

21. Oliver, *Portable Kristeva*, xxii.

22. Ibid.

23. Oliver, *Reading Kristeva*, 69.

24. Ibid., 79.

25. Ibid., 80.

26. Ibid., 79.

27. Martha J. Reineke, *Sacrificed Lives: Kristeva on Women and Violence* (Bloomington: Indiana University Press, 1997), 21.

28. Oliver, *Portable Kristeva*, xxi.

29. Ziarek, "At the Limits of Discourse," 98.

30. Oliver, *Portable Kristeva*, xv.

31. Ibid., xviii.

32. Reineke, *Sacrificed Lives*, 22.

33. Ibid., 27.

34. Noëlle McAfee, "Abject Strangers: Toward an Ethics of Respect," in Oliver, ed., *Ethics, Politics, and Difference*, 121.

35. Ibid.

36. Reineke, *Sacrificed Lives*, 30. For a discussion of the ways in which the process of abjection affects boys and girls differently, see Oliver, *Reading Kristeva*, 55–65.

37. Julia Kristeva, "Women's Time," in Toril Moi, ed., *The Kristeva Reader* (New York: Columbia University Press, 1986), 199.

38. Kristeva, "Stabat Mater," 257.

39. Ibid., 234.

40. Oliver, *Reading Kristeva*, 52; Kristeva, "Stabat Mater," 259.

41. Reineke, *Sacrificed Lives*, 166.

42. Julia Kristeva, "Motherhood according to Giovanni Bellini," in Leon S. Roudiez, ed., *Desire in Language: A Semiotic Approach to Literature and Art*, trans. Thomas Gora, Alice Jardine, and Leon S. Roudiez (New York: Columbia University Press, 1980), 237.

43. For a discussion of Kristeva's fraught relationship with feminism, see Kelly Oliver, "Julia Kristeva's Feminist Revolutions," *Hypatia* 8, no. 3 (1993): 94–114.

44. Fanny Söderbäck, "Motherhood according to Kristeva: On Time and Matter in Plato and Kristeva," *PhiloSOPHIA* 1, no. 1 (2011): 65–87.

45. Oliver, "Introduction," 4.

46. Ziarek, "At the Limits of Discourse," 102.

47. Kristeva, "Stabat Mater," 255.

48. Ibid.

49. Ibid.

50. Oliver, *Portable Kristeva*, 298.

51. Julia Kristeva, *Strangers to Ourselves*, trans. Leon S. Roudiez (New York: Columbia University Press, 1991).

52. Reineke, *Sacrificed Lives*, 171.

53. Oliver, "Introduction," 17.

54. Ibid.

55. Allison Weir, "Identification with the Divided Mother: Kristeva's Ambivalence," in Oliver, ed., *Ethics, Politics, and Difference*, 89.

56. Ibid.

57. Kristeva, *Powers of Horror*, 2.

58. Ibid.

59. Kristeva, "Stabat Mater," 254.

60. Kristeva might be a stranger to herself, but she is no stranger to feminist criticism. For a discussion of feminist critiques of Kristeva's work, see

Tina Chanter, "Kristeva's Politics of Change: Tracking Essentialism with the Help of a Sex/Gender Map," in Oliver, ed., *Ethics, Politics, and Difference,* 179–95. See also Gayatri Spivak, "In a Word," *Differences* 1, no. 2 (1989): 124–56; Judith Butler, "The Body Politics of Julia Kristeva," *Hypatia* 3, no. 3 (1989): 104–18; Jacqueline Rose, "Julia Kristeva: Take Two," in Oliver, ed., *Ethics, Politics, and Difference,* 41–60.

61. Sara Ruddick, "Remarks on the Sexual Politics of Reason," in Eva Feder Kittay and Diana T. Meyers, eds., *Women and Moral Theory* (Totowa, N.J.: Rowman & Littlefield, 1987), 237–60; Bonnie Miller-McLemore, *Also a Mother: Work and Family as Theological Dilemma* (Nashville, Tenn.: Abingdon Press, 1994), 20, 23.

62. Anne Carr and Mary Stewart Van Leeuwen, eds., *Religion, Feminism, and the Family* (Louisville, Ky.: Westminster John Knox Press, 1996), 6.

63. Christine Gudorf, "Sacrificial and Parental Spiritualities," in Carr and Van Leeuwen, eds., *Religion, Feminism, and the Family,* 300.

64. Carr and Van Leeuwen, eds., *Religion, Feminism, and the Family,* 6.

65. Reineke, *Sacrificed Lives,* 28.

66. Ibid.

67. Ibid., 30.

68. Ibid., 29.

69. Ibid., 174.

70. Marilyn Edelstein, "Metaphor, Meta-Narrative, and Mater-Narrative in Kristeva's 'Stabat Mater,'" in David Crownfield, ed., *Body/Text in Julia Kristeva: Religion, Women, and Psychoanalysis* (Albany: State University of New York Press, 1992), 33.

71. Kristeva, "Stabat Mater," 263.

72. John 1:14.

73. Matthew 21:12–13; Luke 8:43–48; and Mark 15:34.

74. Oliver, *Reading Kristeva,* 57.

75. Kristeva, "Stabat Mater," 249.

76. Ibid., 249–50.

77. See Rita Bradley, "Patristic Background of the Mother Similitude in Julian of Norwich," *Christian Scholars Review* 8 (1978): 101–13; and Marsha Bradley, "'When I Was a Child': Spiritual Infancy and God's Maternity in Augustine's *Confessiones,*" in Joseph C. Schnaubelt and Frederick Van Fleteren, eds., *Collectanea Augustiniana* (New York: Lang, 1990), 113–40.

78. Augustine, *Questionum Evangeliorum,* 2.26.

79. Clement of Alexandria, *Pœdagogus,* 1.6.

80. Ambrose, *De Virginibus,* 1.5.

81. On medieval symbolizations of divine maternity and Jesus as mother, see Eleanor McLaughlin, "Christ My Mother: Feminine Naming and Meta-

phors in Medieval Spirituality," *St. Luke's Journal of Theology* 18 (1975): 228–48; Caroline Walker Bynum, *Jesus as Mother: Studies in the Spirituality of the High Middle Ages* (Berkeley: University of California Press, 1982); Robert Boenig, "The God-as-Mother Theme in Richard Rolle's Biblical Commentaries," *Mystical Quarterly* 10 (1984): 171–74; and Valerie Lagorio, "Variations on the Theme of God's Motherhood in Medieval English Mystical and Devotional Writings," *Studia Mystica* 8 (1985): 15–37.

82. Bynum, *Jesus as Mother*, 114.

83. Ibid., 117.

84. Ibid., 122.

85. Julian of Norwich, *Showings*, trans. and into. Edmund Colledge, O.S.A., and James Walsh, S.J. (New York: Paulist Press, 1978), 295.

86. Ibid., 294, 296–97. For discussions of Julian of Norwich's use of maternal imagery, see Rita Bradley, *Julian's Way: A Practical Commentary on Julian of Norwich* (London: HarperCollins, 1992), 134–49; Grace Janzten, *Julian of Norwich, Mystic and Theologian* (London: SPCK, 1987), 115–24; Jennifer Heimmel, "'God Is Our Mother': Julian of Norwich and the Medieval Image of Christian Feminine Divinity," *Elizabethan and Renaissance Studies* 92, no. 5 (1982): 46–102; Brant Pelphrey, *Christ our Mother: Julian of Norwich* (Wilmington, Del.: Michael Glazier, 1989); Margaret Anne Palliser, *Christ Our Mother of Mercy: Divine Mercy and Compassion in the Theology of the Showings of Julian of Norwich* (Berlin: De Gruyter, 1992); and Kerry Dearborn, "The Crucified Christ as the Motherly God: The Theology of Julian of Norwich," *Scottish Journal of Theology* 55, no. 3 (2002): 283–302.

87. Julian of Norwich, *Showings*, 297–99.

88. Ibid., 283.

89. Ibid., 292.

90. Ibid., 298.

91. Ibid., 299; Patricia Donohue-White, "Reading Divine Maternity in Julian of Norwich," *Spiritus* 5, no. 1 (2005): 28.

92. Anders Nygren, *Agape and Eros*, trans. Philip S. Watson (Philadelphia: Westminster Press, 1953); Reinhold Niebuhr, *Nature and Destiny of Man: a Christian Interpretation*, vol. 2 (New York: C. Scribner's Sons, 1943), Chap. 3; and Gene Outka, *Agape: An Ethical Analysis* (New Haven, Conn.: Yale University Press, 1972).

93. Søren Kierkegaard, *Works of Love: Some Christian Reflections in the Form of Discourses*, trans. Howard and Edna Hong (New York: Harper Torchbooks, 1962), 328.

94. Valerie Saiving Goldstein, "The Human Situation: A Feminine View," *Journal of Religion* 40, no. 2 (1960): 100–112.

95. Ibid., 108.

186

96. Ibid., 100.

97. Ibid., 109.

98. Gudorf, Christine. "Parenting, Mutual Love, and Sacrifice," in Barbara Hilkert Andolsen, Christine E. Gudorf, and Mary D. Pellauer, eds., *Women's Consciousness and Women's Conscience: A Reader in Feminist Ethics* (Minneapolis: Winston Press, 1985), 181.

99. Ibid., 185.

100. Ibid., 186.

101. Sallie McFague, "God as Mother," in Judith Plaskow and Carol P. Christ, eds., *Weaving the Visions: New Patterns in Feminist Spirituality* (San Francisco: Harper & Row, 1989), 143.

102. Sally Purvis, "Mothers, Neighbors, and Strangers: Another Look at Agape," *Journal of Feminist Studies in Religion* 7 (Spring 1991): 26.

103. Ibid., 33; Purvis, "Christian Feminist Ethics and the Family," in Carr and Van Leeuwen, eds., *Religion, Feminism, and the Family*, 114.

104. Ibid., 121.

105. Carr and Van Leeuwen, eds., *Religion, Feminism, and the Family*, 3.

106. Jeffrey J. Kripal, *The Serpent's Gift: Gnostic Reflections on the Study of Religion* (Chicago: University of Chicago Press, 2007), 11–12.

107. Ibid., 11.

108. Kristeva, "Stabat Mater," 241.

109. Kripal, *Serpent's Gift*, 124.

110. Robert Orsi, ed., *The Cambridge Companion to Religious Studies* (Cambridge: Cambridge University Press, 2011), 103.

111. Kripal, *Serpent's Gift*, 125.

Afterword/Afterward

1. Marie de l'Incarnation, "Lettre CCXI," in *Marie de l'Incarnation: Correspondance*, ed. Dom Guy-Marie Oury (Sablé-sur-Sarthe, France: Solesmes, 1971), 725.

2. Jeffrey J. Kripal, *The Serpent's Gift: Gnostic Reflections on the Study of Religion* (Chicago: University of Chicago Press, 2007), 141.

3. Ibid., 150.

4. Ibid., 124.

5. Ibid., 130.

Bibliography

Abruzzese, John. *The Theology of the Hearts in the Writings of St. Francis de Sales.* Rome: Institute of Spirituality, Pontifical University of St. Thomas Aquinas, 1985.

Ahlgren, Gillian. *Teresa of Avila and the Politics of Sanctity.* Ithaca, N.Y.: Cornell University Press, 1996.

Ancelet-Hustache, Jeanne, ed. "Les 'Vitae Sororum' d'Unterlinden." *Archives d'histoire doctrinale et littéraire du moyen âge* 5 (1930): 317–509.

Ariès, Philippe. *Centuries of Childhood: A Social History of Family Life.* Translated by Robert Baldick. New York: Vintage Books, 1962.

Atkinson, Clarissa. *Mystic and Pilgrim: The Book and the World of Margery Kempe.* Ithaca, N.Y.: Cornell University Press, 1983.

———. *The Oldest Vocation: Christian Motherhood in the Middle Ages.* Ithaca, N.Y.: Cornell University Press, 1991.

Augustine. *The Sermons of S. Augustine upon the Feast of SS. Perpetua and Felicity.* Translated by Edmund Hill and edited by John E. Rotelle. Hyde Park, N.Y.: New City Press, 1994.

Beck, Martha. *Expecting Adam: A True Story of Birth, Rebirth, and Everyday Magic.* New York: Times Books, 1999.

Bergamo, Mino. *La science des saints: Le discours mystique au XVIIe siècle en France.* Edited by Jacques Le Brun. Grenoble: Millon, 1992.

Berriot-Salvadore, Evelyne. *Les femmes dans la société française.* Geneva: Droz, 1990.

Bérulle, Pierre de. *Bref discours de l'abnegation interieur.* Edited by F. Nef. *Le Nouveau Commerce* 79–80 (1991): 91–133.

Bevegnati, Fra Giunta. *The Life and Miracles of Saint Margaret of Cortona (1247–1297).* Translated and introduction by Thomas Renna. Edited by Shannon Larson. St. Bonaventure, N.Y.: Franciscan Institute, 2012.

Birgitta of Sweden. *Den Heliga Birgitta Revelaciones Extravagantes.* Edited by Lennart Hollman. Uppsala: Almqvist & Wiksells, 1967.

———. *The Revelations of St. Birgitta of Sweden.* 3 vols. Translated by Denis Searby. Introduction by Bridget Morris. New York: Oxford University Press, 2006.

Boenig, Robert. "The God-as-Mother Theme in Richard Rolle's Biblical Commentaries." *Mystical Quarterly* 10 (1984): 171–74.

Bossuet, Jacques-Bénigne. *Oeuvres Complètes de Bossuet, évèque de Meaux.* Vol. 3. Paris: Lefèvre, 1856.

Boswell, John. *The Kindness of Strangers: The Abandonment of Children in Western Europe from Late Antiquity to the Renaissance.* New York: Pantheon Books, 1988.

Bourdieu, Pierre. *Algeria: 1960, the Disenchantment of the World, the Sense of Honor, the Kabyle House or the World Reversed.* Translated by Richard Nice. Cambridge: Cambridge University Press, 1979.

———. *Distinction: A Social Critique of the Judgment of Taste.* Translated by Richard Nice. Cambridge, Mass.: Harvard University Press, 1984.

———. *Homo Academicus.* Translated by Peter Collier. Stanford, Calif.: Stanford University Press, 1988.

———. *In Other Words: Essays towards a Reflexive Sociology.* Cambridge: Polity Press, 1990.

———. *Language and Symbolic Power.* Edited by John B. Thompson and translated by Gino Raymond and Matthew Adamson. Cambridge: Polity Press, 1991.

———. *The Logic of Practice.* Cambridge: Polity Press, 1990.

———. *Outline of a Theory of Practice.* Translated by Richard Nice. Cambridge: Cambridge University Press, 1977.

Bradley, Marsha. "'When I Was a Child': Spiritual Infancy and God's Maternity in Augustine's *Confessiones.*" In *Collectanea Augustiniana*, edited by Joseph C. Schnaubelt and Frederick Van Fleteren, 113–40. New York: Lang, 1990.

Bradley, Rita. *Julian's Way: A Practical Commentary on Julian of Norwich.* London: HarperCollins, 1992.

———. "Patristic Background of the Mother Similitude in Julian of Norwich." *Christian Scholars Review* 8 (1978): 101–13.

Brémond, Henri. *Histoire littéraire du sentiment religieux en France depuis la fin des guerres de religion jusqu'à nos jours.* 11 vols. Grenoble: J. Millon, 2006.

Brodeur, Raymond, ed. *Femme, mystique et missionnaire. Marie Guyart de l'Incarnation.* Quebec: Presses de l'Université Laval, 2001.

———. *Marie de l'Incarnation: Entre Mère et Fils.* Quebec: Presses de la Université de Laval, 2000.

Brown, Peter. *Body and Society: Men, Women, and Sexual Renunciation in Early Christianity.* New York: Columbia University Press, 1988.

Brundage, James A. *Law, Sex, and Christian Society in Medieval Europe.* Chicago: University of Chicago Press, 1987.

Bruneau, Marie-Florine. "Le sacrifice maternel commun alibi à la production de l'écriture." *Études littéraires* 27, no. 2 (1994): 67–76.

———. *Women Mystics Confront the Modern World: Marie de l'Incarnation (1599–1672) and Madame Guyon (1648–1717)*. Albany: State University of New York Press, 1998.

Bunge, Marcia J. *The Child in Christian Thought*. Grand Rapids, Mich.: W. B. Eerdmans, 2001.

Burgess, Ernest Watson, Harvey James Locke, and Mary Margaret Thomes. *The Family, from Institution to Companionship*. New York: American Book Co., 1963.

Burguière, André, Christiane Klapisch-Zuber, Martine Segalen, and Françoise Zonabend, eds. *Histoire de la Famille*. Paris: A. Colin, 1986.

Burrus, Virginia. *The Sex Lives of Saints: An Erotics of Ancient Hagiography*. Philadelphia: University of Pennsylvania Press, 2004.

Butler, Judith. "The Body Politics of Julia Kristeva." *Hypatia* 3, no. 3 (1989): 104–18.

———. *Excitable Speech: A Politics of the Performative*. New York: Routledge: 1997.

———. *Gender Trouble: Feminism and the Subversion of Identity*. New York: Routledge, 1990.

Bynum, Caroline Walker. *Fragmentation and Redemption: Essays on Gender and the Human Body in Medieval Religion*. New York: Zone Books, 1991.

———. *Holy Feast and Holy Fast: The Religious Significance of Food to Medieval Women*. Berkeley: University of California Press, 1987.

———. *Jesus as Mother: Studies in the Spirituality of the High Middle Ages*. Berkeley: University of California Press, 1982.

———. *The Resurrection of the Body in Western Christianity, 200–1336*. New York: Columbia University Press, 1995.

Calvert, Karin Lee Fishbeck. *Children in the House: The Material Culture of Early Childhood, 1600–1900*. Boston: Northeastern University Press, 1992.

Carpenter, Jennifer. "Juette of Huy, Recluse and Mother (1158–1228): Children and Mothering in the Saintly Life." In *Power of the Weak: Studies on Medieval Women*, edited by Jennifer Carpenter and Sally-Beth MacLean, 57–93. Urbana: University of Illinois Press, 1995.

Carr, Anne, and Mary Stewart Van Leeuwen, eds. *Religion, Feminism, and the Family*. Louisville, Ky.: Westminster John Knox Press, 1996.

Castelli, Elizabeth. "Virginity and Its Meaning for Women's Sexuality in Early Christianity." *Journal of Feminist Studies in Religion* 2, no. 1 (1986): 61–88.

Cazelles, Brigitte. *The Lady as Saint: A Collection of French Hagiographic Romances of the Thirteenth Century*. Philadelphia: University of Pennsylvania Press, 1991.

Cobb, L. Stephanie. *Dying to Be Men: Gender and Language in Early Christian Martyr Texts*. New York: Columbia University Press, 2008.

Cognet, Louis. *Post-Reformation Spirituality*. Translated by P. Hepburne Scott. New York: Hawthorne Books, 1959.

Collet, François. "Does Habitus Matter? A Comparative Review of Bourdieu's Habitus and Simon's Bounded Rationality with Some Implications for Economic Sociology." *Sociological Theory* 27, no. 4 (2009): 419–34.

Collins, Patricia Hill. "Shifting the Center: Race, Class, and Feminist Theorizing about Motherhood." In *Representations of Motherhood*, edited by Donna Bassin, Margaret Honey, and Meryle Mahrer Kaplan, 56–74. New Haven, Conn.: Yale University Press, 1994.

Collins, Randall. "Cultural Capitalism and Symbolic Violence." In *Sociology since Midcentury: Essays in Theory Cumulation*, 173–82. New York: Academic Press, 1981.

Couchman, Jane, and Ann Crabb, eds. *Women's Letters across Europe, 1400–1700: Form and Persuasion*. Aldershot: Ashgate, 2005.

Crownfield, David, ed. *Body/Text in Julia Kristeva: Religion, Women, and Psychoanalysis*. Albany: State University of New York Press, 1992.

Cunningham, Hugh. *Children and Childhood in Western Society since 1500*. London: Longman, 1995.

Davis, Natalie Zemon. *Women on the Margins: Three Seventeenth-Century Lives*. Cambridge, Mass.: Harvard University Press, 1995.

Daybell, James, ed. *Early Modern Women's Letter Writing, 1450–1700*. New York: Palgrave, 2001.

Dearborn, Kerry. "The Crucified Christ as the Motherly God: The Theology of Julian of Norwich." *Scottish Journal of Theology* 55, no. 3 (2002): 283–302.

De Caussade, Jean-Pierre. *L'abandon à la providence divine*. Edited by Dominique Salin. Paris: Desclée de Brouwer, 2005.

De Chantal, Jeanne-Françoise Frémyot. *Sa vie et ses oeuvres*. Vol. 1. Paris: Plon, 1874.

DeJean, Joan E. *Tender Geographies: Women and the Origins of the Novel in France*. New York: Columbia University Press, 1991.

Delooz, Pierre. *Sociologie et canonisations*. Liège: Faculté de droit, 1969.

———. "Toward a Sociological Study of Canonized Sainthood in the Catholic Church." Translated by Jane Hodgkin. In *Saints and Their Cults: Studies in Religious Sociology, Folklore, and History*, edited by Stephen Wilson, 189–216. Cambridge: Cambridge University Press, 1985.

DeMause, Lloyd. *The History of Childhood*. New York: Harper & Row, 1975.

De Sales, Francis. *Introduction à la vie dévote*. Edited by André Ravier with the collaboration of Roger Devos. Paris: Gallimard, 1969.

———. *On the Love of God*. Vol. 2. Translated and introduction by John K. Ryan. Garden City, N.Y.: Image Books, 1963.

Desan, Suzanne and Jeffrey Merrick, eds. *Family, Gender, and Law in Early Modern France*. University Park: Pennsylvania State University Press, 2009.

De Voragine, Jacobus. *The Golden Legend*. Vol. 2. Translated by William Granger Ryan. Princeton, N.J.: Princeton University Press, 1993.

Donohue-White, Patricia. "Reading Divine Maternity in Julian of Norwich." *Spiritus* 5, no. 1 (2005): 19–36.

Dunn, Mary. " 'But an Echo'?: Claude Martin, Marie de l'Incarnation, and Female Religious Identity in Seventeenth-Century New France." *Catholic Historical Review* 100, no. 3 (2014): 459–85.

Dunning, Benjamin H. *Specters of Paul: Sexual Difference in Early Christian Thought*. Philadelphia: University of Pennsylvania Press, 2011.

Dupâquier, Jacques, ed., *Histoire de la population française*. Vol. 2. Paris: Presses Universitaires de France, 1988.

Elliot, Dyan. *Fallen Bodies: Pollution, Sexuality, and Demonology in the Middle Ages*. Philadelphia: University of Pennsylvania Press, 1998.

———. *Spiritual Marriage: Sexual Abstinence in Medieval Wedlock*. Princeton, N.J.: Princeton University Press, 1993.

Eudes, Jean. *Vie et royaume de Jésus*. Paris, 1924.

Farrell, Michèle Longino. *Performing Motherhood: The Sévigné Correspondence*. Hanover, N.H.: University Press of New England, 1991.

Fénelon, François. *Selected Writings*. Edited by Chad Helms. Mahwah, N.J.: Paulist Press, 2006.

Flandrin, Jean-Louis. *Families in Former Times: Kinship, Household, and Sexuality*. Translated by Richard Southern. Cambridge: Cambridge University Press, 1979.

———. *Sex in the Western World: The Development of Attitudes and Behaviors*. Philadelphia: Harwood Academic Publishers, 1991.

Foskett, Mary. *A Virgin Conceived: Mary and Classical Representations of Virginity*. Bloomington: Indiana University Press, 2002.

Foucault, Michel. *The History of Sexuality*. 3 vols. Translated by Robert Hurley. New York: Vintage Books, 1990.

Fuchs, Rachel Ginnis. *Abandoned Children: Foundlings and Child Welfare in Nineteenth-Century France*. Albany: State University of New York Press, 1984.

Furey, Constance M. "Body, Society, and Subjectivity in Religious Studies." *Journal of the American Academy of Religion* 80, no. 1 (2012): 7–33.

Gaca, Kathy L. *The Making of Fornication: Eros, Ethics, and Political Reform in Greek Philosophy and Early Christianity*. Berkeley: University of California Press, 2003.

Gaffney, Phyllis. *Constructions of Childhood and Youth in Old French Narrative*. Burlington, Vt.: Ashgate, 2011.

Gerber, Matthew. *Bastards: Politics, Family, and Law in Early Modern France*. Oxford: Oxford University Press, 2012.

Gill, Sam. "No Place to Stand: Jonathan Z. Smith as *Homo Ludens*, the Academic Study of Religion *Sub Specie Ludi*." *Journal of the American Academy of Religion* 66, no. 2 (1998): 283–312.

Gilmore, Leigh. *Autobiographics: A Feminist Theory of Women's Self-Representation*. Ithaca, N.Y.: Cornell University Press, 1994.

Godineau, Dominique. *Les femmes dans la société française, XVIe–XVIIIe siècle*. Paris: Armand Colin, 2003.

Goldsmith, Elizabeth C. *Publishing Women's Life Stories in France, 1647–1720: From Voice to Print*. Aldershot: Ashgate, 2001.

———, ed. *Writing the Female Voice: Essays on Epistolary Literature*. Boston: Northeastern University Press, 1989.

Goldstein, Valerie Saiving. "The Human Situation: A Feminine View." *Journal of Religion* 40, no. 2 (1960): 100–112.

Gregory, Brad S. *The Unintended Reformation: How a Religious Revolution Secularized Society*. Cambridge, Mass.: Belknap Press, 2012.

Greenberg, Mitchell. *Baroque Bodies: Psychoanalysis and the Culture of French Absolutism*. Ithaca, N.Y.: Cornell University Press, 2001.

Greenspan, Kate. "The Autohagiographical Tradition in Medieval Women's Devotional Writing." *A/B: Auto/Biographical Studies* 6 (1991): 157–68.

Griffith, R. Marie. *God's Daughters: Evangelical Women and the Power of Submission*. Berkeley: University of California Press, 1997.

Gudorf, Christine. "Parenting, Mutual Love, and Sacrifice." In *Women's Consciousness and Women's Conscience: A Reader in Feminist Ethics*, edited by Barbara Hilkert Andolsen, Christine E. Gudorf, and Mary D. Pellauer, 175–91. Minneapolis: Winston Press, 1985.

Guibert of Nogent. *A Monk's Confession: The Memoirs of Guibert of Nogent*. Translated and introduction by Paul J. Archambault. University Park: Pennsylvania State University Press, 1996.

Guyon, Jeanne. *Autobiography of Madame Guyon*. Chicago: Moody Press, 1960.

———. *Selected Writings*. Translated and edited by Dianne Guenin-Lelle and Ronney Mourad. New York: Paulist Press, 2012.

Hanigsberg, Julia E., and Sara Ruddick, eds. *Mother Troubles: Rethinking Contemporary Maternal Dilemmas*. Boston: Beacon Press, 1999.

Hardwick, Julie. "Seeking Separations: Gender, Marriages, and Household Economies in Early Modern France." *French Historical Studies* 21, no. 1 (1998): 157–80.

———. "Widowhood and Patriarchy in Seventeenth-Century France." *Journal of Social History* 26 (1992): 133–49.

Harnack, A. *Die Akten des Karpus, des Papylus und der Agathonike: Eine Urkunde aus der Zeit Mark Aurels, Texte und Untersuchungen* 3. Leipzig, 1888.

Harrington, Joel. *The Unwanted Child: The Fate of Foundlings, Orphans, and Juvenile Criminals in Early Modern Germany*. Chicago: University of Chicago Press, 2009.

Harvey, Tamara. *Figuring Modesty in Feminist Discourse across the Americas, 1633–1700*. Aldershot: Ashgate, 2008.

Hays, Sharon. *The Cultural Contradictions of Motherhood*. New Haven, Conn.: Yale University Press, 1996.

Heimmel, Jennifer. "'God Is Our Mother': Julian of Norwich and the Medieval Image of Christian Feminine Divinity." *Elizabethan and Renaissance Studies* 92, no. 5 (1982): 46–102.

Herlihy, David. "The Making of the Medieval Family: Symmetry, Structure, and Sentiment." *Journal of Family History* 8 (1983): 116–30.

———. *Medieval Households*. Cambridge, Mass.: Harvard University Press, 1985.

———. *Women, Family, and Society in Medieval Europe*, edited by A. Molho. Providence, R.I.: Berghahn Books, 1995.

Holler, Claudia, and Martin Klepper, eds. *Rethinking Narrative Identity: Person and Perspective*. Amsterdam: John Benjamins, 2013.

Hollywood, Amy. *Sensible Ecstasy: Sexual Difference and the Demands of History*. Chicago: University of Chicago Press, 2002.

Houdard, Sophie. "Le cri public du fils abandonné ou l'inexprimable secret de la cruauté d'une mere." *Littératures classiques* 68 (Summer 2009): 273–84.

Hunt, David. *Parents and Children in History: The Psychology of Family Life in Early Modern France*. New York: Basic Books, 1970.

Hufton, Olwen. "Le travail and la famille: La maternité." In *Histoire des femmes en occident*, edited by Georges Duby and Michelle Perrot, 25–63. Paris: Plon, 2002.

Hugh of Floreffe. *The Life of Yvette of Huy*. Edited and translated by Jo Ann McNamara. Toronto: Peregrina, 1999.

Janzten, Grace. *Julian of Norwich, Mystic and Theologian*. London: SPCK, 1987.

———. *Power, Gender, and Christian Mysticism*. Cambridge: Cambridge University Press, 1995.

Jenkins, Richard. *Pierre Bourdieu*. London: Routledge, 2002.

———. "Pierre Bourdieu and the Reproduction of Determinism." *Sociology* 16, no. 2 (1982): 270–81.

Joppin, Gabriel. *Fénelon et la mystique du pur amour*. Paris: Beauchesne, 1938.

Julian of Norwich. *Showings*. Translated and introduction by Edmund Colledge, O.S.A., and James Walsh, S.J. New York: Paulist Press, 1978.

Katz, Steven T. "Language, Epistemology, and Mysticism." In *Mysticism and Philosophical Analysis*, edited by Steven T. Katz, 22–74. Oxford: Oxford University Press, 1978.

———. "Mysticism and the Interpretation of Sacred Scripture." In *Mysticism and Sacred Scripture*, edited by Steven T. Katz, 7–67. New York: Oxford University Press, 2000.

Kertzer, David and Marzio Barbagli, eds. *Family Life in Early Modern Times, 1500–1789.* New Haven, Conn.: Yale University Press, 2001.

Kierkegaard, Søren. *Works of Love: Some Christian Reflections in the Form of Discourses* Translated by Howard and Edna Hong. New York: Harper Torchbooks, 1962.

Kiett, Andrew W. *Inventing the Sacred: Imposture, Inquisition, and the Boundaries of the Supernatural in Golden Age Spain.* Leiden: Brill, 2005.

Klapisch-Zuber, Christiane. "The 'Cruel Mother': Maternity, Widowhood, and Dowry in Florence in the Fourteenth and Fifteenth Centuries." In *Women, Family, and Ritual in Renaissance Italy*, 117–31. Chicago: University of Chicago Press, 1985.

Knibiehler, Yvonne and Catherine Fouquet. *L'histoire des mères, du moyen-âge à nos jours.* Paris: Montalba, 1980.

Kripal, Jeffrey J. *Kali's Child: The Mystical and the Erotic in the Life and Teachings of Ramakrishna.* Chicago: University of Chicago Press, 1995.

———. *The Serpent's Gift: Gnostic Reflections on the Study of Religion.* Chicago: University of Chicago Press, 2007.

Kristeva, Julia. *Black Sun: Depression and Melancholia.* Translated by Leon S. Roudiez. New York: Columbia University Press, 1989.

———. "Motherhood according to Giovanni Bellini." In *Desire in Language: A Semiotic Approach to Literature and Art*, edited by Leon S. Roudiez and translated by Thomas Gora, Alice Jardine, and Leon S. Roudiez, 237–70. New York: Columbia University Press, 1980.

———. *Powers of Horror: An Essay on Abjection.* Translated by Leon S. Roudiez. New York: Columbia University Press, 1982.

———. *Revolution in Poetic Language.* Translated by Margaret Waller. Introduction by Leon S. Roudiez. New York: Columbia University Press, 1984.

———. "Stabat Mater." In *Tales of Love*, translated by Leon S. Roudiez, 234–62. New York: Columbia University Press, 1987.

———. *Strangers to Ourselves.* Translated by Leon S. Roudiez. New York: Columbia University Press, 1991.

Lacan, Jacques. "The Mirror Stage as Formative of the Function of the I as Revealed in Psychoanalytic Experience." In *Écrits: A Selection*, translated by Bruce Fink, 3–9. New York: Norton, 2002.

Lagorio, Valerie. "Variations on the Theme of God's Motherhood in Medieval English Mystical and Devotional Writings." *Studia Mystica* 8 (1985): 15–37.

A Legend of Holy Women: A Translation of Osbern Bokenham's Legends of Holy Women. Translated and introduction by Sheila Delany. Notre Dame, Ind.: University of Notre Dame Press, 1992.

The Life of Blessed Birgitta by Prior Peter and Master Peter. In *Birgitta of Sweden: Life and Selected Revelations,* edited by Marguerite Tjader Harris, translated by Albert Ryle Kezel, and introduction by Tore Nyberg. New York: Paulist Press, 1990.

The Life of Marie d'Oignies by Jacques de Vitry. Translated by Margot H. King. Saskatoon: Peregrina, 1986.

Lincoln, Bruce. *Gods and Demons, Priests and Scholars: Critical Explorations in the History of Religions.* Chicago: University of Chicago Press, 2012.

Louth, Andrew. "The Body in Western Catholic Christianity." In *Religion and the Body,* edited by Sarah Coakley, 111–30. Cambridge: Cambridge University Press, 1997.

Mackenzie, Catriona, and Kim Atkins, eds. *Practical Identity and Narrative Agency.* New York: Routledge, 2008.

Mahmood, Saba. *Politics of Piety: The Islamic Revival and the Feminist Subject.* Princeton, N.J.: Princeton University Press, 2005.

Mâle, Emile. *L'art religiuex de la fin du XVIe siècle, du XVIIe siècle et du XVIIIe siècle.* Paris: A. Colin, 1951.

Mali, Anya. *Mystic in the New World: Marie de l'Incarnation (1599–1672).* Leiden: E. J. Brill, 1996.

Marie de l'Incarnation. *Marie de l'Incarnation: Correspondance.* Edited by Dom Guy-Marie Oury. Sablé-sur-Sarthe, France: Solesmes, 1971.

———. *Relation de 1633.* In *Marie de l'Incarnation: Écrits spirituels et historiques,* edited by Dom Albert Jamet. Vol. 1. Paris: Desclée-de Brouwer, 1929.

———. *Relation de 1654.* In *Marie de l'Incarnation: Écrits spirituels et historiques,* edited by Dom Albert Jamet. Vol. 2. Paris: Desclée-de Brouwer, 1929.

Martin, Claude. *La Vie de la Vénérable Mère Marie de l'Incarnation.* Sablé-sur-Sarthe, France: Solesmes, 1981.

McCutcheon, Russell T., ed. *The Insider/Outsider Problem in the Study of Religion: A Reader.* London: Continuum, 2005.

———. *Manufacturing Religion: The Discourse on Sui Generis Religion and the Politics of Nostalgia.* New York: Oxford University Press, 1997.

McFague, Sallie. "God as Mother." In *Weaving the Visions: New Patterns in Feminist Spirituality,* edited by Judith Plaskow and Carol P. Christ, 139–50. San Francisco: Harper & Row, 1989.

McGinn, Bernard. "The Language of Love in Jewish and Christian Mysticism." In *Mysticism and Language,* edited by Steven T. Katz, 202–35. London: Oxford University Press, 1990.

——. "Mystical Consciousness: A Modest Proposal." *Spiritus* 8, no. 1 (2008): 44–63.

McInerney, Maud Burnett. "In the Meydens Womb: Julian of Norwich and the Poetics of Enclosure." In *Medieval Mothering*, edited by John Carmi Parsons and Bonnie Wheeler, 157–82. New York: Garland, 1996.

McLaughlin, Eleanor. "Christ My Mother: Feminine Naming and Metaphors in Medieval Spirituality." *St. Luke's Journal of Theology* 18 (1975): 228–48.

McNamara, Jo Ann, ed. *Sainted Women of the Dark Ages*. Translated by Jo Ann McNamara and John E. Halborg with E. Gordon Whately. Durham, N.C.: Duke University Press, 1992.

Merrim, Stephanie. *Early Modern Women's Writing and Sor Juana Inés de la Cruz*. Nashville, Tenn.: Vanderbilt University Press, 1999.

Meyers, Kathleen, ed. *Word from New Spain: The Spiritual Autobiography of Madre Marie de San Jose (1656–1719)*. Liverpool: Liverpool University Press, 1993.

Milcent, Paul. *Saint Jean Eudes*. Paris: Bloud & Gay, 1964.

Miller-McLemore, Bonnie. *Also a Mother: Work and Family as Theological Dilemma*. Nashville, Tenn.: Abingdon Press, 1994.

Moi, Toril, ed. *The Kristeva Reader*. New York: Columbia University Press, 1986.

Moore, Brenna. "Friendship and the Cultivation of Religious Sensibilities." *Journal of the American Academy of Religion*. Forthcoming.

Mulder-Bakker, Anneke B. *Lives of the Anchoresses: The Rise of the Urban Recluse in Medieval Europe*. Philadelphia: University of Pennsylvania Press, 2005.

——, ed. *Sanctity and Motherhood: Essays on Holy Mothers in the Middle Ages*. New York: Garland, 1995.

Newman, Barbara. *From Virile Woman to WomanChrist: Studies in Medieval Religion and Literature*. Philadelphia: University of Pennsylvania Press, 1995.

Niebuhr, Reinhold. *Nature and Destiny of Man: A Christian Interpretation*. New York: C. Scribner's Sons, 1943.

Nygren, Anders. *Agape and Eros*. Translated by Philip S. Watson. Philadelphia: Westminster Press, 1953.

Obeyesekere, Gananath. *The Work of Culture: Symbolic Transformation in Psychoanalysis and Anthropology*. Chicago: University of Chicago Press, 1990.

O'Faolain, Julia, and Lauro Martines, eds. *Not in God's Image: Women in History from the Greeks to the Victorians*. New York: Harper & Row, 1973.

Oliver, Kelly, ed. *Ethics, Politics, and Difference in Julia Kristeva's Writing*. New York: Routledge, 1993.

——. "Julia Kristeva's Feminist Revolutions." *Hypatia* 8, no. 3 (1993): 94–114.

——, ed. *The Portable Kristeva*. New York: Columbia University Press, 2002.

——. *Reading Kristeva: Unraveling the Double-Bind*. Bloomington: Indiana University Press, 1993.

Olphe-Galliard, M. "L'abandon a la providence divine et la tradition salesian." *Revue d'Ascétique et de Mystique* 38 (1962): 324–53.

Orsi, Robert. "2+2=5, or the Quest for an Abundant Empiricism." *Spiritus: A Journal of Christian Spirituality* 6, no. 1 (2006): 113–21.

———. *Between Heaven and Earth: The Religious Worlds People Make and the Scholars Who Study Them.* Princeton, N.J.: Princeton University Press, 2005.

———, ed., *The Cambridge Companion to Religious Studies.* Cambridge: Cambridge University Press, 2011.

Oury, Dom Guy-Marie. *Dom Claude Martin: Le Fils de Marie de l'Incarnation.* Sablé-sur-Sarthe, France: Solesmes, 1983.

———. *Marie Guyart (1599–1672).* Translated by Miriam Thompson. Sablé-sur-Sarthe, France: Solesmes, 1978.

Outka, Gene. *Agape: An Ethical Analysis.* New Haven, Conn.: Yale University Press, 1972.

Ozment, Steven. *Ancestors: The Loving Family in Old Europe.* Cambridge, Mass.: Harvard University Press, 2001.

Pagels, Elaine. *Adam, Eve, and the Serpent.* New York: Random House, 1988.

Paige, Nicholas D. *Being Interior: Autobiography and the Contradiction of Modernity in Seventeenth-Century France.* Philadelphia: University of Pennsylvania Press, 2000.

Palliser, Margaret Anne. *Christ Our Mother of Mercy: Divine Mercy and Compassion in the Theology of the Showings of Julian of Norwich.* Berlin: De Gruyter, 1992.

The Passion of Perpetua and Felicity. Translated by Thomas J. Heffernan. New York: Oxford University Press, 2012.

The Passion of SS. Perpetua and Felicity. Translated by W. H. Shewring. London: Sheed & Ward, 1931.

Pellegrin, Nicole, and Colette H. Winn, eds. *Veufs, Veuves, et Veuvage dans la France d'ancien régime.* Paris: Champion, 2003.

Pelphrey, Brant. *Christ Our Mother: Julian of Norwich.* Wilmington, Del.: Michael Glazier, 1989.

Pender, Patricia. *Early Modern Women's Writing and the Rhetoric of Modesty.* New York: Palgrave Macmillan, 2012.

Perrier, Sylvie. "Logique patrimoniale et relations sociales: Les familles recomposées dans la France d'Ancien Régime." In *La valeur des liens: Hommes, femmes et comptes familiaux,* edited by Agnès Martial and Agnès Fine, 69–90. Toulouse: Presses Universitaires du Mirail, 2007.

Petroff, Elizabeth. *Consolation of the Blessed.* New York: Alta Gaia Society, 1979.

Pollock, Linda. *Forgotten Children: Parent–Child Relations from 1500 to 1900.* New York: Cambridge University Press, 1983.

Proudfoot, Wayne. *Religious Experience.* Berkeley: University of California Press, 1985.

Purvis, Sally. "Mothers, Neighbors, and Strangers: Another Look at Agape." *Journal of Feminist Studies in Religion* 7 (Spring 1991): 19–34.

Rayez, A. "La spiritualité d'abandon chez saint Jean-Baptiste de la Salle." *Revue d'Ascétique et de Mystique* 121 (1955): 47–76.

Reineke, Martha J. "Our Vital Necessity: Julia Kristeva's Theory of Sacrifice." In *Religion in French Feminist Thought: Critical Perspectives*, edited by Morny Joy, Kathleen O'Grady, and Judith L. Poxon, 101–16. London: Routledge, 2003.

———. *Sacrificed Lives: Kristeva on Women and Violence*. Bloomington: Indiana University Press, 1997.

Rich, Adrienne. *Of Woman Born: Motherhood as Experience and Institution*. New York: Norton, 1976.

Ricoeur, Paul. *Oneself as Another*. Translated by Kathleen Blamey. Chicago: University of Chicago Press, 1992.

Roberts, Tyler. "All Work and No Play: Chaos, Incongruity, and *Différance* in the Study of Religion." *Journal of the American Academy of Religion* 77, no. 1 (2009): 81–104.

Ruddick, Sara. "Remarks on the Sexual Politics of Reason." In *Women and Moral Theory*, edited by Eva Feder Kittay and Diana T. Meyers, 237–60. Totowa, N.J.: Rowman & Littlefield, 1987.

———. *Maternal Thinking: Toward a Politics of Peace*. Boston: Beacon Press, 1989.

Ruether, Rosemary Radford. *Christianity and the Making of the Modern Family*. Boston: Beacon Press, 2000.

———. "Misogyny and Virginal Feminism in the Fathers of the Church." In *Religion and Sexism: Images of Woman in the Jewish and Christian Tradition*, edited by Rosemary Radford Ruether, 150–83. New York: Simon and Schuster, 1974.

Sahlin, Claire. *Birgitta of Sweden and the Voice of Prophecy*. Rochester, N.Y.: Boydell Press, 2001.

Schaff, Philipm and Henry Wace, eds. *Nicene and Post-Nicene Fathers*. Buffalo, N.Y.: Christian Literature Publishing Co., 1893.

Schechtman, Marya. *The Constitution of Selves*. Ithaca, N.Y.: Cornell University Press, 1996.

Schulenburg, Jane Tibbets. *Forgetful of Their Sex: Female Sanctity and Society, ca. 500–1100*. Chicago: University of Chicago Press, 1998.

Shahar, Shulamith. *Childhood in the Middle Ages*. London: Routledge, 1990.

Shorter, Edward. *The Making of the Modern Family*. New York: Basic Books, 1977.

Smith, Jonathan Z. *Imagining Religion: From Babylon to Jonestown*. Chicago: University of Chicago Press, 1982.

———*Map Is Not Territory: Studies in the History of Religion*. Leiden: Brill, 1978.

———. *Relating Religion: Essays in the Study of Religion*. Chicago: University of Chicago Press, 2004.

Söderbäck, Fanny. "Motherhood according to Kristeva: On Time and Matter in Plato and Kristeva." *PhiloSOPHIA* 1, no. 1 (2011): 65–87.

Spangler, Jonathan. "Benefit or Burden? Elite Widows in Seventeenth-Century France." *Proceedings of the Western Society for French History* 31 (2003): 65–83.

Spivak, Gayatri. "In a Word." *Differences* 1, no. 2 (1989): 124–56.

Stone, Alison. "Against Matricide: Rethinking Subjectivity and the Maternal Body." *Hypatia* 27, no. 1 (2012): 118–38.

Stone, Lawrence. *The Family, Sex and Marriage in England, 1500–1800.* London: Weidenfeld & Nicolson, 1977.

Stopp, Elizabeth. *Madame de Chantal: Portrait of a Saint.* Westminster, Md.: Newman Press, 1963.

Streete, Gail Corrington. *Redeemed Bodies: Women Martyrs in Early Christianity.* Louisville, Ky.: Westminster John Knox Press, 2009.

Sulkunen, Pekka. "Society Made Visible: on the Cultural Sociology of Pierre Bourdieu." *Acta Sociologica* 25, no. 2 (1982): 103–15.

Vásquez, Manuel A. *More Than Belief: A Materialist Theory of Religion.* New York: Oxford University Press, 2011.

Vauchez, André. *La sainteté en Occident aux derniers siècles du Moyen Age.* Rome: École française de Rome, 1981.

Wacquant, Loic, J. D. "Toward a Reflexive Sociology: A Workshop with Pierre Bourdieu." *Sociological Theory* 7, no. 1 (1989): 26–63.

Warner, Lyndan. "Widows, Widowers and the Problem of 'Second Marriages' in Sixteenth-Century France." In *Widowhood in Medieval and Early Modern Europe*, edited by Sandra Cavallo and Lyndan Warner, 84–107. London: Longman, 1999.

Weber, Alison. *Teresa of Avila and the Rhetoric of Femininity.* Princeton, N.J.: Princeton University Press, 1990.

Weinstein, Donald, and Rudolph Bell, *Saints and Society: The Two Worlds of Western Christendom, 1000–1700.* Chicago: University of Chicago Press, 1982.

Weisner, Merry. *Christianity and Sexuality in the Early Modern World: Regulating Desire, Reforming Practice.* New York: Routledge, 2000.

Wheaton, Robert, and Tamara K. Hareven, eds. *Family and Sexuality in French History.* Philadelphia: University of Pennsylvania Press, 1980.

Wiethaus, Ulrike, ed. *Maps of Flesh and Light: The Religious Experience of Medieval Women Mystics.* Syracuse, N.Y.: Syracuse University Press, 1993.

Wilkin, Rebecca. "L'Algonquin par abjection: Une mystique aborde le Nouveau Monde." In *L'Autre au XVIIème siècle: Actes du 4e colloque du Centre International de Rencontres sur le XVIIème siècle*, edited by Ralph Heyndels and Barbara Woshinsky, 31–46. Tübingen: Gunter Narr Verlag, 1999.

Wolf, Kenneth Baxter. *The Life and Afterlife of St. Elizabeth of Hungary: Testimony from Her Canonization Hearings.* New York: Oxford University Press, 2011.

Wolff, Larry. "Religious Devotion and Maternal Sentiment in Early Modern Lent: From the Letters of Madame de Sévigné to the Sermons of Père Bourdaloue." *French Historical Studies* 18 (1993): 359–95.

Wright, Wendy. *Bond of Perfection: Jeanne de Chantal and François de Sales.* New York: Paulist Press, 1985.

Ziarek, Ewa. "At the Limits of Discourse: Heterogeneity, Alterity, and the Maternal Body in Kristeva's Thought." *Hypatia* 7, no. 2 (1992): 91–108.

Žižek, Slavoj. *Jacques Lacan: Society, Politics, Ideology.* London: Routledge, 2003.

Index

CATHOLIC PRACTICE IN NORTH AMERICA

James T. Fisher and Margaret M. McGuinness (eds.), *The Catholic Studies Reader*

Jeremy Bonner, Christopher D. Denny, and Mary Beth Fraser Connolly (eds.), *Empowering the People of God: Catholic Action before and after Vatican II*

Christine Firer Hinze and J. Patrick Hornbeck II (eds.), *More than a Monologue: Sexual Diversity and the Catholic Church. Volume I: Voices of Our Times*

J. Patrick Hornbeck II and Michael A. Norko (eds.), *More than a Monologue: Sexual Diversity and the Catholic Church. Volume II: Inquiry, Thought, and Expression*

Jack Lee Downey, *The Bread of the Strong:* Lacouturisme *and the Folly of the Cross, 1910–1985*

Mary Dunn, *The Cruelest of All Mothers: Marie de l'Incarnation, Motherhood, and the Christian Tradition*